CHOOSING A SELF

CHOOSING A SELF

Young Women and the Individualization of Identity

Shelley Budgeon

Westport, Connecticut
London

Library of Congress Cataloging-in-Publication Data

Budgeon, Shelley, 1967–
    Choosing a self: young women and the individualization of identity /
  Shelley Budgeon.
      p.   cm.
    Includes bibliographical references and index.
    ISBN 0–275–97637–8 (alk. paper)
    1. Young women—Psychology.   2. Women—Identity.   3. Individuality.   4. Femi-
ninity.   I. Title.
    HQ1229.B83 2003
    155.3'33—dc21   2002030744

British Library Cataloguing in Publication Data is available.

Library of Congress Catalog Card Number: 2002030744
ISBN: 0–275–97637–8

First published in 2003

Praeger Publishers, 88 Post Road West, Westport, CT 06881
An imprint of Greenwood Publishing Group, Inc.
www.praeger.com

Printed in the United States of America

The paper used in this book complies with the
Permanent Paper Standard issued by the National
Information Standards Organization (Z39.48–1984).

10 9 8 7 6 5 4 3 2 1

Copyright Acknowledgments

Excerpts from *Modernity and Self Identity*, Anthony Giddens. Copyright © 1991. Reprinted
with permission of Blackwell Publishing Ltd., Oxford, United Kingdom.

Excerpts from *Inventing Our Selves, Psychology, Power, and Personhood*, Nikolas Rose.
Copyright © 1996. Reprinted with permission of Cambridge University Press, Cambridge,
United Kingdom.

Excerpts from "Emergent Feminist(?) Identities: Young Women and the Practice of Micropolitics," Shelley Budgeon. Copyright © 2001, *The European Journal of Women's Studies*, Vol. 8 (1).
Reprinted with permission of Sage Publications Ltd., London.

For Myrna, Joan, Grace, and Pat in recognition and gratitude.

Contents

Acknowledgments

I would like to recognize a wide network of people who have contributed in various ways to the writing of this book. First, I am deeply indebted to James, Thomas, Anna, Kajsa, Ola, Carl, Joanne, the Beechwood Collective, Gav, Lara, Ian, and Jennifer for their friendship and generosity. Special thanks to Simon for his encouragement, ongoing inspiration, and kindness, given freely and often. Appreciation is extended to my family for their support and understanding, who despite geographical challenges have never been absent in my life; and to Carol and Sasha for their guidance, direction, and good advice. Finally, the enthusiasm of the young women who participated in the interviews and their willingness to share their stories made this project possible.

Funding for this project was provided by a doctoral fellowship from The Social Sciences and Humanities Research Council of Canada.

Chapter 7 initially appeared in *The European Journal of Women's Studies* 8 (1), February 2001. Reprinted by permission of Sage Publications Ltd. (© Sage Publications Ltd. 2002).

A version of chapter 4 initially appeared in *Body and Society* 9 (1), March 2003.

Chapter 1

Choosing a Self

This book arose from an interest in theorizing the relationship between the lived experiences of young women and the varied cultural representations that organize definitions and practices of femininity. It became apparent that this was part of a much larger question about young women and self-identity—that is, about how young women actively negotiate possible ways of being in the course of constructing a self. As such, this is a book about processes of self-enunciation. More specifically, it is about the self-enunciation of young women who are embedded within particular social relations, practices, knowledges, and technologies that constitute a specific historical and cultural context. It is within this context—defined by, among other things, significant social change, expansion of choice, and increased emphasis on individuality—that the enunciation of self is explored throughout the following chapters. For example, Shannon is eighteen years old and attending a course in health and social care at a further-education college. She is trying to decide what she will do after she completes the course at the end of the year. In thinking about her options, she emphasizes individual choice and responsibility:

You grow up all through high school, go through changes, go through puberty and everything and that is a big change but then you realise you're not in this little circle of school and teachers taking care of you. You're in the outside world now it's you that's got to get it right.

Laura is seventeen years old and is finishing her first year of A-levels[1] at a private all-girl school where she has studied since she was eight. She is thinking about her future, what she might like to do after completing school—about who she is:

I'm trying to be what I want to be and not what everyone else wants me to be. Try-ing to find my own feet.

Claire is eighteen years old and has been involved in a variety of youth training programs but is still unsure about what kind of job she wants to do. Again, her reflections upon the available choices are intrinsically linked to an individualized identity:

I don't think there is a definition of the ideal woman. People say, "I'm normal" and what is normal? Nobody is normal. Everybody's got to be who they are and re-spect who they are because before you can respect anybody else, you've got to re-spect yourself.

These examples of self-enunciation provide a rich backdrop for engag-ing with questions of self-identity. How is it that through negotiating choices in day-to-day life a particular understanding of who we are and what we might (be)come arises? What does it mean to say that you are whoever you choose to be? In what ways are definitions of self located within a wider social and historical context? What are the implications of the relationship between transformations to the social order and the iden-tities that are fashioned within?

This set of questions introduces three key aspects of theorizing the self that provide the basis for issues explored in this book: choice, identity, and social change. The core of the argument undertaken throughout the fol-lowing chapters is constituted by a close examination of what identities are possible for individualized selves and how these constructed identi-ties are understood by those who create and enact them in everyday life. Moreover, it is argued that the questions posed above are particularly salient if one is to understand the lives of young women at the turn of the twenty-first century.

Identity, as a topic of investigation, has become fundamentally tied to debates surrounding the nature of social and cultural transformations. Re-cent arguments have centered upon the assertion that within postmoder-nity the individual is increasingly freed from the constraints of ascribed identities that once were more tightly organized through relations of class, race, sexuality, ethnicity, and gender, and must, therefore, construct his or her own internally referential identity within conditions of expanded choice. Questions surrounding how to live one's life have not only become central to identity, but the process of having to confront increased uncer-tainty and choice is itself productive of self-identity. Theorizing the pro-cesses through which identities are forged, as well as the nature of identities under construction, has proceeded from different strategies: those falling under the rubric of reflexive modernization (Beck 1992; Gid-dens 1991) and those that are informed by poststructuralist cultural the-ory, most notably theorists such as Michel Foucault and Judith Butler. This book explores how different lines of inquiry make different assumptions about subjectivity and how these assumptions have significant implications for the ways we can come to understand that choices about how to live one's life are located within interrelationships between social institutions, social relations, self/other, and the individual who is an active and creative subject.

Often lacking within debates about theorizing identity is a more grounded understanding of the relationship between choice and identity within contemporary social and cultural conditions. This elision can only be addressed through a close examination of lived experiences, which in turn requires working through some of the contradictions and limitations posed by different strategies for theorizing identity. This must proceed in relation to concrete individuals living in contemporary society. The aim of this book, therefore, is to examine the tension between various theoretical perspectives and to explore and challenge strategies of theorizing identity in postmodernity by undertaking a grounded examination of emergent modes of femininity—that is, ways of being a young woman within a cultural moment often referred to as "Girl Power."

Throughout the following chapters, assumptions underlying dominant approaches to theorizing identity are interrogated where increased choice about how to live one's life is perceived as being central to the formation of the self. The wider contexts addressed, therefore, are social conditions,[2] which have transformed in such a way that identities now emerge in a context characterized by a greater degree of uncertainty, flux, and individualized culture. First, this book aims to address the suggestion that young women at the turn of the twenty-first century are making choices about their lives within a set of conditions that increasingly allow for expanded options and alternatives about how to live. Interviews provide the basis for exploring what it means to be a young woman in contemporary Britain and how the lives of young women are organized around notions of choice across a number of different sites.

Second, this book takes as a central concern the understanding and engagement with lived experiences as a means for developing strategies for theorizing the construction of identities. The narratives that young women construct about themselves and their lives, therefore, are used strategically to critically interrogate assumptions that underpin ways of theorizing the relationship between choosing a self-identity and social conditions described as postmodern. This involves engaging critically with existing theories, particularly reflexive modernization, poststructuralism, and feminist perspectives. Here the focus is upon understanding how to theorize what it means to be a "choosing, autonomous self."

The remainder of this introduction serves to provide the background context for examining the choosing self as a particular relation to the self. This involves a discussion of the emergence of individualized identity, an outline of the social conditions that both allow and demand individuals to engage in constructing a self-identity, and a discussion of the relevance of these issues for understanding what it means to be a young woman at the turn of the twenty-first century.

SETTING THE CONTEXT

In theorizing a transition from modernity to postmodernity, identity has been identified as a central topic of investigation because it is suggested that an emerging set of conditions now provides the context for the creation of new forms of identity. However, in order to engage with this suggestion, the debate, and confusion, about what the terms "postmodernity," "postmodernism," and "poststructuralism" refer to demands acknowledgment. Postmodernity within the context of this book is used as a designation for a specific set of historical social conditions characteristic of the post–World War II era. Postmodernism and, in particular, poststructuralism refer to ways of theorizing our relation to those conditions. This set of conditions reflects both continuity and discontinuity with the conditions that constituted modernity, and as such, postmodernity cannot be seen as a radical departure from modernity.[3] Postmodernity is a historical era rooted in modernity, where "modern ideas, practices, and politics continue, to some extent, to exist alongside postmodern ones" (Roseneil 1999, 164). It is located at the historical moment when modernity becomes self-conscious and begins to reflect upon itself. Therefore, postmodernity does not represent a new era as much as a new situation to the extent that we can now, for the first time, look back on modernity and reflect upon it from a perspective that allows particular questions to be asked (Bauman 1992, 23–24, 187; Huyssen 1990, 267–68; Kumar 1995, 140–42).[4]

It is precisely this possibility of being able to take stock of modernity, that is, to be able to reflect upon its central assumptions, practices, and accomplishments or consequences, which has been identified as symptomatic of a postmodern condition. (Smart 1997, 398)

The main analytical and political assumptions distinctive to modernity—that knowledge is progressive, cumulative, holistic, universal, and rational—have been made deeply problematic by a postmodern radicalization of the reflexive potential of modernity (Smart 1997, 397). The result has been the development of what is referred to in this study as a postmodern perspective—that self consciously questions and, thereby, renders problematic particular assumptions that underlay modernity. Thus, a postmodern perspective redefines our relation to those conditions. The position taken here is that postmodern society is defined by several distinct characteristics and that questions of identity are embedded in this set of conditions. Those relevant to this analysis of identities are

- A fragmentation of the social order into a set of relations characterized by increased fluidity and contingency so that heterogeneity and multiplicity undermine the belief in a unified, single reality
- The end of grand narratives, for example, the belief progress can be achieved through the right application of reason
- A critique of the rational, self-constituting subject where the "death of the subject"[5] means enacting a challenge to the ideology of the universal modern subject (male, White, and middle-class), in order to develop alternative notions of subjectivity
- A shift from universals to questions of difference
- A shift from the production of knowledge from a so-called objective, universal position to that of the local and everyday
- An increased importance of knowledge and culture with an emphasis upon language as constitutive rather than reflective of the social order
- A recognition that identities are not essential or unitary but are constituted from multiple sources and assume multiple forms across time and place

INDIVIDUALIZED IDENTITY

The importance accorded to the individual and increasing individual autonomy are defining features of modernity (Calhoun 1994, 9). The assertion that identity is inextricably linked to the social conditions within which it is produced is itself a modern notion. Indeed the discourse of identity is distinctly modern, intrinsic to and partially constitutive of modernity, which is often characterized by a transformation in which the individual, in contrast to the collective, becomes of increasing importance. The recognition of and increased value placed upon the individual are outcomes of processes of modernization such that it is with the development of modern social conditions that the imperative to "know oneself" outside of the constraints of tradition arises. Individualization, as a defining characteristic of late modernity, translates into an enhanced potential of individuals to be freed from external forces that limit the kinds of identities possible. Individualization, therefore, is part of the process of detraditionalization for which Heelas (1996, 2) provides the following working definition:

Detraditionalisation involves a shift of authority: from "without" to "within." It entails the decline of the pre-given or natural orders of things. Individual subjects are themselves called upon to exercise authority in the face of disorder and contingency which is thereby generated. "Voice" is displaced from established sources, coming to rest with the individual.

From this perspective, in traditional societies the individual was embedded in a pre-given order in which external sources of authority determined, to a large extent, the destiny of the individual who exercised only a limited autonomy. Traditions, by providing an ordering framework for existence, worked to satisfy existential and ontological questions. For example, religion, kinship systems, and the local community played a significant role in shaping the scope and direction of individual lives (Giddens 1991). Processes of modernization, however, effect a demystification and dissolution of external sources of authority. Privileges of rank and religions lose their force and ascriptive statuses increasingly disappear as sources of identity, thereby leaving the individual with more autonomy to confront an expanding range of options about how to live.

The modern era brought an increase in the multiplicity of identity schemes so substantial that it amounted to a qualitative break, albeit one unevenly distributed in time and space. In the modern era, identity is always constructed and situated in a field and amid a flow of contending cultural discourses. (Calhoun 1994, 12)

The very notion of self-identity is made possible by the modernization of tradition, but the processes that bring it into being also make it increasingly problematic to create and sustain. As Giddens states, in premodern societies, "tradition is a means of handling time and space, which inserts any particular activity or experience within the continuity of past, present and future, these in turn being structured by recurrent social practices" (Giddens 1990, 37–38). In contrast, modernity is rife with discontinuities, ruptures, and rapid change—all characteristics that enhance the development of reflexivity. Loss of external authority, the freeing up of life courses circumscribed by ascriptive categories, and a growing awareness by individuals of their own distinct sense of self contribute to less stable identities that are constantly in a process of reconstruction. As in the transformation from traditional to modern social forms, Giddens (1991, 1992) maintains that the transformation to late modernity[6] similarly exhibits an intensification of individualization and reflexivity such that self-identity becomes an ever more individualized project.

These arguments illustrate how locating particular forms of selfhood within the social and understanding the dynamics of this relationship have been important aspects of analyzing social conditions. This focus is evident in recent debates concerning the nature of contemporary society, notably in the work by Bauman (1996b), Beck (1992), Beck and Beck-Gernsheim (1995), Castells (1997), Giddens (1991, 1992), and Rose (1998). Identity "is constituted within a historical process of consciousness, a process in which one's history is interpreted or reconstructed by each of us within the horizon of meanings and knowledges available in the culture at given historical moments" (de Lauretis 1986, 8). The historically specific social and material conditions that influence how identities are formed and maintained affect how we make sense of social relations and practices, as well as how we then live out identities in relation to others (Woodward 1997, 12). Identity is about the relationship between the individual and society, agency and structure, the link between the self and the social, the self and other.

Responses to theorizing identity within this set of transformed conditions have followed two main strategies:[7] The first strategy, one associated with social theory, offers a "historicized narrative of the development of identity, which is conceptualised as *self*-identity, the individual's conscious sense of self" (Roseneil and Seymour 1999, 3). The other strategy, based within cultural theory, focuses on "the problematic of identity and cultural difference, and in the theoretical deconstruction of identity categories" (Roseneil and Seymour 1999, 3). The former position includes theorists of reflexive modernization, particularly Giddens (1991) and Beck (1992),[8] who argue that identity becomes more important in late modernity because as the social order fragments, reflexivity increases and identities are less likely to be built within the parameters of ascribed categories.

Like Giddens (1991, 1992), Beck argues that "just as modernisation dissolved the structure of feudal society in the nineteenth century and produced the industrial society, modernisation today is dissolving industrial society and another modernity is coming into being" (1992, 10). This argument rests upon the assertion that reflexivity, which is a key characteristic of modernity, works to dissolve the parameters of industrial society—gender roles, family and occupation, the belief in science and progress. Beck asserts that industrial society is based upon a fundamental contradiction between the universal principles of modernity—civil rights, equality, functional differentiation, methods of argumentation, and skepticism—and the structure of institutions that allow these principles to be achieved in only a limited and partial way (Beck 1992, 14). The result is the destabilizing of industrial society through its very establishment. Modernity, therefore, is being released from its industrial design and the individual is now, more than ever before, left to negotiate an ever-widening expanse of choices. Identity is established and maintained through the ongoing development of a reflexively ordered self-biography and the ability to keep a particular narrative going.

From a perspective influenced by cultural theory, most notably poststructuralism, theories of identity share with reflexive modernization theory the premise that identities are not fixed. However, there is a more explicit focus on the inherent instability of identity categories, the processual nature of identity formation, and the heterogeneity of the self—

assumptions that challenge the humanist conception of the unified and essential subject (Butler 1990, 1992, 1993; Rose 1998; Weedon 1997). Poststructuralism launches an attack on assumptions underlying the modernist subject—namely, that the subject is the origin of meaning and the essential ground of knowledge.[9] Instead, in poststructuralist theory, the subject is conceived as a construct of linguistic practices (Kumar 1995, 131). Although many of the theorists labeled as poststructuralist differ in key respects, one "common theme is that the self-contained, authentic subject conceived by humanism to be discoverable below a veneer of cultural and ideological overlay is in reality a construct of that very humanist discourse" (Alcoff 1988, 415). An analysis of the operation of power is also explicit in this approach, where "truth" is seen as the product of the operation of power. As Butler and Scott (1992, xiv) argue, "poststructuralism is not, strictly speaking, *a position,* but rather a critical interrogation of the exclusionary operations by which 'positions' are established." Attention is given to the cultural context of the production of the subject as opposed to the "ontologically intact reflexivity" of the subject emphasized by theorists of reflexive modernization (Butler 1992, 12). Poststructuralism offers useful tools for theorizing the self within postmodernity because it shares an emphasis on pluralization and fragmentation, the refusal of positing totalities, and an incredulity toward grand narratives (Kumar 1995).

These two strategies for theorizing identity rely on different ontological assumptions. Understanding how they differ requires a consideration of the specific types of selfhood they focus on. The modern intellectual history of selfhood revolves around three dimensions through which the self is constructed: the material/bodily, the relational/social, and the reflexive/self-positing.[10] As Seigel (1999, 285) points out, "how each is conceived, which one is emphasised, and what relations are posited between them are the central questions determining what a given view of the self will be like." Proponents of reflexive modernization tend to emphasize the self-positing self, while poststructuralists focus upon relational aspects of identity where meanings of subjectivity are organized discursively through operations of difference.

Finally, while it is acknowledged that detraditionalizing forces are a significant characteristic of late modernity, the *extent* to which this leads to a set of conditions within which the individual is free to construct or choose a self-identity is often disputed (Luke 1996; Thompson 1996). An argument against the individualization thesis asserts that modern societies may undergo processes of differentiation and pluralization, thereby becoming more fragmented, but that the extent to which tradition is disintegrated in the process remains open for debate. Rather than modernity being fundamentally about the eradication of tradition, the argument has been made that processes of detraditionalization coexist with processes that lead to the rejuvenation, reconstruction, and maintenance of tradition within modern forms of life. The result is a social condition shaped by both tradition and individualization. To fail to take both processes into account is to fail to adequately understand the complex nature of late modernity. Therefore, it is argued that because tradition continues to operate drawing a clear contrast between past and present, or tradition and modernity, it is a misrepresentation of social processes that occur simultaneously rather than as discrete social forms. For individuals, this means that the authority of the self exercised autonomously in constructing a biography is always held in tension with external sources of authority that operate to limit or shape that autonomy.

If detraditionalization means the individual is able to live a more autonomous existence and choose from a wider array of possibilities in seeking self-fulfillment, the individual also comes to experience an effect that contradicts and counteracts this freedom yet has its origins in the same source. "Individuation"[11] makes reference to the tendency within modern society for increased surveillance and control of individual subjects.[12] Processes that result in more importance being accorded to the individual also make it "meaningful to tell individuals apart, to identify them, to register them and ultimately to control them; the uniqueness of the individual is his or her subordination" (Abercrombie, Hill, and Turner 1986, 151). Thus, there is a tension inherent in conditions that permit increased autonomy to individuals who are at the same time embedded in relations and institutions that seek to inscribe the subject in specific ways. Throughout the chapters that follow, this tension between the subject who freely chooses and the subject who is made knowable through particular modes of subjectification provides a backdrop for discussions of the ways the young women interviewed made choices about their own identities.[13] In examining the narratives young women construct about choosing a self-identity, it becomes apparent that understanding this tension between constraint and freedom inherent in choosing an identity requires the development of theoretical strategies.

These issues provide the backdrop to questions that are explored herein. The aim is to examine in detail the tensions and contradictions inherent in theorizing identity and to interrogate assumptions underlying theoretical explanations of how the relation of self and other is being constructed and lived in late/postmodern social conditions by young women for whom choice is an important aspect of daily life. This endeavor necessitates a critical engagement with those theorists who are located within the framework of reflexive modernization—Beck and Giddens—and those who argue from a position defined by poststructuralist critiques (Butler 1990; Foucault 1988; Grosz 1994; Rose 1998; Weedon 1997). The ontological assumption from which this project begins is that social reality is produced and reproduced by social actors. It is not an object that exists outside of discourses, representations, interpretations, social constructions, and the practices that these organize. It is not singular in form but a multiplicity of realities where sets of meanings and relations provide the basis for processes through which the individual assembles a representation of the self in the form of identity. The representations that give meaning to who we are do not emerge from within the self-constituting individual but through a continuous process, an ongoing renewal based in an interaction with the outside world—that is, a subjective engagement with practices, discourses, and institutions that lend significance (value, meaning, affect) to the self and daily events (de Lauretis 1986).

YOUNG WOMEN, INDIVIDUALIZATION, AND CHOICE

In this research, thirty-three young women age sixteen to twenty were interviewed in a northern city in England.[14] The purpose of the interviews was to listen to the ways young women talked about themselves and their lives in order to gain an understanding of how they were actively constructing a self-identity within late modern social conditions. The interviews were conducted across a range of sites that reflect the spaces in which young women confront decisions about their lives following the completion of compulsory education. These sites also represent how young women differ in relation to each other regarding their access to educational resources, their different needs and goals, and the different trajectories they are on in making a transition into adulthood.[15] At each site these young women were embedded within activities and practices oriented toward decisions about the next stages of their lives primarily in relation to education and career plans. However, in discussing these decisions and the options they perceived as being available to them, many other areas of their lives, such as views on marriage, emerged. The interviews were conducted in

- A private all-girl school sixth form[16]
- A mixed-sex state-run comprehensive sixth form[17]
- A further-education vocational qualification program in health and social work
- A career guidance center for school leavers
- A youth outreach project designed to provide services to young women who had "fallen through the cracks in the system" and who had a wide spectrum of needs ranging, for example, from drug addictions to single parenting to lack of education or employment opportunities

Young women are of particular interest in relation to debates surrounding choice and identity because since the mid-1970s a number of significant social transformations have impacted greatly on the life choices and trajectories available to them. As McRobbie (1994) suggests, young women have been "unhinged" from their traditional social position organized through gender relations and that the impact of feminism

Has made issues around sexual inequality part of the political agenda in both the private sphere of the home and in domestic relations, and in the more public world of work. Likewise, institutions themselves (particularly in education) have been alerted to the question of women and young women as economic agents, participating in the economy for the greater part of their lives. Altogether this kind of heightened activity around questions of gender has radically undermined what might be described as the old domestic settlement which tied women (and young women's futures) primarily to the family and to low-paid or part-time work. There is, as a result, a greater degree of uncertainty in society as a whole about what it is to be a woman, and this filters down to how young women exist within this new *habitus* of gender relations. (McRobbie 1994, 157)

The uncertainty to which McRobbie refers formed a central concern of the interviews undertaken here. Transformations to the social have resulted in a set of conditions where more options and possibilities for defining the self exist than for any previous generation of women. Contributing factors to these historical transformations include post-industrialization, the restructuring of the economy, revisions to state welfare provision, the expansion of post-compulsory education, and the impact of feminism and new social movements.

One of the most important outcomes produced by these changes to the social order is that the route from school into the workplace, the traditional notion of transition from youth to adulthood, has become de-standardized and individualized.[18] For example, Furlong and Cartmel (1997, 1) argue that over the last two decades the experiences of young people in industrialized society have altered dramatically, having consequences for relationships with family and friends, experiences in education and the labor market, leisure pursuits and lifestyles options, and the ability to become established as independent adults. By the 1990s, it was apparent that all of these structural changes combined to have a profound impact on the experiences of young people. The reorganization of the economy had resulted in limited employment opportunities, but also opened up a range of training programs as an alternative to further education. Due to a need for skilled workers, it became increasingly important to acquire qualifications, and new vocational programs were made available to young people in response. The pursuit of noncompulsory education became more prevalent while the number of young people leaving school at age sixteen to go into full-time employment diminished. In Britain, the viability of leaving school was further curbed by changes made to the provision of benefits by the conservative government. Such policies, reflecting the rise of New Right political ideologies, were part of an overall social environment where meritocracy and individualism had become prominent. The values and worldview of young people began to reflect this. In summary, the route to adulthood was no longer as straightforward as it once it had been. Young people were faced with having to choose from more options in an environment that placed emphasis upon individual choice and acceptance of responsibility for success as well as failure.

Since the transition of youth into adulthood has always been socially organized and constructed by gender, the ways in which structural changes have altered this transition have had a significant gendered dimension. There have been a number of structural transformations since the early 1970s that have impacted gender relations and are particularly relevant to understanding the position of young women at the turn of the twenty-first century. Women have increasingly moved from the private into the public sphere—this movement being most apparent within the realms of education and paid employment. Within the area of paid employment there has been a significant restructuring of job opportunities available for women. The percentage of female employees in Britain rose from 38 percent in 1971 to 49.6 percent in 1995, indicating a substantial increase in women's economic activity.[19] The wage gap between men and women has also declined steadily since the early 1970s, although this has happened primarily in full-time work. In 1970 women earned only 63 percent of men's full-time wage, but by 1995 this gap had narrowed to 80 percent (Walby 1997, 31).

The restructuring of employment opportunities for women is further reflected in the decline of occupational segregation within certain areas. Significantly, in the period between 1975 and 1994, men's monopolization of the top professional and managerial positions decreased. Women have been able to move into the upper socioeconomic levels of managerial, administrative, and professional jobs for which university qualifications constitute an effective entry prerequisite. This increase in women's participation in upper-level socioeconomic positions has been accompanied by a decrease in sex segregation in the lower levels (Walby 1997, 34–35).[20] The higher the occupational order, the more likely there is an increase in both the absolute and relative numbers of women.

Walby (1997, 38) argues that the dramatic transformation of the position of women within paid employment can be attributed to three key structural changes. First, equal opportunity legislation and policies have reduced discrimination against women. A variety of these sex equality legislation measures have been passed since the early 1970s as a result of a number of factors that include pressure from organized women's trade unions, pressure to ratify the 1951 International Labour Organisation on equal pay, the support of a woman minister of state, and the requirements of membership of the European Union.

Second, transformations in employment opportunities for women are directly linked to their increased educational participation and acquisition of qualifications. Girls in the contemporary context are gaining more educational qualifications than their male counterparts. This is an important point, as knowledge is an increasingly significant factor in social change and economic development (Drucker 1993). There is a significant relationship between level of education and likelihood of involvement in paid work. In 1994 among women aged twenty to twenty-nine with higher educational qualifications, 89 percent were working, with only 4 percent inactive. However, among the same age group lacking educational qualifications, only 33 percent were active and 56 percent economically inactive (Walby 1997, 41).

Historically, the underachievement of young women in academic settings provided the focus of concern for educators and policymakers. Girls performed better than boys at the primary school level but were then surpassed, never again regaining their advantage. In the 1970s, the tendency was for young women to acquire fewer school-leaving qualifications than young men and they were underrepresented in universities (Furlong and Cartmel 1997, 22). However, this is no longer the case. Young women are now outperforming young men at primary and secondary schools by getting better results in both the General Certificate of Secondary Education exams (GCSEs) and A-levels. In addition, they are making gains in entry to traditionally male-dominated fields (Roberts 1995, 47).[21] Finally, as recently as ten years ago it was young men who held the advantage in educational attainment, but now young women are more likely than men to participate in further education (Walby 1997, 44).

Increasing educational achievements by women, however, do not apply uniformly. The decreasing gender gap in educational attainment pertains primarily to younger women and is less relevant in the case of older women. Walby (1997) stresses the significance of age in assessing the impact of structural transformations on the position of women. Young women have been able to more readily gain access to education than older women, and the younger the age at which a woman attains her qualifications, the better off her position tends to be in relation to men. Therefore, the advantages brought by educational attainment to women's position in employment are restricted primarily to younger women, as they are more likely to have acquired qualifications. Among older men and women, the differences in qualifications remain. For example, in 1994 in the age group fifty to fifty-nine, 54 percent of women held no formal educational qualification compared to only 33 percent of men. Among sixteen- to twenty-four-year-olds, however, the number of women holding no educational qualifications was 19 percent and for men 20 percent (Walby 1997, 47). Walby concludes that there can be no sweeping statement about women catching up with men but that this is a generationally specific phenomenon.

The third factor that has contributed to women's improved position within employment is the declining significance of domestic activities for some women, in particular, younger women who are moving into top jobs (Walby 1997, 50). Events such as marriage, childbirth, and child care have traditionally played a key role in determining women's participation in paid employment, but Walby (1997) argues that this influence has less impact in today's context. For example, the economic activity rate of women with dependent children has increased from 49 percent in 1974 to 65 percent in 1994.[22]

These are some of the main components of an environment where gender relations have significantly transformed and contributed to a set of conditions in which young women are constructing their identities in relation to a diverse range of opportunities, within the realms of education and training, career paths, domesticity, relationships, and consumer culture. Young women today *must* confront a set of choices that for the most part were unknown to their parents. The lessening influence of ascribed identities has resulted in a more individualized experience of the transition to adulthood and the routes to follow out of secondary schooling have become less predictable. Opportunities have expanded, a greater degree of options are offered, and materials from which to construct an identity have multiplied.

THE SELF AND AUTONOMY

A consideration of transformations to social structures and the emergence of theoretical perspectives which posit that self-identity has become more fluid and individualized were used as a basis for the construction of interview questions that were designed to elicit a self-narrative by the young women who participated. The questions focused on several topics—including educational plans, career goals, intentions regarding marriage and child rearing—all of which contributed to the construction of a life narrative. Within these narratives it was also possible to discern attitudes toward a number of identity issues: the nature of available choices and opportunities; the importance of being able to choose; understandings of limits to choices available; the relationship between self and body; and perceptions of social change and relations of inequality, particularly with regard to feminism.

An initial analysis of the interview material revealed a remarkable degree of uniformity in the nature of the self-narratives and identities that were produced, the kinds of attitudes and values expressed, and the manner in which decisions were being negotiated. The similarity in the self that was being constructed can be characterized as a self that is free to choose, is in control of one's destiny, and is individually responsible for the outcome of one's choices. An analysis of this so-called autonomous self raised questions about the effects this construction has for the narratives young women are able to produce about their lives. It also raised questions about the implications this kind of self-identity has for ways in which young women live their identities. Finally, questions were also raised about how to theorize the relations that work to constitute the identities under construction.

These concerns became central to the subsequent analysis and, therefore, the following chapters do not constitute a study of the lives of the young women interviewed. The goal is not to deliver a detailed account of their lives per se, but instead to engage with the particular form of selfhood they constructed within a specific site and context of making choices about their lives.[23]

OVERVIEW OF CHAPTERS

Throughout the remainder of this book, a sustained engagement with core assumptions of theories of individualization, detraditionalization, and reflexive modernization is undertaken with the aim of understanding how identity is connected to and produced through choice. Beginning in chapter 2, strategies for theorizing identity within the context of transforming social conditions are examined from within the framework of reflexive modernization through a close examination of the work of Anthony Giddens. The argument is made that an alternative approach—a "genealogy of subjectification"—can provide a useful reorientation to some of the problems posed by reflexive modernization, particularly the notion of the autonomous, choosing self.

In chapter 3, the construction of the idea of choice within life narratives forms the basis for a discussion of young women's decisions about their future. From an analysis of these narratives about choice, it is argued that the young women interviewed constructed a relation to the self that is organized by the ideal of autonomy and the freedom to be whatever one wants to be, but that analytically this process is not detached from a context formed by relations of gender, class, and ethnicity. The emphasis placed by theories of reflexive modernization upon choice, authenticity, and coherence, and the implication of this perspective that young women are self-authoring selves is evaluated and countered by a reading using a genealogical framework. Emphasis is placed upon contextualizing the identities under construction within the local context of schools, career guidance centers, and youth outreach programs. Recognition of this embeddedness is significant as relations, practices, and knowledges that organize these sites also work to organize the possible selves that young women can construct and inhabit.

The centrality of embodiment to identity formation is explored in chapter 4. This chapter examines young women's experiences with regard to their own bodies, as well as the bodies that are represented to them in media and popular culture. The analysis begins with the suggestion that the body is incorporated into the reflexive project of the self as it becomes less of a natural given and more an object of human intervention. The mind/body dualism implicit in this argument and the privileging of the mind over the body is problematized. The aim of this chapter is to establish the relevance of transcending mind/body schemas for feminism and to introduce the body as a borderline concept (neither subject nor object), as ultimately this allows for thinking in nondichotomous terms. This way of thinking is central to understanding women's embodied agency. Through an exploration of interview material, the body is established as exceeding a surface inscribed by culture via the consumption of images. An examination of how the meaning of self and body arises out of practices like cosmetic surgery is undertaken, and the argument is made that in order to understand the relation between identity and embodiment and to devise a strategy for theorizing young women's embodied identity, it is useful to see the body as an event—as a site of production rather than as an effect of representation.

The focus in chapter 5 is on how difference organizes narratives of the self and relations to others through an examination of the young women's engagement with the idea that choice can be limited by forces external to the self. The goal is to understand the operation of difference in the construction of identity and what implications a self defined by autonomy and freedom of choice have for social relations that are organized hierarchically. The ways that youth practitioners positioned young women within discourses about class, gender, and ethnicity are compared with how the young women positioned themselves, and other young women, within unequal social relations. Particular attention is given to the construction of the self/other relation in these accounts and through this, the emergence of difference as a source of one's own separate uniqueness.

Chapter 6 explores the discursive construction of heterosexual relations and practices via an examination of how young women incorporated intimacy into the construction of their life narratives. Their mothers' lives, used as a point of comparison, were viewed as having been dominated by constraint associated with a commitment to marriage, domesticity, and child rearing. Several conflicts were produced by trying to reconcile intimacy and autonomy. The contradiction between being an autonomous self and having an obligation or commitment to a partner required discursive management, and these strategies are examined in detail.

In chapter 7, the nonidentification by young women with the feminist movement is explored. Intergenerational difference has been a significant problem for the political project of feminism, as has the lack of subjective identification with the category "feminist." In the discussion, "postfeminism" is defined as a moment of transformation in ways women relate to social conditions that has repercussions for the value of a nonfoundational politics. The identity narratives of young women are used as a basis for challenging the definition of a feminist identity and to question prescriptions for what constitutes feminist action. Through a close reading of the interview material, it is suggested that a micropolitics of everyday life is evident and that this coincides with a localized engagement in resistant practices. Here the autonomous self allows young women to inhabit a position from which they can critically understand, challenge, and ultimately transform their positioning within relations of inequality.

The goal throughout these chapters is to follow through a process of theorizing identities by moving back and forth between theory and the empirical in order to develop strategies for rendering discernible the identities constructed here and to develop ways of thinking about processes of self-enunciation. This process also lends insight into the identities that young women are producing within a particular historical moment, as well as indicates what some of the implications are for the types of selves under construction.

NOTES

1. A-levels are the equivalent of grades 11 and 12 in the American system.

2. These social conditions are sometimes described as postmodern and at others, late modern. The concern for this study is a particular historical era to which both of these terms apply—the latter half of the twentieth century. Characteristics of the historical era in question are explained further in this chapter.

3. This is a position shared by Bauman (1992); Beck, Giddens, and Lash (1994); Giddens (1991); and Roseneil (1999).

4. This position is common to theorists of reflexive modernization for whom expanded reflexivity is central to their theorization of contemporary social conditions.

5. The demise of the modern subject is a concept influenced by the work of Foucault, Derrida, and Barthes. See discussion in Kumar (1995, 129).

6. The terms "late modern" and "postmodern" often refer to the same set of sociohistorical conditions. For purposes of this study, the two terms are be used to indicate the same historical era, that is, post–World War II, but where specific theorists are discussed, their usage is employed. For example, although Giddens does not use the term "postmodern" but instead uses late modernity or reflexive modernity, his characterization of this historical era shares many of the points of a postmodern position. The defining features of this historical social condition are provided in chapter 1.

7. This idea is taken from Roseneil and Seymour (1999, 2–5).

8. Although theorists who fall under this rubric differ in certain respects, their position is similar to the extent that it is appropriate to group them together in this way.

9. The main assumptions regarding the poststructuralist theorization of the subject are explained in Barrett (1992, 202–4).

10. These categories are not wholly discrete from each other but form sufficiently different aspects such that a distinction is helpful. As Seigel (1999, 284) points out, at different moments any one of these dimensions may either nurture or limit the others, allowing for the self either to expand or to become constrained.

11. This idea is also expressed in Foucault's work on subjectification, particularly in the concepts of disciplinary power, normalization, and surveillance where the individual becomes an object of knowledge. These ideas are developed in his discussion of "the panoptican" (Foucault 1977). Also see the discussion in Abercrombie, Hill, and Turner (1986). The term "individuation" is also used as a psychological concept; however, this is not how the concept is being deployed here.

12. This argument is not universally supported. See Maffesoli (1996), who maintains that in late modernity, group identification or so-called tribes increase in importance. This viewpoint follows in the tradition of Durkheim.

13. The central premises of reflexive modernization, particularly Giddens's theorization of the choosing subject, are addressed in chapter 2. An alternate approach also is outlined, "a genealogy of subjectification," which is influenced by Foucault's work and developed by Rose (1996a, 1996b, 1998).

14. Practitioners within each site were also interviewed about their understandings of the choices available to young women, and how the young women they worked with negotiated identity formation. Interviews were conducted from May 1997 to August 1998. Please refer to the appendix for a description of the interview sites.

15. Of the thirty-three interviewed, five were of Asian descent and the rest were White. Four had children, and all were single. It is interesting to note that while these young women came from a variety of backgrounds that are in some measure reflected in the institutional sites in which they were located, they were remarkably similar in the nature of the self-narrative produced. The defining characteristic apparent across other differences was the value placed on autonomy. To engage with this construction, as is done in the analysis here, is not to suggest that these young women constitute a uniform category. They do occupy different positions within social relations that are hierarchically organized, and this may have an effect on the extent to which they will be able to enact the particular relation to the self that they are constructing in the present.

16. The sixth form is the equivalent of grades 11 and 12 in the American system.

17. A comprehensive school takes all children of the appropriate age that live in a given district, regardless of ability.

18. The scope of these issues lies outside the space of this discussion. For detailed analyses of youth transitions, please refer to Bates and Riseborough (1993), Furlong and Cartmel (1997), Griffin (1993), Hollands (1990), Irwin (1995), and Roberts (1995).

19. This increase is mainly due to an increase in women's participation in part-time work, which generally is lower paid than full-time work and involves poorer working conditions. However, as Walby (1997, 34) argues, "for the purposes of understanding changing gender relations in people's lives and experiences, it is more important to focus on the experience of having a job. Part-time work should not be dismissed as something done by 'grateful slaves' who have little commitment to work, but recognised as a distinctive form of employment with its own significance for the position of women in society and for the restructuring of employment relations for both women and men."

20. While sex segregation has decreased in the upper-level jobs, significant sex segregation in employment remains. In many occupations, employees are still of the same sex. See the discussion by Walby (1997, 34–36).

21. Despite their significant entry into these nontraditional areas, women are still underrepresented in certain subjects, such as sciences (Furlong and Cartmel 1997, 22).

22. See discussion in Walby (1997, 50–51) for detailed statistics.

23. For studies that do offer ethnographic accounts of young women's lives, please refer to Griffin (1985), Hey (1997), Lees (1986, 1993), McRobbie (1991), and Sharpe (1976, 1994).

Chapter 2

Theorizing Identity

The tension between the choosing self and a self that is made knowable through regimes of subjectification is examined in this chapter through a critical interrogation of the assumptions of reflexive modernization. Many of the points made in this critique reappear throughout the following chapters, as the identity narratives of the young women are further explored. Following an explanation of the shortcomings of Giddens's theory of reflexive modernization, an alternate approach to self-identity is developed at the end of the chapter. Rather than accept the self-constituting subject of Giddens's modernity, it is proposed that a "genealogy of subjectification," in which the subject is decentered from the origin of meaning, constitutes a challenge to the self-positing self and supplies a useful reorientation to questions about how a particular relation to the self is formed. The tension between the self-positing self and the self that is made knowable through relations of power and knowledge is exemplified in the contrast between the following quotations:

Each of us not only "has," but *lives* a biography reflexively organised in terms of flows of social and psychological information about possible ways of life. Modernity is a post-traditional order, in which the question, "How shall I live?" has to be answered in day-to-day decisions about how to behave, what to wear and what to eat—and many other things—as well as interpreted within the temporal unfolding of self-identity. (Giddens 1991, 14)

Power applies itself to immediate everyday life which categorises the individual, marks him by his own individuality, attaches him to his own identity, imposes a law of truth on him which he must recognise and which others have to recognise in him. It is a form of power which makes individuals subjects. There are two meanings of the word *subject:* subject to someone else by control and dependence, and tied to his own identity by a conscience or self-knowledge. Both meanings suggest a form of power which subjugates and makes subject to. (Foucault 1982, 212)

The processes through which one comes to know oneself, that is, becomes a particular kind of subject, are a central theme here. Indeed, both of these quotes draw attention to a self that becomes known; however, the contrast is in the emphasis on the source of that understanding of self. In the following chapters, this question underpins the reading of the narratives that these young women produced.

REFLEXIVE MODERNIZATION

Throughout a significant number of theoretical works, Anthony Giddens has sought to identify, analyze, and elucidate the distinctive characteristics that together are constitutive of the condition of modernity. In so doing, he has been particularly interested in the "crucial contradictions of modern existence: the enabling and constraining impact of social embeddedness, dialectics of power and freedom, trust and risk, autonomy and dependence in identity formation" (Bauman 1993, 363). His attention has focused on questions regarding the nature of modern identity and how it is that a distinct form of identity is associated with late modern social conditions. While reaction to this body of theory is mixed, it is generally acknowledged that the issues he addresses are of central importance to contemporary social theory. Indeed, theorizing identity has become a principal problem within social theory—a problem whose significance has been increasing particularly as a central theme in debates about whether or not a postmodern condition describes the contemporary social world.

Giddens's position in debates about contemporary forms of identity begins with an "interpretation of the current era which challenges the usual views of the emergence of post-modernity" (Giddens 1990, 149). Central to the challenge he presents to those who advance theories of postmodernity is the concept of "radicalized" or "reflexive" modernity. This current stage of modernity into which, he asserts, we are now entering is distinct from the previous stage of modernity as a result of an intensification of processes immanent in modernity. He argues that this does not constitute a radical break with modernity, but a further stage brought into being by its own logic. The consequences of modernity itself are becoming more radicalized and universalized.

At the core of modernity is this principle of reflexivity, which in the Weberian tradition identifies the growth of rationalization and rationality in the orientation of actors as a key to understanding modern social forms. For Giddens, reflexivity is a key structuring property of modernity that accounts for its dynamic character at both the individual and institutional level. At the individual level, reflexivity refers to the monitoring of activity in everyday life that is central to processes of structuration;[1] however, on a more significant level, reflexivity also accounts for the dynamic processes by which knowledge about social life is used in ways that work to organize or transform social life:

The reflexivity of modernity has to be distinguished from the reflexive monitoring of action intrinsic to all human activity. Modernity's reflexivity refers to the susceptibility of most aspects of social activity, and material relations with nature, to chronic revision in the light of new information or knowledge. Such information or knowledge is not incidental to modern institutions but constitutive of them. (Giddens 1991, 20)

In this way, reflexivity is the key to the notion of duality central to Giddens's theoretical ontology. In his theory of structuration, the social world is produced and reproduced through the actions and interactions of skilled and knowledgeable actors. Structural properties of social systems are both the medium and outcome of the practices they recursively organize. Structures, therefore, do not exist externally to the actions, knowledge, and routines that constitute them. They are a "virtual order" because "social systems, as reproduced social practices, do not have 'structures' but rather exhibit 'structural properties' and that structure exists, as time-space presence, only in its instantiations in such practices and as memory traces orienting the conduct of knowledgeable human agents" (Giddens 1984, 17).

While reflexivity is characteristic of all human activity for Giddens, his theory of modernity rests upon the assertion that modernity is distinct from premodern society in that the quantity and quality of reflexivity in modern societies is unique. He posits that modernity is an inherently transformational social order that is in a constant process of renewal and reproduction in which the potential for change is immanent to any and every interaction (O'Brien 1999, 23). The state of constant flux characteristic of modernity is often interpreted as a desire for novelty, but to Giddens what is characteristic of modernity is not "embracing of the new for its own sake, but the presumption of wholesale reflexivity" (Giddens 1990, 39). This movement into a thoroughly reflexive social order is a distinctive quality of late modernity.

In the modern world, accepted habits, norms, and conduct are continuously subject to revision in light of new information, knowledge, or resources, thereby generating a mutable order (O'Brien 1999, 25). This contrasts with traditional societies in which reflexivity is in operation but within more rigid parameters. For example, social reproduction in traditional societies is circumscribed by place. Existence is bound to the local both in terms of spatial territory and access to distant events or persons.

Institutions, therefore, are grounded in local customs and habits. Within these settings, tradition operates as a structuring principle because it is a means of integrating present experience with the past. Reflexivity in this process is largely limited to the reinterpretation and clarification of tradition so that the past retains a significant influence on the present and future (Giddens 1990, 37). Authority in the form of tradition operates as a framework of external rule, and there is minimal reflexive examination or questioning of established rules of conduct, beliefs, practices, or institutions.

The dynamic nature of modernity resides in three main elements: the separation of time and space, disembedding mechanisms, and institutional reflexivity. All of these interact to both radicalize and globalize the traits of modernity, thereby transforming the content and nature of daily life. In traditional society, time was bound to space as both were experienced within the context of place—the location of day-to-day life. Experience for the majority of the population, therefore, was always within a space of time linked to a specific place. Modern social organization, however, is characterized by a separation of time and space; or an "emptying" through the development of mechanisms for marking time, such as calendars and clocks, which remove the experience of time from place. This emptying coincided with the advent of modernity, as well as the separation of space from place. Modernity

increasingly tears space away from place by fostering relations between "absent" others, locationally distant from any given situation of face-to-face interaction ... place becomes increasingly phantasmagoric: that is to say, locales are thoroughly penetrated by and shaped in terms of social influences quite distant from them. (Giddens 1990, 18–19)

The significance of these separations is that the local context is increasingly structured not only by that which is present, but also by that which is not visible. These separations also allow for the coordination of social organization across time and space, as social activity is no longer constrained by the framework of local habits and practices.

The second element, disembedding mechanisms, is integrally linked to the emptying of time and space. These processes make reference to the "lifting out" of social relations from local contexts of interaction and their restructuring across indefinite spans of time and space (Giddens 1990, 21). Two types of such mechanisms are: symbolic tokens (e.g., money) and expert systems (e.g., law, medicine). Both types of abstract systems function to bracket time and space. For instance, money operates as a medium of exchange with a standard value across multiple contexts. Expert systems bracket time and space by assembling various forms of technical knowledge that have validity regardless of the individuals who make use of them (Giddens 1991, 18). In short, disembedding mechanisms remove social relations from the immediacies of local context. They imply that trust becomes a feature of social organization as they require a vesting of confidence in the abstract rather than the local and immediate.

The third element identified by Giddens relates to reflexivity at the institutional level:

Modernity is essentially a post-traditional order. The transformation of time and space, coupled with the disembedding mechanisms, propel social life away from the hold of pre-established precepts or practices. This is the context of the thorough going reflexivity which is the third major influence on the dynamism of modern institutions ... *the susceptibility of most aspects of social activity, and material relations with nature, to chronic revision in the light of new information or knowledge.* (Giddens 1991, 20, emphasis added)

Although new information and knowledge provides the basis for the reconstitution and renewal of social institutions, the employment of reason, in this configuration, does not guarantee certainty. Indeed, detraditionalization is driven by the constant scrutinizing and revision of knowledge, which introduces doubt alongside trust as features of late modernity. In this regard, post-traditional societies are characterized by a lack of external authority vested in a uniformly accepted set of core values and norms, which are able to provide direction for individual decisions, actions, and conduct. Traditional sources of authority, in the form of values or standards that are passed down to further generations, are increasingly questioned via reflexive engagement (Bagguley 1999, 68–69). Social systems thereby become internally referential—autonomous systems determined by their own constitutive effects.

A fundamental consequence of all these processes is that "for the first time in human history, 'self' and 'society' are interrelated in a global milieu" (Giddens 1991, 32). Traditions, which once clearly staked out the parameters of identity, lose hold and the individual's immediate context is defined by an expanding array of social contexts or so-called lifeworlds. Daily life becomes a combination of the local and the global, where experience is increasingly mediated such that events, regardless of their location, have an immediacy within local contexts. Giddens stresses the point that reflexive awareness, which is characteristic of all human action in late modernity, becomes constitutive of the self. The reflexivity inherent in the constitution of modern institutions extends fully to the individual so that the self becomes a "reflexive project" that must continually be remade in light of information about the many possible ways of life made available. The construction of a self-reflexive biography is governed by the moral imperative of authenticity, for it is up to the individual to gain self-knowledge to ensure that one is "being true" to oneself and it is one's obligation to pursue this self-actualization.

The self is reflexively understood by the person in terms of her or his own biography and the awareness of this biography having a coherence and continuity across time and space (Giddens 1991, 53). So although a multitude of choices and opportunities for self-definition may be available, the individual achieves coherence through the capacity to keep certain narratives consistent. The project of the self involves the continuous integration of events occurring in the external world into this ongoing story of the self (1991, 54). Through continuous self-observation a coherent and rewarding identity is constructed and reconstructed in light of both past events and an anticipation of the future. This "trajectory of the self" assumes a narrative form—an interpretative self-history. Whereas in premodern society the life span was governed by preordained or institutionalized "rites of passage" which the individual passively encountered, in late modernity, the life course loses this external structuring. The development of self is no longer tied to external structures but is increasingly internally referential as the points of reference to which the self-narrative is oriented in order to establish coherence are set within that narrative according to how the individual constructs her own life history. For instance, many life transitions are now initiated by the individual whom they affect rather than being standardized points of reference along the life course. This negotiation, however, must be done within conditions of increased risk and uncertainty so that self-actualization becomes a balance of opportunities against risk:

Negotiating a significant transition in life, leaving home, getting a new job, facing up to unemployment, forming a new relationship, moving between different areas or routines, confronting illness, beginning therapy—all mean running consciously entertained risks in order to grasp the new opportunities which personal crises open up ... such transitions are drawn into, and surmounted by means of, the reflexively mobilised trajectory of self-actualisation. (Giddens 1991, 79)

A central feature of the reflexively organized biography of the self is choice. For Giddens, choice is a fundamental element of day-to-day life. He states, "modernity confronts the individual with a complex diversity of choices and, because it is non-foundational, at the same time offers little help as to which options should be selected" (1991, 80). As a consequence, one's daily routines and practices become oriented to questions such as, who am I? or, who do I want to be? From among the options available, an integrated and routinized set of practices is chosen as an expression of one's self-narrative. Such clusters constitute a particular lifestyle, which is then subject to further revision in light of new experiences or information. Lifestyles are composed of choices made in the areas of styles of dress, diets, modes of conduct, social settings, types of people one socializes with, and so on. Lifestyles connect and integrate these elements so that the choices made exhibit some unity and consistency in regard to one's reflexively organized biography. Part of adopting a particular lifestyle involves projections of oneself into the future, and this planning for the future is just as integral as reflecting on the past in constructing a self-narrative.

THE BODY, PURE RELATIONSHIPS, AND LIFE POLITICS

The implications for increasingly reflexive identities are drawn out by Giddens in relation to a number of issues. He argues specifically that the "wholesale" reflexivity of modernity extends to the body, intimate relationships, and the realm of politics, producing specific effects unique to conditions of late modernity.

The Body

According to Giddens, in conditions of late modernity, the body becomes less a "given" that functions outside of internally referential systems and instead is increasingly subject to reflexive processes. On a basic level, the self is embodied in the sense that throughout daily activity and interaction the individual must be aware of the movements and appearance of the body. Routinized control of the body in this regard is a central aspect of agency. More than a passive object, the body is, Giddens argues, "an action-system, a mode of praxis, and its practical immersion in the interactions of day-to-day life is an essential part of the sustaining of a coherent sense of self-identity" (1991, 99). Within late modernity, reflexivity extends beyond the basic awareness and monitoring that is necessary for individuals to operate as competent social actors.

Four aspects in particular bear significance for the relationship between the self and the body: appearance, demeanor, sensuality, and regimes. Appearance refers to the outer surface of the body that is visible to the self and others. Demeanor concerns the ways in which appearance is used within daily settings. Sensuality refers to "dispositional handling of pleasure and pain." Regimes are the practices to which the body is made subject. As the individual encounters a plurality of different social settings and engages in a wide variety of social relations, both appearance and demeanor have to be adjusted. Despite this constant realignment, an inner core of self is maintained through reflexive monitoring of identity. Bodily practices and routines are carried out in ways that are consistent with the biographical narrative of the actor. In this way, the self and the body are integrated and lived as a unity. It is argued in chapter 4 that this formulation of the self and the body implicitly retains a separation of the subject and object or mind/body relation and a privileging of the mind over the

body in such a way that prevents an understanding of the mutually constituting and irreducible nature of the relation.

Giddens argues that as the body in late modernity becomes immersed
in the ever-increasing reflexive organization of social life, like other aspects of life, it also becomes subject to the notion of choice. Like the self,
the body becomes a project constructed and cultivated reflexively in view
of options made available through a multitude of lifestyle options and in
accordance with the self-narrative. These options are made manifest in
areas such as clothing styles, self-help health guides, diets, and exercise
regimes through which the individual assumes responsibility for the design of his or her body. In this regard, "body planning" is a central part of
the internally referential system of the self.

These assumptions raise questions about where the meaning of the body
comes from and what it means to choose a body. In Giddens's formulation,
it is seemingly chosen as part of one's reflexive self-management, but it
is argued in chapter 4 that the body and the self are embedded in local
practices and relations whereby the body's meaning and its relation to
the self emerge as a complex event rather than as an object of reflexive
choice.

Intimacy and the "Pure Relationship"

Giddens argues that there is a "direct (although dialectical) connection
between the globalising tendencies of modernity" and what he terms "the
transformation of intimacy" within daily life (1990, 114). The significance
he attaches to intimate relationships derives from the recursive relationship between the personal and wider social context—transformations in
the nature of one area impact upon the other. As intimacy becomes subject
to both reflexive processes and the dynamics of the internally referential
project of the self, conditions are created for the emergence of the "pure relationship."

The pure relationship is "a social relation which is internally referential,
that is, depends fundamentally on satisfactions or rewards generic to that
relation itself" (Giddens 1991, 244). The basis for intimate relationships
within this context becomes that which it can deliver to each of the parties
involved, replacing external criteria such as kinship, social duty, and traditional obligations. These dissolve as anchors for interrelationships, and
intimate ties instead become subject to voluntary selection. Because this
form of relationship is no longer tied to external references it must be reflexively organized, made and remade against a backdrop of continuous
social changes and transformations. Reflexive engagement and interrogation is oriented specifically to what the relationship is delivering or, for
that matter, not delivering.

Within this reflexive form of relationship there is constant balance between autonomy and the kind of self-disclosure that is necessary to build-

ing and sustaining trust. Like other aspects of the pure relationship, trust has to be worked at and cannot be taken for granted. At its very core, the pure relationship is chosen and entered into voluntarily, which ultimately means it can be exited on the very same grounds. Self-reflexivity is integral to building trust, as being true to oneself depends upon such activity, and it is only this implied authenticity that can provide the basis for mutual trust. The discovery of self that is undertaken by each partner and shared through processes of mutual self-disclosure, therefore, forms the basis for the ongoing cultivation of trust.

This transformation of intimacy in Giddens's formulation would seem to make intimacy increasingly difficult to find, let alone foster and sustain, but he argues that the loss of external influences and a recognition of the tensions inherent in relationships based on choice by individuals is offset by commitment. Here, commitment is linked directly to choice because to commit to someone or to a relationship implies that it is an option. Commitment means that despite the problems inherent in modern relationships the individual is willing to take a chance, to work at it, but only insofar as the relationship remains rewarding according to internal references. Reflexivity, therefore, introduces an element of tension between the ordering by individuals of their own self-biographies and the pure relationships into which the self may enter. For Giddens, "self-identity is negotiated through the linked processes of self-exploration and the development of intimacy with others where individuals commit to creating and sustaining a meaningful connection, a 'quality of relationship'" (1991, 97). However, as in other aspects of his analysis, he suggests that pure relationships, while providing opportunities, also imply risks.

Considering further the ways that intimate relationships have been transformed by the expansion of reflexivity, Giddens addresses the issues of love and sexuality. In particular, he ties the "sexual revolution" of the past thirty or forty years to a revolution in female sexual autonomy and to the flourishing of homosexuality (1992, 28). Freed from prior constraints "decentered" sexuality becomes "plastic." The development of new reproductive technologies and birth control techniques sever the connection between reproduction and sex, allowing sex to become truly autonomous—wholly a quality of individuals and their interactions.

A related notion is that of "confluent love," which has developed not completely in opposition to romantic love but definitely in tension with it. The ideals of romantic love such as "forever" and "one-and-only" collapse beneath the pressure of female sexual emancipation so that love becomes more active and contingent in nature. This form of love presumes equality in emotional give and take; therefore, love, like intimacy, develops only in so far as each partner is willing to engage in self-disclosure, thus making him or herself vulnerable. The significance of this reciprocity for Giddens is that, to a certain extent, romantic love does not require this of men. Confluent love, however, is rooted in the assumption of gender equality.

Confluent love develops as an ideal in a society where almost everyone has the chance to become sexually accomplished; and it presumes the disappearance of the schism between so-called respectable women and those who in some way lie outside the pale of orthodox social life. Unlike romantic love, confluent love is not necessarily monogamous in the sense of sexual exclusiveness but is held together through the acceptance on the part of each partner that "until further notice," each gains sufficient benefit from the relationship to make its continuance worthwhile (Giddens 1992, 63).

In his analysis of intimate relationships, Giddens draws out the implication that "the possibility of intimacy means the promise of democracy" because confluent love and the pure relationship are based on autonomy. The principles such as autonomy that have transformed the personal realm are consistent with the realization of democratic principles in the wider social context. Giddens argues that autonomy "means the successful realisation of the reflexive project of the self—the condition of relating to others in an egalitarian way" (1992, 189). The establishment of these sorts of relations in the private sphere has the potential to translate into a transformation of relations within the public sphere where the creation of a democratic order depends upon the recognition that others are not a threat.

Giddens's theorization begs the question of how individuals actually practice intimacy and the associated reflexive negotiations he presumes. Issues around autonomy, authenticity, choice, and intimacy played a central part in the narratives of the young women interviewed, as did the principle of gender equality. Indeed, the incorporation of intimate relationships into their narratives required the negotiation of often-contradictory positions. These were discursively managed through the production of various models of intimacy, which are analyzed in chapter 6.

Life Politics

In Giddens's view, the processes that underlie the dynamics of modernity ultimately point toward the possibility of a distinctly reformed social order. Throughout his analysis of self-identity in late modernity, Giddens argues that the expansion of institutional reflexivity, the disembedding of social relations by abstract systems, and the consequent interpenetration of the local and the global underlie crucial transitions in the modern social order. These transitions force acknowledgment of the existential issues that institutions of modernity have excluded and so contribute to a new form of political engagement concerned with human self-actualization at both the individual and collective levels. These contours of late modern "life politics" are best discerned against the contrast provided by the nature of politics Giddens associates with modernity.

Emancipatory politics, which Giddens associates with modernity, are defined as "a generic outlook concerned above all with liberating individuals and groups from constraints which adversely affect their life chances" (Giddens 1991, 210). The principles central to this outlook are the same ones that have been fundamental to the development of modern institutions, primarily the ideal of freeing individuals and social life from the constraints of tradition through the subjection of the social and natural worlds to human control. The orientation to freedom and liberty expressed in emancipatory politics involves casting off the constraints of the past to allow the creation of a better future and, more specifically, the aim of overcoming the domination of some individuals or groups by others (Giddens 1991, 211). In this form of politics, power is conceived as hierarchical and is expressed through its exertion of one individual or group over others. As such, the main concerns of emancipatory politics have been to reduce or abolish exploitation, inequality, and oppression. This vision is guided by the imperatives of justice, equality, and participation, as well as the mobilizing principle of autonomy, which privileges the right of the individual to exercise freedom and independent action. Giddens does not suggest that this form of politics ceases in late modernity but coexists alongside a different form—life politics.

Life politics "concerns political issues which flow from processes of self actualisation in post-traditional contexts, where globalising influences intrude deeply into the reflexive project of the self, and where converse processes of self-realisation influence global strategies" (Giddens 1991, 214). The emergence of such a form of politics presumes that a certain level of emancipation from the constraints of tradition and conditions of hierarchical domination has been achieved. The emphasis shifts away from a definition of power as hierarchical to a focus on its transformative capacities. Within this context, political concerns begin to be restructured around issues of lifestyle choices and self-actualization. Political issues arise from reflexively ordered biographies as people search for answers to questions such as, how should we live? Life politics are, therefore, explicitly oriented toward the future and the anticipation of "the development of forms of social order on 'the other side' of modernity" (Giddens 1991, 214). Where emancipatory politics are derived from the belief characteristic of modernity that humans can seize control of the natural and the social in order to improve the quality of life for all humans, life politics arise when the effects produced from those very efforts are questioned. The goal becomes finding ways to create morally justifiable ways of life that will promote self-actualization within a global context of interdependence (Giddens 1991, 215). The types of concerns that are addressed by life politics are very much at the individual level, but because of the globalizing processes of modernity, decisions made at this level have consequences on a much greater scale.

Giddens characterizes the concerns of life politics as those of the reflexive subject because "the more we reflexively 'make ourselves' as persons, the more the very category of what a 'person' or 'human being' is comes to the fore" (1991, 217). These issues raise the question of how self-reflexive biographies can be associated with political engagement or politicized identities. Indeed, for feminism, the nonidentification by young women with second-wave feminism has often been seen as a problematic feature of a post-feminist social climate. In chapter 7, these themes are taken up in a discussion of how the identities being constructed by the young women in this study are indicative of a form of politicized agency at the local level of everyday life. The implication for the project of feminist politics is a necessary reflexive engagement with its own assumptions about what constitutes a feminist identity.

CRITIQUING REFLEXIVE MODERNIZATION

Giddens's rendering of the social world in late modernity has been the subject of much scrutiny, and while his work provokes considerable debate, there are clearly areas that prove problematic. His commitment to a modernist ideal of rationality leads to a series of shortcomings that warrant attention, and the ontological assumptions upon which he relies, particularly regarding the subject, raise problems for the analyses of identity as a specific kind of relationship to the self. Many of Giddens's assumptions limit an understanding of how identity is formed within specific, local, and historical contexts. In the following critique, these issues are reviewed providing a point of departure for the further examination of some of these problems in relation to the identities that were constructed by the young women interviewed.

In a highly critical treatment of Giddens's work, Mestrovic argues that Giddens's message is distinctly modernist and, therefore, implicitly inadequate for theorizing the condition of the contemporary social order. This is apparent in his tendency to develop a single theory to encompass all other attempts at social theory and in his dependence on the "rational Enlightenment-based trajectory of cognition and rationality as the unifying element" (Mestrovic 1998, 31). Indeed, Giddens's reliance on reflexivity and the purposes he has for the notion presents a series of problems. At the very core of his theory of structuration is the idea that "the human agent is skilled and knowledgeable and uses structure in an enabling fashion" (Mestrovic 1998, 32). For Giddens, reflexivity is a structuring principle of modernity, which accounts for its dynamic character, its constant movement, and its displacement of tradition. In the transition from traditional to modern society, and the transformation from modernity to late modernity, individualization, or the freeing of individuals from the constraints of tradition, provides the motor for social change (Lash 1994, 112). It is also the basis for Giddens's normative agenda because it underlies the rational basis for freedom and provides an orientation toward personal and social development (Penna, O'Brien, and Hay 1999, 8). One consequence of invoking the notion of reflexivity to such a significant extent is an over-reliance on the rational, instrumental, individualistic agent.

Self-identity according to Giddens depends upon the active production of self by the individual in which the self becomes the object of reflexivity (Bagguley 1999, 70), for as he argues, the self is "routinely created and sustained in the reflexive activities of the individual" (Giddens 1991, 52). This social agent is not dissimilar to the self-authoring, calculating, goal-oriented subject of the liberal tradition associated with Western thought throughout modernity. This subject is "unambiguously sovereign in conception and exercises powerful interpretative skills as an author of conditions, qualities and events" (May and Copper 1995, 78). The intentionality implicit in his theorization of the subject excludes consideration of those moments where unintentional events or actions produce a more significant effect upon identity than moments where the subject is consciously and reflexively choosing a self. The emergence of self-identity out of such moments suggests that a significant share of identity emerges out of a much more haphazard process. Bagguley takes up this argument in relation to transformations of self-identity that occur within the context of social movements where it is more likely that transformations to self-identity follow an unintentional path rather than result as the product of the individual's realized intentions (1999, 82). Giddens's privileging of rational intent limits an understanding of the dynamics of social processes that are due in some part to irrational, random, or unexpected phenomena.

This point, taken up by Mouzelis (1999), leads to a questioning of Giddens's formulation of reflexivity, and more specifically to thinking about reflexivity in terms that do not rely upon a construction of the agent as essentially rational and goal-oriented. The starting point for Giddens is the distinction between the reflexivity characteristic of traditional contexts and that which operates in late modern contexts. In traditional contexts, reflexivity is limited by the fact that tradition to a large extent defines the parameters of an individual's social existence. Within late modern contexts, Giddens states that reflexivity is significantly less constrained by extrinsic factors, therefore requiring the individual to actively negotiate questions about how to live. The qualitative difference between these two modes of reflexivity has been challenged by some of Giddens's critics; however, Mouzelis makes the important point that attention would be better placed in examining the qualitative distinctions that can be drawn between different forms of reflexivity that coexist *within* late modernity. The formulation of reflexivity offered by Giddens tends toward a one-sided treatment of a complex process. According to Mouzelis, what remains to be considered is whether there might be other ways of reflexively reacting to the conditions created by detraditionalization—ways that are not so thoroughly activistic:

Following the Protestant-ethic tradition, the reflexive individuals' relation to their inner and outer worlds is conceptualised in ultra-activistic, instrumental terms: subjects are portrayed as constantly involved in means-ends situations, constantly trying reflexively and rationally to choose their broad goals as well as the means of their realization. (Mouzelis 1999, 85)

It is likely that setting goals and devising means of achieving them are governed by reflexive processes organized along less rational and instrumental lines. Thrift, drawing on de Certeau's (1988) account of everyday life, argues that a "make-it up-as-you-go-along" world of pliable, opaque, and stubborn spaces undermines the known and determinate appearance of daily, routinized life (Thrift 1993, 114). For Giddens, however, the only other alternative to reflexive conduct is the pathological engagement in compulsive behaviors. This begs the possibility of a "reflexive attitude that does not seek (via rational choices) actively to construct life orientations, but rather allows in an indirect, passive manner life orientations and other broad goals to emerge" (Thrift 1993, 114). This analysis opens up the possibility that individuals make their way through the post-traditional field of choices in front of them in a more arbitrary manner than Giddens suggests.

Exploring this issue further, Mouzelis endeavors to show that individual goals and life plans can be emergent in nature and not necessarily the product of rational calculation. He makes this point by exploring how nonsecular mystical traditions have emphasized the impossibility of relating to the divine via rational or cognitive methods. In these traditions, reason can only be useful for developing awareness of the inner obstacles that impede the soul from opening up to divine grace. This form of reflexivity has its secular parallel in forms of psychoanalysis and therapies in which the development of awareness of defense mechanisms that prevent nonpathological patterns from emerging is the objective. In this form of reflexivity, "life-goals 'appear' or 'emerge' rather than having to be actively constructed" (Mouzelis 1999, 87).

Giddens's means-ends reflexivity may, therefore, be incompatible with many areas of social life in which individuals develop identity. To some degree it is incompatible with Giddens's own approach to the "pure relationship." He maintains that pure relationships depend upon a form of intimacy freed from external obligations, grounded instead in ongoing dialogue, mutual disclosure, and trust, but reflexivity, in Giddens's usage, involves an instrumental relationship to the self in which the self is an objectified project.[2] The pure relationship as formulated by Giddens,

Mouzelis argues, is supposed to be based on an inter-human relationship in which the self and other are treated non-instrumentally. Giddens states:

The pure relationship depends upon mutual trust between partners, which in turn is closely related to the achievement of intimacy.... Such trust presumes the opening out of the individual to the other, because knowledge that the other is committed, and harbours no basic antagonisms towards oneself, is the only framework for trust when external supports are largely absent. (Giddens 1991, 96)

Indeed, if pure relationships are entered into by individuals who actively construct reflexive biographies in the way argued by Giddens, then it is more likely that the pure relationships they enter into are based on "mutual distrust and the mutual manipulation of each other's weaknesses and insecurities" (Mouzelis 1999, 92). In summary, all these arguments support the value of recognizing the limits of Giddens's use of reflexivity and the need to consider ways in which reflexivity may best be understood as a less unitary and instrumental relation to the self.[3] This theme recurs throughout the following chapters, particularly in relation to how subjects come to understand the self and their available choices for constructing a self within conditions of embeddedness—that is, within multiple, contradictory local practices and relations.

The limits of Giddens's instrumental reflexivity also become apparent when considering the relationship between the self and group identifications. It is within settings shaped by collective processes and sentiments that identities often find expression. Giddens's ideal type, however, is a singular subject. Hetherington (1998) locates this ideal type within the Weberian tradition of the autonomous, bourgeois, male subject who occupies a privileged position that presumes objectivity. Despite postmodern critiques, Giddens retains a commitment to a humanist conception of the subject, which leads to an underestimation of the affective dimension of identity that finds expression in gatherings based on shared emotion. According to Hetherington:

Revolutionary action, solidarity and comradeship, the symbolism of revolt, and so on all call upon the feelings of people and seek to ground a sense of moral right and wrong in that realm of feeling and expression rather than in reason alone. To have an identity is to find ways of expressing oneself through identifying with others, and that identification is based in the expressive world of feeling and emotion and forms of collective sentiment. (Hetherington 1998, 51)

Giddens follows the dominant trend in sociology of overlooking emotional experiences in favor of privileging rationality, which means that this approach fails to adequately analyze the basis of collective movements characteristic of late modernity and their implications for identity (Bagguley 1999; Hetherington 1998; Maffesoli 1996).[4] While Giddens outlines the implications of increased reflexivity for the political realm, the form of "life politics" he offers up is still to a large extent designed according to highly individualized terms, whereas Hetherington, among others, points out that deindividualizing processes arise alongside detraditionalization and are just as significant in their effects as individualizing ones. As identifications based on ascriptive categories like class break down, new sorts of social groupings emerge and provide the basis for identifications and lifestyles. Detraditionalization, therefore, might dilute and dissolve communal ties, but elective communities arise in the space provided. At the same time, as the individual becomes the central social actor, there is a return of the "repressed we" (Lash 1994, 111). This is true in the sense of the emergence of social movements, but also in regard to ethnic cleansing, neo-Nazi movements, and surges of nationalist sentiment.

Furthermore, reflexivity as formulated by Giddens fundamentally undermines his own theory of structuration duality. If, as he argues, structures are a "virtual" system made up of rules and resources instantiated as agents draw upon and use them, then structures are not fully external to the agent—they are something "out there" confronted by the subject—but are both the means and the outcomes of interaction. This understanding is at the core of his subversion of the problem of agency-structure dualism. However, his notion of "duality" versus "dualism" is difficult to retain once the subject is said to reflect upon the plurality of life worlds and choices, as this implies a distancing between the subject (knowledgeable agent) and the object (external social conditions). Reflexivity depends upon awareness; once it is reached, the subject is able to observe, analyze, manage, and make choices, but this awareness is contingent upon a dualism of subject and object. It seems more likely, therefore, that only under routine conditions would the subject/object and agent/structure dualities remain in place because in these mundane, taken-for-granted conditions, the carrying through of actions involves less reflexive engagement. As soon as the subject engages reflexively, however, the dual relation between agent and structure comes into being. Therefore, Giddens's notion of a reflexively constructed self creates a contradiction within this overall theoretical project (Bagguley 1999; Mouzelis 1999).

Questions about human agency also follow from the critique of Giddens's reflexive project of the self. In a world that is increasingly complex and fragmented due to the very processes that Giddens claims bring about late modern social conditions, his confidence in the free, knowledgeable, and skilled agent may seem somewhat exaggerated. Mestrovic (1998, 34) proposes that the massive proliferation of information to which individuals are subject creates a complex world in which most people function on autopilot for most of the time because they simply cannot engage knowledgeably with these conditions. A similar challenge is made to the inherent knowledgeability and skill of Giddens's social agent by considering the many people who do not fall into this category: children, mentally ill persons, and the mentally disabled, for example, fall outside of his "emancipatory vision" (Mestrovic 1998, 23). Clearly, for many people, the suggestion of reflexively engaging with and thereby transforming one's social conditions implies the operation of freedom and, therefore, power.

One area where this critique has relevant application is Giddens's notion of the pure relationship in which each partner invests in the relationship as long as it serves his or her individual interest. Partners are able to hold such an attitude because individuals in late modernity enjoy a level of autonomy made possible by the separation of sex from reproduction. But, as Bauman effectively points out, if sex has been freed from reproduction, "it is also true that so far reproduction has not been separated from sex and pair relationships in general" (1993, 366). Therefore, there is another category of persons, "third persons" who have a stake in the preservation of the relationship but do not enjoy the autonomy that Giddens emphasizes.[5] These people are affected deeply by the outcomes of intimate relationships, but possess very little choice about what these outcomes should be and, furthermore, lack the resources they would need to shield themselves against the impact of the pure relationship's outcome. Such an example is only one that brings forth the complex nature of choice and freedom that Giddens overlooks. According to Bauman:

As with all freedom, this one deepens the dependence of those acted upon and mortgages the future of the actors. As with all freedom, X's choice is Y's fate. In this game as in others, the most consequential decisions are made by those with the biggest hand, not by those with the biggest stakes. (Bauman 1993, 367)

Giddens's failure to deal adequately with issues of power, domination, and social inequality leaves a consequential gap in his theorizing. If late modernity is about openness, the diversity of authorities, and the expansion of lifestyle choices as the basis for the constitution of self-identity, is this a uniform phenomenon? Disembedding of social relations, the increase of mediated experience, the pluralization of life worlds, and the contingency of knowledge might create conditions in which individuals have wider parameters within which to create self-identities, but Giddens seems to conflate the possibility of doing so with the actuality. Acknowledgment is made that "class divisions and other fundamental lines of inequality, such as those connected with gender or ethnicity, can be partly defined in terms of differential access to forms of self-actualisation and empowerment," but Giddens argues it would be a major error to suppose that this phenomenon is restricted to those in more privileged material circumstances (1991, 6). It is the existence of widely divergent material circumstances characteristic of late modernity that Giddens has been criticized for glossing over. Critics maintain that material conditions and access to economic resources underpin to a large extent any construction

of self-identity or the realization of a "life project." It seems that his analysis is operating primarily outside of the material realm. May and Cooper
suggest that:

The activity and sovereignty attributed to these subjects—unhindered as they are
by the absence of structural and infrastructural resources—might lead us to suppose that what Giddens is outlining here is a theory of self-maximisation for the
middle classes, or "free floating" individuals. (May and Cooper 1995, 82)

Giddens's undertheorization of these concerns may be due in some part
to his explicit interest in arguing that human beings are active agents who
never passively accept external conditions and that social systems do not
form an uncontrollable context for social action. Indeed, his central notion
of institutional reflexivity depends upon social actors incorporating new
knowledge into environments of action that are thereby reconstituted or
reorganized (Giddens 1991, 243). Movement within structuration theory is
categorically recursive. Giddens's commitment to arguing for the recursive relationship between individuals and their environment is a useful
way of subverting structural determinism, but at times he may privilege
self-constituted agency at the expense of examining social conditions that
continue to produce social divisions. This commitment to individual
agency is the basis for Giddens's rejection of Foucauldian analyses of the
discursive construction of the subject because he sees this analysis strip-
ping the subject of agency. These themes emerge in chapters 3 and 4,
where the subject is located within particular practices and sites—positions from which a relation to the self is formed—thereby problematizing
Giddens's "free floating" social agent.

Part of the problem with using Giddens's theory of self-identity to understand social divisions returns to his theory of the subject. A subject that
is unitary is difficult to locate within the multiple, intersecting dimensions
that constitute relations of power and domination. Anthias, in her critique
of Giddens, starts with the argument that:

It could be argued that the self in high modernity is constituted in the different existential or ontological places of class location, sexual difference and collective or
ethnic belongingness at the global as well as national levels. These do not take any
necessary social forms but are intertwined in complex new ways that produce contradictory social locations, arising from the differential positionings of persons
within the hierarchical orders of each existential location. The self is thus constructed in terms of multiplicity and contextuality rather than as a unitary process.
(Anthias 1999, 157)

When Giddens theorizes the self of late modernity, he constructs a "collective" agent and proceeds to explain processes of identity formation as
though these are universal. Differentiation fragments modernity, producing, in Giddens's estimation, more choices and options, but he fails to come

to terms with the other implications of differentiation—namely, that it is characterized by and reproduces hierarchies and inequalities within social relations. In this regard, identities are about the outcomes of differential positioning across a range of locales. It has become increasingly important to recognize difference and divisions in understanding the dynamic of modernity, particularly under the influence of postmodern analyses in which the social world is said to be fundamentally about difference. To understand the implications of difference for identities and social relations, it is necessary to move beyond thinking through these issues within the confines of binaries such as structure/agency, modernity/tradition, and subject/object (Anthias 1999, 159). Such binaries restrict understanding because the multiplicity and contradictions that are at play cannot be adequately captured in mutually exclusive categories, but only through and across multiple positionings (Braidotti 1994).

While postmodernism in many ways has influenced recognition and even celebration of difference, it is important to recognize that difference is not politically neutral. Evaluation and assigning value are intrinsic to the processes of classifying, thereby producing categories which then form the basis of social stratification. Anthias argues "once individuals are placed into categories … across different dimensions, the relational terms of otherness and sameness are constructed. In the process notions of self and other, identity, identification and division come into play" (1999, 163). Thus, social divisions are at the "very heart of the social order and of culture. They are central to the constructions of identity and otherness and the production of differentiated and complex social outcomes for individuals and groups" (Anthias 1999, 162). These arguments suggest the need for examining how difference operates to define, limit, and demarcate the parameters of identity narratives. These issues arise in chapters 3 and 4, where the relation to the self that young women construct is a process mediated and shaped by the operation of difference.

The combination of a reflexive, self-authoring subject; social conditions marked by an easing of external constraints on the individual; an undertheorization of power relations; and the favoring of universalism over difference make Giddens's theorization of late modern a highly optimistic account. Modernity for Giddens is driven by processes that allow individuals to exercise more control over their lives. Disembedding processes lead to a condition of empowerment, that is, the "power of human beings to alter the material world and transform the conditions of their own actions" thereby providing "generic opportunities not available in prior historical eras" (Giddens 1991, 139). This confidence in social transformation is evident when Giddens proposes that the democratizing effects of intimacy will transform the public sphere, but May and Cooper argue that this is one of many examples of how he relies upon an exaggerated model of human agency and "neglects the ways in which collective, rather than individual action is the primary source of political change" (May and Cooper 1995, 81).

Finally, Giddens has been criticized for not granting enough significance to the chaos and irrationality that is at play within modernity. He attempts to construct a social theory on solely cognitive grounds, which leaves out people's histories, habits, customs, feelings, and other aspects of non-agency, all of which are essential to understanding social processes and human behavior (Mestrovic 1998, 25). Some commentators suggest that his optimism rings unrealistic in the face of continued inequality and divisions at both the local and global levels:

Giddens and many other mainstream sociologists have been singing a merry tune of global democratisation even as genocide raged in Bosnia, Russians expressed a nostalgia for Communism, the European Community began unravelling almost as soon as it was formed, and "ethnic cleansing" became a metaphor for our times. (Mestrovic 1998, 5)

The critique developed here continues to unfold, as aspects of these debates are pursued in detail through a reading of the self-identities young women constructed in the interviews. The narratives they produced provide a lens through which we may interrogate ways of theorizing identity in late modernity, particularly a form of self-identity defined through choice. Theories of reflexive modernization are central to analyzing the young women's self-identity narratives; however, before proceeding with such an analysis, the assumptions underlying another approach are briefly outlined. A "genealogy of the subject" provides a useful counterpoint to reflexive modernization and serves as a site from which to engage with Giddens.

FROM BIOGRAPHIES TO TECHNOLOGIES OF THE SELF

Rather than accept that individuals are the reflexive, goal-oriented agents of late modernity that Giddens suggests, could it be that this construction of the subject as autonomous, sovereign, and freely choosing is instead a regulative illusion? Rose (1998, 2) proposes an alternative theorization that this understanding of the self represents a *particular way of thinking*—a "certain way of understanding and relating to ourselves and others, to the making of human beings intelligible and practicable under a certain description":

We have been freed from the arbitrary prescriptions of religious and political authorities, thus allowing a range of different answers to the questions of how we should live. But we have been bound into relationships with new authorities, which are more profoundly subjectifying because they appear to emanate from our individual desires to fulfil ourselves in our everyday lives, to craft our personalities, to discover who we really are. Through these transformations we have "invented ourselves" with all the ambiguous costs and benefits that this invention has entailed. (Rose 1998, 17)

From this perspective, individualized responses to a detraditionalized world are the specific product of a historically contingent regime of the self that produces notions of what it means to be a human being. In this conceptualization, the freely choosing, autonomous individual is actually a mode of subjectification that provides a way of relating to, understanding, and thereby governing the self. It is a way of recognizing oneself as a particular type of person—the subject of free will. What Rose challenges is the suggestion that a singular form of subjectivity inhabits a singular cultural configuration. Instead, he proposes that a heterogeneity of forms of personhood are assumed in different practices and that there are diverse possibilities for codes of conduct that orient any one human being in different fields of thought and action (Rose 1996a, 303). If this is taken as the starting premise for theorizing identity, then questions arise as to why particular forms of identity emerge in specific locales at particular moments.

Rose proposes a "genealogy of subjectification" as a means of accounting for the heterogeneous processes and practices by which individuals in modern Western societies comprehend the person as "a natural locus of beliefs and desires, with inherent capacities, as the self-evident origin of actions and decisions, as a stable phenomenon exhibiting consistency across different contexts and times" (1998, 22). This genealogy is concerned with the relations that human beings have established with themselves—relations in which they come to understand and see themselves as selves. A genealogy of subjectification aims to focus directly on the practices within which (in both historical and contemporary contexts) human beings have been made subjects. Such a project would "address itself to those heterogeneous authorities that have, at different times and places, problematised human conduct and developed more or less rationalised programmes and techniques for its shaping and re-shaping" and study "the connections between the truths by which human beings are rendered thinkable—the values attached to images, vocabularies, explanations, and so forth—and the techniques, instruments and apparatuses which presuppose human beings to be certain sorts of creatures, and act upon them in that light" (Rose 1996a, 296).

This project relies upon a fundamentally different set of principles compared to Giddens's framework because it does not conceptualize changing forms of identity as the consequence of wider social and cultural transformations. To interpret changing forms of selfhood as the result of transformations brought about by technological advances or changes in systems of production, for instance, is to presume that these influences change ways of being because of some experience they produce. This would presuppose that humans are essentially equipped with the capacity for endowing meaning, but the counterargument maintains that ways of giving meaning do not come ready-made. There are different ways of giving meaning to an experience, and it is, in fact, these ways of giving meaning that produce experience, not vice versa (Rose 1998, 25). This point raises questions about how meaning is produced within specific historical, cultural, and local contexts.

The concern of a genealogical approach is the history of ways in which humans give meaning to experience. Techniques of constructing meaning produce experience because they provide the meanings and discourses that are available to the individual to employ in constructing the self and the social world (Dean 1994; Joyce 1994; Rose 1998, 25). The aim is to uncover "mundane everyday practices that try to shape the conduct of human beings in particular sites" to understand how they are organized and enacted (Rose 1996a, 298). Hence the need to examine the specific practices, techniques, knowledges, and programs that seek to govern human beings "through inciting them to reflect upon their conduct in a certain manner" (Rose 1996a, 300) across a multiplicity of heterogeneous sites. Rose argues:

Our present ways of understanding ourselves are not the culmination of a unified narrative of real time—a singular linear chronicity which, despite advances and lags, moves from fixity to uncertainty, from habit to reflexivity across all domains of existence and experience. *We must imagine time in ways that are more multiple than are dreamt in the temporalities of tradition and detraditionalisation.* (Rose 1996a, 303–4, emphasis added)

Here, Rose is advocating that our relation to our selves is a question of technologies that shape and guide our ways of "being human." He rejects the notion of the detraditionalized self because it does not engage with the ways in which different localized practices presuppose, represent, and act upon human beings as if they were certain sorts of subjects. For example, he considers that the contemporary problematics of risk have not emerged out of novel existential features of the current moment, but as a novel way of reflecting upon that experience (Rose 1996a, 320).

An account of the self defined by autonomy, rationality, and authenticity demonstrates a relation to the self that Rose argues is constituted through a variety of "rationalised schemes," which seek to influence the form self-understanding takes and the enactment of this particular understanding in the name of certain objectives. Such objectives include manliness, femininity, honor, modesty, propriety, civility, discipline, distinction, efficiency, harmony, fulfillment, virtue, and pleasure (Rose 1998, 24). These technologies are spatialized—that is, human beings are rendered knowable across a range of different sites, each with a localized repertoire of habits, routines, and images of self-understanding and self-cultivation. The ways individuals come to understand themselves as certain types of subjects are inscribed in the practices that act upon the "conduct of conduct." These practices are organized within specific locations such as the school, the family, the prison, the church, and so on, all of which work upon persons as particular types. Self-understanding becomes a way of governing the self in relation to the achievement of the objectives set within each of these sites. These "technologies of the self" work as self-steering devices because they inform the ways in which individuals experience, perceive, evaluate, and conduct themselves, thus bringing particular types of human beings into being (Foucault 1988).

In a whole variety of different locales—not just in sexuality, diet, or the promotion of goods for consumption, but also in labor and in the construction of political subjects—the person is presumed to be an active agent, wishing to exercise informed, autonomous, and secular responsibility in relation to his or her own destiny. The language of autonomy, identity, self-realization, and the search for fulfillment acts as a grid of regulatory ideals, not in an amorphous cultural space, but in the doctor's consulting room, on the factory floor, and in the personnel manager's office, in the training of unemployed youth and the construction of political programs (Rose 1996a, 320).

Techniques of the self operate to organize conduct in the context of everyday life and to orient this conduct toward a consideration of the kind of person one should aspire to be and the kind of life one should aim to lead (Rose 1996a, 296–97). These techniques, therefore, bear an inescapable normative function, and this normativity is dependent upon the problematization of conduct.[6] The ideals of self-responsibility and self-control are established and enacted in relation to those who are marginalized in such a way as to impede the possibility of taking up such a position. These individuals continue to be problematized and made subject to a range of experts and sources of authority who seek to reeducate or empower them through skills training, group relations, and various psychological techniques so that they can enact this type of relation to the self.

Central to Rose's conceptualization of subjectification is that the way in which one understands one's self and others involves a specific relation to authority. Authority is not a centralized power, but is spread across heterogeneous locations. The steering of one's conduct is always done under a real or imagined authority of a particular system of truth (Rose 1996b, 135). The aim of genealogy is to differentiate the "diverse persons, things, devices, associations, mode of thought, types of judgement that seek, claim, acquire, or are accorded authority" (Rose 1998, 27). How is it, though, that external authorities come to produce certain types of persons? Rose seeks to avoid an answer to this question, which would posit human beings having an essential basis to subjectivity:

The human being, here, is not an entity with a history, but the target of a multiplicity of types of work, more like a latitude and longitude at which different vectors of different speeds intersect. The "interiority" which so many feel compelled to diagnose is not that of a psychological system, but of a discontinuous surface, a kind of enfolding of exteriority. (Rose 1996b, 142)

Drawing on Deleuze's (1992) notion of the fold or pleat, Rose argues that this metaphor allows us to think of human beings in certain ways without postulating an essential interiority. The inside is merely a folding in of that which is exterior, thereby incorporating without totalizing, internalizing without unifying, collecting together discontinuously in the forms of pleats, making surfaces, space, flows, and relations (Rose 1996b, 143). In such an analysis of subjectification, that which is enfolded is anything that can acquire authority. Examples include injunctions, advice, techniques, habits of thought and emotion, an array of routines, and norms of being human—in short, all the practices and relations through which being constitutes itself (Rose 1996b, 143). The contemporary regime of the self, Rose argues, is to be located within the proliferation of authorities on human conduct over the past one hundred years. Examples include economists, managers, accountants, lawyers, counselors, therapists, medics, anthropologists, political scientists, and social policy makers. But underlying all these kinds of expertise regarding human conduct are the "psy" disciplines, which presume an interiority of the subject. Arising in the nineteenth century, psychology invented the so-called normal individual, and within contemporary society it is a discipline that forms the basis for the elaboration of a complex of emotional, interpersonal, and organizational techniques by which the practices of everyday life can be arranged according to an ethic of authentic, autonomous selfhood (Rose 1998, 17).

The influence of the "psy" disciplines derives from their generosity—that is, the multiple ways they lend themselves to practices within which individuals come to develop a relation to the self. Rose points out that "contrary to conventional views of the exclusivity of professional knowledge, psy has been happy, indeed eager, to 'give itself away'—to lend its vocabularies, explanations and types of judgement to other professional groups and to implant them within its clients" (Rose 1996b, 139). This knowledge forms the "psychology of everyday life" and is found in the practices developed by authorities such as schoolteachers, social workers, and nurses, as well as being inscribed in magazine advice columns, television talk shows, and self-help books. These technologies of the self work as a form of governance. Rose draws on the work of Foucault to suggest that government pertains to a "certain perspective from which one might make intelligible a diversity of attempts by authorities of different sorts to act upon the actions of others in relation to objectives," which include the objectives of national prosperity, harmony, virtue, productivity, social order, discipline, emancipation, and self-realization, to name a few (Rose

1996b, 135). Technologies of the self, therefore, are about the ways in which individuals come to regulate themselves and the conduct of others in relation to certain truths.

Rose argues that the development of disciplinary knowledge is linked to the wider social context of liberal democratic traditions whose legitimacy depends upon "free individuals." All such programs of government have been defined by the problem of "how free individuals can be governed such that they enact their freedom appropriately" (Rose 1998, 29). The government of others in liberal and democratic systems has always been, in some form, linked to specific strategies for inducing "free individuals" to govern themselves as "subjects simultaneously of liberty and responsibility—prudence, sobriety, steadfastness, adjustment, self-fulfilment, and the like" (Rose 1998, 12). At the turn of the twenty-first century, the regime of the self in the context of "postwelfare" nations depends upon instrumentalizing the capacities and properties of the "subjects of government." In contemporary advanced liberal programs of government, freedom is presumed as the desire of each individual to conduct his or her existence as a project for the maximization of quality of life and as such, responsibility for this quality of life becomes individualized (Rose 1996b, 146). This regime is expressed across a range of locales in which it is presumed that each subject is an active agent who wishes to exercise "informed, autonomous, and secular responsibility in relation to his own destiny" (Rose 1996b, 145). It is somewhat paradoxical then that language associated with freedom, such as self-realization, autonomy, and self-identity, actually forms an integral part of contemporary modes of subjectification.

Regimes of subjectification, however, should not be interpreted as deterministic. Resistance to a form of personhood that one is enjoined to take up is made possible because across a range of locations and practices persons are addressed as different sorts of human beings. Demands on the individual are always heterogeneous, competing and conflicting. According to Rose:

The "question of agency" as it has come to be termed, poses a false problem. To account for the capacity to act one needs no theory of the subject prior to and resistant to that which would capture it—such capacities for action emerge out of the specific regimes and technologies that machinate humans in diverse ways … agency itself is an effect, a distributed outcome of particular technologies of subjectification that invoke human beings as subjects of a certain type of freedom and supply the norms and techniques by which that freedom is to be recognised, assembled, and played out in specific domains. (Rose 1998, 186–87)

In summary, Rose stresses that the self in late modernity should not be approached as a question about the distinctiveness of this historical moment defined by features such as reflexivity, self-scrutiny, and individualization. Instead, what should be questioned is whether or not

There has been a transformation in the ontology through which we think our-selves, in the techniques through which we conduct ourselves, in the relations of authority by means of which we divide ourselves and identify ourselves as certain kinds of persons, exercise certain kinds of concern in relation to ourselves, are gov-erned and govern ourselves as human beings of a particular sort. (Rose 1996a, 319–20)

If new modes of subjectification have appeared today, then through which practices and in relation to which problematizations does this self emerge? In which locales is this regime of the self operating and according to which codes of truth? What techniques constitute this mode of subjecti-fication and in relation to which general strategies of government?

CONCLUSION

While Giddens has explored important issues regarding the relation-ship between transformed social conditions and late modern forms of self-hood, the kinds of questions that can be asked and/or answered within the context of his framework are limited. To think instead about the self as a particular historical and spatial relation—in effect to decenter the sub-ject—begins to open up possibilities for thinking about how current forms of self-identity emerge. The origin of what it means to be a self is not the rational, sovereign subject of liberal humanism. Indeed, this interiority of the self is a historical fiction. Decentering this subject—the unitary self-au-thor of social conditions—requires the thinking of self-identity as a ge-nealogical question. Meanings attached to being are embedded in specific practices through which individuals come to know themselves as particu-lar sorts of human beings. One advantage of this approach is that it ex-plicitly entails relations of power between authorities having the legitimacy to say what constitutes "personhood" and those who seek to understand themselves in that way. The effects of subjectification are not unitary—they may be empowering or disciplinary—thus account is given to the operation of discontinuous and simultaneous positionings of indi-viduals. In short, where Giddens's theoretical account is lacking, a ge-nealogical approach to subjectification can be used as a way into an investigation of the intricate relationship between self and the social where selves are both embodied and embedded.

In relation to the kind of self-identity being constructed by young women, this approach provides a framework within which to ask about the ways they construct a relation to the self that is embedded in everyday practices and techniques. How are the selves of young women produced and organized across a range of sites? In what ways does this relationship to the self operate as a form of governance? What are the sources of au-thority that are enfolded into the self to effect this relation? In what ways are young women and their lives problematized and therefore the object of normalization? What resistances are made in response to processes that seek to govern their lives? This set of questions and the assumptions underlying them are used as a broad framework for theorizing the relations between a decentered subject and the construction of identity defined by autonomy and created through the act of encountering choices about who to be and how to live.

In the following chapters, identity construction is located within a social context where young women have more choices and options available to them. The aim is to take into account the criticisms outlined here and suggest ways in which some of these shortcomings may be addressed. The main emphases that flow through this analysis are an engagement with Giddens's self-constituting, reflexive subject; his reliance on binary thinking; his neglect of the relation of difference and identity; and his under-theorization of the multiple embeddedness of the subject in the social—an issue that is apparent in the extent to which he constructs processes as internally referential. These points have implications for how we understand the ways young women are engaging with the choices available to them, how they position themselves within sets of relations, and how they enact a particular relation to the self.[7]

The narratives that the young women produced in the interviews are introduced in chapter 3 to establish the kinds of issues that were of central importance to them at the time they were interviewed. This discussion locates these young women within particular contexts, practices, and relations. The narratives are interpreted in terms of the kind of self that is being produced and provide some insight into the lives of the young women at the time of the interviews, specifically the ways they engaged with having to make choices about their futures. Through a close reading of the narratives, it is argued that a particular relation to the self is under construction—a self that is autonomous and self-constituting with an authentic interiority. This is not a free-floating self, however, but a self that is historically and culturally located within specific practices, knowledges, relations, and institutions, all of which contribute to the ways the self is constituted. The assumptions of reflexive modernization are employed in a reading of the narratives, but the reflexive, self-constituting subject is problematized in order to locate individualized narratives as indicative of a particular regime of subjectification.

NOTES

1. Giddens refers to "structuration" as the mutual dependency of human agency and social structures, where social structures both constrain and enable human action. Social structures provide the means necessary for human agency and at the same time are also the outcome of those actions.

2. Mouzelis means that the self becomes to the subject an object of strategies. This is apparent, for example, in attempts undertaken to maximize self-actualization through the use of self-help manuals or therapy where specific ideas are applied to the self as an object of knowledge. It is a relation, therefore, governed by instrumentality. Mouzelis maintains that operating from this position of instrumentality in the context of intimate relationships would likely prevent open, mutual disclosure and trust (1999, 92).

3. The notion of reflexivity as formulated by Giddens or Mouzelis, as well as the different forms of pure relationships discussed in their work, are ideal types. Therefore, it is important to acknowledge that these types more likely occur in combinations.

4. Furthermore, this construction ignores the relational aspects of reflexivity. For a useful discussion of an alternative to the privileging of this individualized, unitary, rational self, see Mason (2000).

5. For a useful development of a critique of this in relation to the changing dynamics of family life, refer to Smart and Neale (1999).

6. In relation to young women, the dominant discourse of femininity works to define what conduct is appropriate and to problematize conduct that falls outside this definition. For example, one of the young women recounted a scenario about her experience at a career guidance center. The male guidance counselor clearly advised against her desire to pursue a career in auto mechanics—a domain traditionally defined as masculine and, as such, deemed by him to be entirely unsuitable for a young woman.

7. For example, this relation to the self has implications for agency. This is apparent in the discussion of intimacy and politics in chapters 6 and 7, where a relation to the self that is defined by the ideal of autonomy offers the possibility for resistance in living out this relation in day-to-day life.

Chapter 3

The Self as Narrative

In order to have a sense of who we are, we have to have a notion of
how we have become, and of where we are going.
                                         Charles Taylor, *Sources of the Self*

To make known one's sense of self is not a process of expressing a self that
is already there, being merely in need of discovery, but a process in which
one's self-concept is achieved through the configuration of personal
events into a historical unity (Polkinghorne 1988, 150). This historical
unity is achieved via the representational conventions of narrative in
which individuals organize their lives and experiences and thereby make
sense of them (Coffey and Atkinson 1996, 68; Jervis 1998; Josselson 1995;
Sarup 1996). Through the acquisition of language, we learn to "give
voice—meaning—to our experience and to understand it according to
particular ways of thinking, particular discourses" such that the positions
that we identify with constitute our consciousness and structure our sense
of ourselves and our subjectivity (Weedon 1997, 32). Constructing a narrative as a form of self-representation takes into account the past in order to
understand the present, while also offering an anticipated outline of the
form the self will take in the future. Taylor explains, "I understand my
present action in the form of an 'and then': there was A (what I am), and
then I do B (what I project to become)" (1989, 47).

To construct a narrative of the self is to locate oneself along a trajectory
that gives a coherent shape to past, present, and future. This trajectory,
structured through the linearity of the narrative form, is the product of a
process in which the past is mined for experiences and events that can account for the present. The construction that is yielded by this process highlights what is significant or meaningful to that individual at the particular

point in time when he or she articulates a narrative of the self. Therefore, the narrative can vary across both time and space, and in this sense, one's self-narrative is never complete or stable. Events or experiences, interpreted retroactively, may acquire different meanings at different moments and across disparate spaces. Thus, the degree of emphasis and interest given to any event or experience is always subject to revision. Giddens relates these processes of interpretation to his theory of the reflexive self such that an individual's reflection on and interpretation of life experiences and events is constitutive of the self:

Self identity is not a distinctive trait, or even a collection of traits, possessed by the individual. It is *the self as reflexively understood by the person in terms of her or his own biography.* Identity here still presumes continuity across time and space: but self identity is such continuity as interpreted reflexively by the agent. (Giddens 1991, 53, emphasis in original)

Despite the impermanence inherent in any specific construction of the self, there is a coherence and continuity within accounts because the narrative form works to join and align experiences and events that are chosen for inclusion in the story, thereby smoothing out any inconsistencies. The criteria for either adding to or omitting events from one's narrative are not only dependent upon the degree of perceived significance of any particular experience, but the extent to which they contribute to this overall sense of continuity. There is a completeness to the story being told, but the totality of the narrative in its present form relies upon what is absent.

Expressions of self-identity are made possible by linguistic conventions—that is, grammatical, rhetorical, and narrative structures that constitute, or impose form upon, the subjects and objects that appear in the order of meaning (Polkinghorne 1988, 158). Because these linguistic forms organize meaning in this way, they have as much reality as the material objects of the physical realm and constitute an effective point of entry into the study of identity. According to Josselson:

The truths inherent in personal narrative issue from real positions in the world—the passions, desires, ideas, and conceptual systems that underlie life as lived. People's narratives are efforts to grapple with the confusion and complexity of the human condition. (Josselson 1995, 32)

These "real positions" refer to social contexts that are structured through relations of class, nation, race, ethnicity, gender, religion, and so forth. The individual actively engages in constructing a self through telling his or her story, but this is done in tension with the effect of such relations—relations that influence, and to a certain extent, circumscribe the narrative. Often, these social dynamics are embedded in the narrative, but the working-out of these dynamics and their interrelationships are not necessarily explicitly mentioned in the story. When telling our stories, we focus on what happened and what we did rather than the possible theoretical causes. Nevertheless, these issues are implied in the story (Sarup 1996, 15). Therefore, the dynamics of relations organized around understandings of race, class, and gender often provide the basis for ascribed statuses and the kinds of narratives that can be constructed. Giddens argues, however, that in late modernity the influence of these dynamics is weakening and the possibility for new kinds of narratives is emerging.

YOUNG WOMEN'S NARRATIVES

Understanding identity as a narrative—as telling stories about the self—is a useful strategy for opening up the concept of identity to investigation. One of the objectives of the interviews conducted with the young women was to have them position themselves within a narrative account of their lives in order to explore how they understood and lived their identities. This was achieved by initially having them locate themselves within a life trajectory defined by the most important decisions that currently faced them. This exercise required them to consider not only their current situation, but also their future direction. This part of the interview also raised issues about the kind of choices the young women viewed as significant and how in negotiating these choices a particular understanding of the self emerges.

In view of this production of self-identity, these narrative accounts of the self can be analyzed according to their constituent elements: content, form, and function.[1] First, the content of the narrative reveals the social actor's interpretation of key events and experiences in her life, which she uses to account for how and why she has arrived at the present moment and, furthermore, gives insight into the direction she projects her life to take. Second, the form of a narrative is relevant because its key features and defining characteristics are due in part to the mediating influence of values, social relations, processes, and knowledges. Analyzing narrative form reveals how narratives are embedded in sites and settings that are located within particular cultural and political contexts. Chase maintains that:

Narrative analysis is grounded in a particular theoretical commitment: understanding general social processes *requires* a focus on their embodiment in actual practises, that is, actual narratives. In other words, life stories themselves embody what we need to study: the relation between *this* instance of social action (*this* particular life story) and the social world the narrator shares with others; the ways in which culture marks, shapes and/or constrains this narrative; and the ways in which *this* narrator makes use of cultural resources and struggles with cultural constraints. (Chase 1995, 20, emphasis in original)

This embeddedness is about social and cultural influences that affect the kind of story that can be told.[2] Third, because narratives are not simply transparent representations of identities that exist independently of the telling, but instead are specific constructions that effect a particular understanding of the self, central to their analysis are questions about how the kind of narrative constructed operates to perform distinct functions. This means first, that the content and form of the narrative reveals a particular relation to the self and, second, that the way the self is constructed produces specific effects. Analyzing narratives from this perspective requires a consideration of the purposes served by constructing a particular story about the self.[3] As Polkinghorne argues, "On the basis of this constructed experience, we understand ourselves and the world, and we make decisions and plans regarding how we will act" (1988, 158).

This chapter draws upon these ideas in order to understand the kinds of narratives produced by the young women who were interviewed. The related concepts of choice, narrative, and ascribed statuses,[4] such as class and gender, are central to developing a strategy for theorizing the production of self-identity by these young women. This analysis establishes the point at which the young women were in planning their lives and indicates the nature of issues that were important to them. By examining content, form, and function, the narratives reveal how the act of choosing affects the production of a particular relation to the self. Using Giddens's theory of reflexive modernization, the narratives are examined as trajectories in which a consistent relation to the self is constructed—a self that is defined by the features of autonomy and authenticity. However, this reading is also analyzed as the production of a particular relation to the self or, as outlined in chapter 2, as the product of a specific regime of subjectification.[5]

LIFE PLANNING: PAST, PRESENT, AND FUTURE

For Giddens, the reflexively constituted narrative of the self is fundamentally about the negotiation of choices required in the making of life plans. He states that life plans are "something of an inevitable concomitant of post-traditional social forms" (1991, 85). These life plans provide the substance of the reflexively organized trajectory in which the self is positioned within an ordered narrative. However, because the life span is less constrained by external factors such as place, social relations, kinship, and traditional rites, it can no longer be taken for granted that external supports and guides will determine the form taken by these life trajectories. Narratives, as a result, become internally referential. The same processes that release the individual from constraints of tradition also intensify the experience of uncertainty and, therefore, choices about lifestyle options exist within the structure of life plans reflexively negotiated under conditions of increased doubt.

The concern here is with how one's relation to choice is configured within a narrative and how this configuration defines a particular kind of self. Asking the young women about their choices provided an effective point of entry into the ways they interpreted their lives and those experiences they identified as being significant to their self-definition.[6] In the following narratives, the young women formulate a variety of relationships to choice in their lives. The discussion of life plans started by asking them to talk about the most important decision they'd had to make in the past twelve months. Because all of the research sites were involved with the organization of young women's lives and future choices, it is not surprising that all of the young women were preoccupied at the time of the interview with their plans for careers, training, and education. The narratives produced reflect the young women's embeddedness within their relations with parents, teachers, career guidance counselors, family members, and friends, all of whom worked to shape the context within which the young women had to think about their future lives. Despite the varied interview locations, they all broadly shared the position of having to confront qualitatively similar decisions about which direction they wanted to pursue.

These decisions were clearly guided by an orientation to the future, and the trajectories they constructed followed a coherent line of progress from past, present, and into the future. However, the form of the trajectories and nature of the narratives varied, reflecting to a certain degree their different understandings of choice. For some of the young women, the narrative told was relatively straightforward; there was little conflict for them because the past, present, and future fit together in a highly consistent manner. One effect of this consistency was that the notion of choice constituted only a minimal aspect of their experience and wasn't as central to the narrative as it was in other cases. For instance, Emilia, who was seventeen years old, had just completed her first year of sixth form and was planning to continue her studies at a university. In her story, choice is less relevant than inevitability because she understands herself as being a particular kind of person:

Shelley: Did you feel any pressure trying to decide which A-levels to take?

Emilia: No, not really because I really didn't have that much choice because I've only ever been good at the arts so sciences weren't really an option anyway. I always knew which path I was going on. *(Emilia, seventeen years old, lower sixth form at Ripley School)*

Michelle, who was sixteen, had left school and was interviewed at a career guidance center. Her goal was to find a job working as a beauty therapist and eventually set up her own business. Like Emilia, her narrative is structured by consistency because her decision to leave school wasn't constructed by her as a choice, but as an inevitability. One effect of consistency within a narrative is that it produces and retains a particular relation to the self. Emilia and Michelle explain their decisions within the context of understanding themselves to be certain kinds of people: people who advance to a university or people who aim to leave school at age sixteen:

Shelley: What was the most important decision you had to make in the past twelve months?
Michelle: What to do after leaving school.
Shelley: At what point did you decide to leave school?
Michelle: All my life. *(Michelle, sixteen years old, career guidance center)*

Consistency such as this contributes to the linearity that the narrative form tends to assume, but in many instances, this must be more actively achieved by the actor in the act of construction. Life events and experiences are not automatically consistent, and many of the narratives told by these young women involved a negotiation of inconsistencies, interruptions, and conflicts in their lives in order for linearity to be accomplished, thus preserving a particular understanding of one's self—a self that, once established, guides how choices are made. Being aware of the existence of different potential trajectories meant that for some young women creating self-narratives involved locating themselves in relation to those other available options. Choices were then evaluated for the effect they would have on the kind of self being constructed and the inconsistency this would produce. Therefore, life planning wasn't simply a case of indiscriminately making a choice among different options. Some options were understood as being less consistent with the self they were creating.

Constructing a self is about managing these kinds of contradictions. For example, in some cases, inconsistencies emerged out of the tension between, on the one hand, an understanding of what one's own life chances were likely to be and, on the other hand, the potential to subvert these expectations. Here, consistency is defined by what one feels able to choose and what one believes ought to be available to "someone like me." The idea of "what is meant to happen to someone like me" refers to the influence trajectories that are in many ways ascribed and often tied to the influence of tradition, norms, routines, and customs defined via family background, ethnicity, or gender.

This process is evident in Georgia's narrative. For Georgia, an eighteen-year-old who was completing a General National Vocational Qualification (GNVQ) in health and social care, her goal of going to a university is consistent with the way that she views her past and present, but it contradicts what her family anticipated. Being able to choose to go to a university was perceived as an option that she would not have available to her because nobody else in her family had pursued higher education. Her decision in the past twelve months to go to a university is seen by her as a choice, but one that is partly defined by its inconsistency with what was expected to be possible. The significance of this choice for Georgia lies in this tension between consistency and inconsistency—consistency with the self she wishes to be and its inconsistency with what someone from her background would normally do:

Shelley: Did you feel any pressure trying to decide which university to go to?

Georgia: No. Not really. It was never really a choice of whether to go to university or get a job. I've always wanted to go to university. It hasn't been my Mum or Dad pressuring me. They would have stood by whatever I wanted to do but I'm the first person in the family to have got this far ever so they're all really proud of me saying, "You're going to go aren't you?" I've always wanted to go but even if I didn't I think I might have gone just because they'd be so proud of me and I'd really be letting them down. (*Georgia, eighteen years old, completing a GNVQ at Pearson College*)

Negotiating inconsistency was also an integral part of Joanne's narrative. She was nineteen years old and had a two-year-old son. At the time of the interview, she was employed as a receptionist in a photography studio. She accounted for what she perceived as her current level of success as due in part to the confidence she developed during her participation in a youth-skills program. In her narrative, she revealed that she is violating the trajectory that as a single mother she is "meant to be on." This inconsistency between an ascribed narrative and one in which she can make choices is an important part of the self she is constructing:

Shelley: Why did you end up getting involved with YouthWorks? What was there about it that you thought was good for you?

Joanne: When I fell pregnant with Jason a lot of people said, "She's not going to do nothing with her life. Now she's ruined her life." But it was like I wanted to get more grades so I've got more things to aim for so I thought I might as well do this. I'm not doing anything else and I should try my hardest at it and it did work out because I got a job through it. (*Joanne, nineteen years old, YouthWorks program*)

Joanne acknowledges that she has escaped a trajectory that, due to her being a young, single mother, was expected. For her, escaping this fate was a matter of choosing to get involved in the life-skills program. Her awareness of the inconsistency in her narrative is also apparent when she compares herself to her cousins who don't have any children and work in a packing factory, which, she says, is what *she should be* doing instead of the relatively higher status of working in a photography studio. Joanne's comments draw attention to other narratives that preexist the individual who comes to be positioned within them and influence the positioning of the self within one's own narrative. Her awareness of the structure of the single-mother narrative that is expected of her is derived from the way she is positioned by others, for example, through media representations. Joanne knows that her narrative involves a conscious contradiction of what is expected from someone who is young, female, and a single mother:

I'm on family credit now because I'm working which is a big relief. I used to hate queuing up for income support and you go home and it's always on TV that young women get pregnant to get money and to get houses where I've done none of that because I've got a job so I'm not on income support and I haven't got my own house. I'm living with my parents so I haven't done none of what they're saying young women are doing.

For Joanne, the violation of an anticipated trajectory produced a positive outcome; however, for Louise, also a single mother, the altering of her anticipated trajectory was experienced as a loss of her sense of self. Louise was twenty-one years old and had a four-year-old daughter whom she had lost custody of because she was addicted to heroin. At the time of the interview, she was living in a hostel, having recently decided to leave an extremely abusive relationship. The decision to leave this man, who introduced her to heroin, and to overcome her addiction were the most important decisions she had made in the past twelve months. Louise began the interview by locating herself in relation to what was once expected for "someone like her" by emphasizing that she was from a good background and wasn't a "snob or anything" but wasn't "hostel material." Reflecting on the past when she had "everything going for her," she constructed a story about having her life "perfectly sorted." Through her introduction to heroin and the treatment of an abusive boyfriend, however, she told a story about "losing everything"—her good job, a flat furnished with nice belongings, her savings, her health, and most importantly, her daughter:

Louise: I still can't believe that I'm living here and everything. It's a total shock. Let's put it this way, if someone would have said to me when I was 18 that when you're 21 you're going to be a heroin addict and have your daughter taken away and be a victim of domestic violence and be completely mentally tortured for a year I would never had believed them.

Shelley: If you look ahead what do you see yourself doing in a year from now?

Louise: I'll have a job, a nice home. I'll be with my daughter. (*Louise, twenty-one years old, YouthWorks program*)

In her story, Louise reorients herself to a future that is much happier than the recent past, but more significantly, it is a future that is more consistent with where she has come from (i.e., "not hostel material"). For her, this is a return to where she feels she should have been if she hadn't met her ex-boyfriend. It is a return to where she is *really meant to be* because in her view, her current trajectory was never something she would have chosen for herself. If it weren't for meeting him, she says, she would now be in her first year at a university, still have her job at a pub, have a nice boyfriend, and still have her daughter, who would be starting Catholic school. Louise has left a trajectory that would have been characterized by choice and entered one in which choice enters only marginally into her narrative because of addiction. The inconsistency between these two different trajectories and the implications for her relation to choice are readily apparent. Louise states:

The next year is most important because a lot of it is going to depend on getting off drugs. You can't do anything when you're an addict. You know you can't do anything because you are a drug addict. Especially with heroin addiction because you wake up one day and you've not got it and you want it. You wake up one day and need it because you are sick. It's like a disease in a way almost. If you've not got it you can't even get up and do anything.

Narratives work as a medium through which to construct and preserve a relation to the self, and this relation then influences how choices are interpreted. How one negotiates consistency or inconsistency in life events is significant because this negotiation works to establish and maintain a particular relation to the self. Choices are engaged with via an understanding of the self as being a particular sort of person. This understanding is influenced by ascribed statuses, but not determined by them. Indeed, there is a tension between the self that is chosen and the self that is conceivable—often the result of external expectations, material circumstances, traditions, and so forth.

The most important decisions these young women identified as having to make also involved preserving an identity particularly with regard to the self they had yet to become. When constructing their narratives, many of the young women spoke of having to reject options that would place them on alternate trajectories. Again, this indicated they were aware that their lives could potentially follow a range of different paths. The criteria for accepting or rejecting these options depended on whether they were consistent with the kind of self under production. Katy, an eighteen-year-old who was just completing her first year of sixth form, said that she decided to stay on at school and do A-levels so that she could go to a university, a goal that is consistent with her desire to have a career. Her choice to do this was informed by the other option she perceived as available—an option that if taken would constitute an inconsistency with the way she sees herself:

Shelley: Why did you decide to stay on at school?
Katy: I think partly because I've seen other people like my Aunties who don't have jobs and they're not educated and I don't want to go the same

route and be unhappy and be a housewife and bring up kids. I want a career. *(Katy, eighteen years old, completing lower sixth form at Ripley School)*

Sasha, a seventeen-year-old who was also finishing her first year of sixth form, said that the most important decision she had to make in the past twelve months was to refuse her consent to an arranged marriage. This decision was heavily influenced by the limits it would put on her life—primarily that it would prevent her from pursuing and achieving the future she was constructing for herself. To accept the conditions of an arranged marriage, which would be consistent with an ascribed trajectory, would be highly inconsistent with the trajectory she is choosing for herself:

Shelley: What were the main factors that you found were influencing you?

Sasha: I didn't really like his father. Well … they're quite a strict family. They're quite strict about what they let women do. They don't really want you to work—not to study. You know, be home based and stuff and I'm not really like that at all. I want a career and stuff … It wasn't like they were going to get me married straight away. It's just a case of saying, "yes in the near future" but I thought "no." It's just that what I want to do in the near future would clash with that. *(Sasha, seventeen years old, completing lower sixth form at Ripley School)*

Sasha talked at length about marriage and the conflict the expectations stemming from her embeddedness in the Asian community caused for her. This conflict and the way it affected her choices formed an important part of her narrative, which to some extent was about forging an identity that was made possible by having choices available—specifically being able to say no to the marriage even though it was expected.

Other young women faced equally difficult choices. Lauren, a nineteen-year-old who was looking for employment, said that the most important decision she had to make in the past year was to have an abortion. Lauren reflected on her experience and constructed her choice to have the abortion as a difficult one, but one that was made in order to carry on with her goals and aspirations for the self-identity she is constructing. Her anticipation of the future was used as the basis for making this decision:

Shelley: What factors did you take into account when you were trying to decide?

Lauren: I would be restricted in terms of the jobs I could go for because of the hours. I would feel bad leaving my baby with my Mum all the time and sorting out the money. I'd have to go for a job which would cover everything. My Mum is on benefits so obviously a lot of money would be going on the baby and I couldn't really give that baby the home I'd wanted to or the life I want so I considered that. I never wanted a child young. My Mum did. She had me when she was twenty but she had an abortion at sixteen as well which her parents forced her into. She knew what kind of stress I was under but in the end it all worked out for the best. Otherwise I wouldn't have been able to travel or anything like that as much as I wanted to. I'm not knocking single mothers, which I would have been, but it's just not for me yet. It was a very hard decision. *(Lauren, nineteen years old, career guidance center)*

Lauren uses her mother as a point of reference to understand her own relationship to choice and acknowledges that, unlike her mother, she has choices available to her. Her decision to have the abortion is formulated through a particular relation to her self—a self that will be able to exercise autonomy.

ORIENTATIONS TO THE FUTURE

Once the young women had located themselves within a narrative based on the decisions they had recently faced, they were then asked to look ahead to the near future and talk about what they saw themselves doing in one year. For nearly all of them, this projection was defined by education or career goals.[7] In general, they constructed a future oriented to goals that they had already begun to work toward. The decisions they had already made—to leave school, to do A-levels, or to enroll in a training scheme, for instance—had begun to lead them down different routes, and the choices available to them and kinds of decisions they faced reflected this. The discussions begin to reveal what kinds of things these young women wanted from life and, quite significantly, what things they thought they could get. These discussions also reveal how their relationship to choices affects the production of their narratives.

Assembling the future was done with a degree of uncertainty, and a considerable amount of tension surrounded these deliberations. Indeed, it is interesting to note that in some cases uncertainty about the future was not due to a lack of choices, but was instead exacerbated by external pressure to engage actively with the range of choices available. All of the young women, regardless of the trajectory they were on, experienced the pressures associated with having to choose. There is somewhat of a normative element emerging in these narratives because making choices is not experienced as value-free. The search is for the right decision and for doing the right thing:

Shelley: Are you concerned right now about making the wrong decision?

Anna: Yeah because it just makes you realise that it's not a game anymore. It's not just like GCSEs. You're older and it's going to affect you for a long time. It's quite frightening. *(Anna, eighteen years old, completing lower sixth form at Ripley School)*

Shelley: What is the most important decision you'll have to make in the next year?

Morgan: The problem of a job. You know like do I go back onto training? Do I go
         for a proper job? Because if you go on training you're working toward
         something aren't you? But my Mom will be giving me grief, saying,
         "But it's only a low wage," so do I go against her wishes and go back on
         training or do I go for a proper job and make her happy? Which will
         make me unhappy really because it's going to be a no hope job isn't it?
         It's going to go nowhere. *(Morgan, eighteen years old, career guidance
         center)*

The final point on their life trajectories that the young women were
asked to describe was what their lives would be like in five years. Some
difficulty was apparent in making this projection because the activities
they were involved in at the time of the interview did not so clearly relate
to that point in the future. Nevertheless, the future was constructed in a
coherent relation to the things they had planned for the next year and was
primarily defined in relation to their career goals. The young women who
were planning to continue their education saw the successful completion
of their qualifications and the beginning of their careers having transpired
in five years. This was also true for the young women who were in training programs or aiming to get into a training program.

Whether their trajectory followed a path through a university into a
profession or through leaving school at sixteen years old to enter the
workplace as soon as possible, the narratives were implicitly about self-
improvement, the pursuit of ambition, and the realization of aspirations.
In the following excerpts, the young women discuss the goal of progress-
ing in their chosen educational and career paths. These narratives function
as stories about achievement and success, thereby supporting a particular
relation to the self—a self founded in the normative expectation of self-
reliance and self-efficacy:

Shelley: What do you see yourself doing in five years from now?

Laura: Oh God! Hopefully, fingers crossed, I'll have my law degree and be
          working as a solicitor in somebody's office and making lots of money!
          But it's not important. Just making a living and doing well. *(Laura,
          seventeen years old, completing lower sixth form, Greenwood School)*

Lianne: Hopefully a manager of a shop or just a little shop of my own. I'd like to
          do something in cars or motorbikes. Retail manager or something like
          that just so that I could have some control over someone else and not be
          doing what everyone else is telling me to do for the rest of my life.
          *(Lianne, sixteen years old, inquiring about training programs at the career
          guidance center)*

Georgia: I'll be twenty-three … If I do well in my psychology degree I would love
         to carry on and do another course to become a psychologist. *(Georgia,
         eighteen years old, completing a GNVQ at Pearson College)*

When these young women spoke about their pursuit of education and
career goals, they revealed that achievement and independence were of

central importance to their self-definitions. These values were apparent in the majority of accounts, regardless of whether the route to their goal was via a university, vocational training programs, or work experience. Central themes in their accounts were about the importance of job satisfaction and progression informed by the underlying value of independence:

Victoria: I'd rather do office work because I want to do something with good prospects that can get you far. Yeah you have to be able to move up in it. I wouldn't like to be a receptionist because in a way I see you as being a slave doing something for other people and you just stay there all the time and you never move up. *(Victoria, seventeen years old, inquiring about training programs at the career guidance center)*

Sarah: If I failed all my exams and didn't have anything else I could do then maybe I would consider working for my Dad. I mean I don't think like that but my best friend is just so laid back that she'd just go work for her Dad but I want to get more. *(Sara, sixteen years old, completing lower sixth form at Greenwood School)*

In these discussions, education, training, achieving qualifications, and planning for careers continued to form the main part of the narrative, but marriage, having children, and thoughts about settling down also began to emerge. Considerations of the impact of marriage on the identities they were creating revealed that generally getting married and having children were regarded as possible choices, but not something they would choose to do. It was perceived that this would prevent them from advancing in their trajectory, again highlighting the centrality of independence and autonomy to their construction of the self:

Shelley: Where do you see yourself in five years?

Shayne: Oh hopefully I'll have a degree by then! Hopefully. I'd really like to get a degree—do my A-levels and get a degree. Not settle down but pursue my career then possibly settle down after that. *(Shayne, seventeen years old, completing lower sixth form at Ripley School)*

Lucy: I'll be twenty-two. I have no idea. No idea. Hopefully ... well it depends on going to university and getting a job or something. I won't be married then hopefully. *(Lucy, seventeen years old, completing lower sixth form at Greenwood School)*

Claire: I don't want to get settled down. Not in five years. I want to have my life to do what I want to do then say mid-twenties settle down and get a house. I want my career and to enjoy my life. *(Claire, sixteen years old, looking for a job at the career guidance center)*

There were exceptions to this skeptical evaluation of the prospect of settling down in five years, though. Joanne, a nineteen-year-old single mother with a two-year-old son, Jason, hoped to continue to work her way up into a higher position in her part-time job so that she would be working full-time once her son was in school. Marriage entered into her narrative not as something incongruous with her goal of progression, but as the only way she could perceive getting her own home, something that was a very important component of her goal of achieving independence. The desire for independence constituted a central part of most of the young women's narratives, but whereas many of them interpreted marriage and having children as a restriction to their independence, Joanne saw her independence as contingent upon finding a partner whom she could depend on for financial support:

I'd like to have my own house I think. It might be expensive and I wouldn't be able to give Jason as much as he does want but I don't want to live on a council estate [low-income government-subsidized housing] on my own. I want my own house and the only way I can do that is to meet someone who loves us both and can support us. So I think I'm going to be at home for a few more years yet which I don't mind but it would be nice to have a bit more independence of my own. *(Joanne, nineteen years old, YouthWorks program)*

If marriage was discussed by most of the young women with ambivalence because of the impact it might have on their independence and building a career, then this was particularly true of the young Asian women interviewed. In these examples, the ascribed trajectory of getting married and having children is derived not only from the embeddedness of young women in gender relations, but also from the intersection of their gender with expectations held by their ethnic community. These young women spoke of the pressure they were under to marry at an early age, and they were all resisting it. Prea, who was nineteen years old, said she wouldn't mind settling down, which for her meant living with a boyfriend before deciding to marry. She admitted that this "won't happen because my parents would just go mental if I said I was going to live with my boyfriend to see what it was like." Prea located the origin of their attitudes within the Asian community's belief system. Katy, a seventeen-year-old and also Asian, was experiencing significant pressure from her mother to pursue both a university education and marriage:

Shelley: Do you see anything else happening in 5 years time?

Katy: Probably marriage. That will be another burden that my Mum is putting on top of me. To get married and have kids.

Shelley: Is that something that you want?

Katy: Well I've told her in maybe seven years and then another seven years after to have kids but she wants it now. My sister has already got married and now she's talking about having children. I don't think I want to do the same. *(Katy, eighteen years old, completing lower sixth form at Ripley School)*

The challenge of incorporating intimate relationships, child rearing, and domesticity into narratives built on independence and individualization is further explored in chapter 6.

In summary, the content of these self-narratives reveals that planning for further education, training, and careers is of particular importance to the young women interviewed. Constructing these narratives entailed a navigation of a range of options that were understood in relation to the kind of story they were trying to coherently create and sustain. The form of the narratives reveals that choices and decisions were made in tension with both the desire to preserve a particular relation to the self, a self that is free to choose, and with the influence of ascribed trajectories—that is, the knowledge of "what a person like me" is able to do or should do. These narratives functioned to preserve a particular relation to the self— the self as autonomous, independent, and goal-oriented. Once established, this relation operated to inform the negotiation of further choices and decisions.

UNCERTAINTY, DOUBT, AND FATEFUL MOMENTS

As alternatives for individual life plans expand in late modernity, more possibilities are created, but according to Giddens, possibility also translates into uncertainty. The individual must choose a lifestyle and assemble a life plan, but without knowing for sure if one plan is better than any of the other possible ones. This pervasive experience of uncertainty, Giddens argues, is manifest in radical doubt, which filters into most aspects of day-to-day life in late modernity (1991, 181). In response, individuals attempt to colonize[8] the future and these attempts become key moments in creating certainty within conditions of contingency.

As it becomes more difficult to see the future as something that will unfold according to fate or predetermination, this system increasingly comes to be governed by a belief in control of the environment at both the individual and collective levels. For Giddens, modernity is "a system geared to the domination of nature and the reflexive making of history" (Giddens 1991, 107). Confronting the future as an open realm that must be colonized, individuals are required to calculate risks as a central part of the construction of life plans. Giddens argues that "the more the individual seeks reflexively to forge a self-identity, the more he or she will be aware that current practices shape future outcomes ... assessment of risk—of the balance of risk and opportunity—becomes the core element of the personal colonising of future domains" (1991, 129).

Individuals are for the most part able to unproblematically engage in a project of the self because they are able to "bracket out" uncertainty through basic trust. Here, Giddens relies on Goffman's (1971) concept of the *Umwelt*—defined as a core of accomplished normalcy with which individuals and groups surround themselves (Giddens 1991, 127). Trust works to secure the ongoing engagement with daily life in such a way that the future, although uncertain and characterized by risk, is experienced as manageable and subject to individual control through the calculation of risk and the concomitant assessment of different life plans and courses of action. Modern anxiety is fundamentally a product of risk calculations and having to screen out contingencies so that life planning can be made a manageable task.

Although the pervasive nature of risk does not lead to a complete breakdown in the construction of coherent identities, Giddens does suggest that at certain moments the experience of risk and uncertainty is intensified and the "protective cocoon" that trust provides to the individual breaks down. It is during these fateful moments that the effects of the loss of external anchoring points are intensified and ontological security comes under strain. During these moments, individuals are called upon to make crucial decisions that carry great consequence for their future. Examples of such moments include: taking examinations, deciding to get married or divorced, deciding on a course of study, going on strike, giving up one job in favor of another, hearing the result of a medical test, losing a large amount of money in a gamble, or winning a large amount of money in a lottery (Giddens 1991, 113). It is during these moments that individuals become particularly aware of the consequences of their decisions, knowing that they "must launch into something new, knowing that a decision made, or a specific course of action followed, has an irreversible quality" (Giddens 1991, 114).

Many of the decisions faced by these young women could be said to constitute such fateful moments. Despite having relatively well-defined goals and trajectories to which they oriented their decisions, they were experiencing some apprehension about choosing a path for their lives. For example, there was some anxiety about not achieving the goals described in their narratives and not knowing what outcomes would be the result of their planning. Uncertainty was expressed in a variety of ways. Lucinda, a seventeen-year-old completing lower sixth form at a private school, expressed concern about the potential for her goals to be thwarted and, similarly, Shannon expressed worries about the possibility that she wouldn't be able to get a job despite the effort she is putting into gaining qualifications at college and university.[9] Here, the uncertainty is about not being sure that a self defined by independence and autonomy will be enough to mitigate external forces:

Shelley: What might prevent you from achieving your future goals?

Lucinda: There'll probably be loads of things I expect. Maybe money could. I might be able to not afford to live or something. You've got to think of everything. You can't just sort of ... you've got to be able to cover yourself. *(Lucinda, seventeen years old, completing lower sixth form at Greenwood School)*

Shannon: I don't think anything is under anyone's control with things changing so fast. I think it is pretty much under your control because you can say what you want to go into but at the end of the day you can't say if you're guaranteed a job within a hospital or guaranteed a nursing job. That is a factor. You're not guaranteed a job which is a hard thing. *(Shannon, eighteen years old, completing a GNVQ at Pearson College)*

Ultimately, mitigation of uncertainty requires a strategy if the individual is to create a particular relation to the self, especially one defined by autonomy. This idea of having to cover oneself within a context of uncertainty was central to almost all of the narratives constructed. This meant developing ways to diminish uncertainty where it was supposed to be made manageable through the effect of individual efforts. One of the ways of seeking to do this was through placing a belief in self-efficacy, often expressed in the form of a desire to take control of one's life. This was a highly individualized solution in which responsibility for success or failure was placed solely on the individual. The value of achieving independence emerged again, expressed here as a belief in the autonomous self:

Shelley: Do you think the future is under your control?

Lucinda: Well, I wouldn't leave it to anyone else! I don't like relying on other people anyway. I think if you're going to do something it's better to do it yourself. You're going to get it done then. *(Lucinda, seventeen years old, completing lower sixth form at Greenwood School)*

Lynn: I wanted to get into nursing so I arranged my courses. I've got the grades which I'm going to deserve at the end of the course so I'm in control of most of my life and how well I do. *(Lynn, eighteen years old, completing a GNVQ at Pearson College)*

Shayne: Oh to a certain extent. I mean you've got self control over yourself if you're out to get what you want then definitely you can do it. If you have strong enough will but sometimes you tend to find that some people are just too reliant upon others, not independent enough and that is what stops them I think. *(Shayne, seventeen years old, completing lower sixth form at Ripley School)*

For a self defined through autonomy, the basis for believing that the future is under one's control is the belief that individual effort, attitude, and action can bring about a desired outcome in one's life. Within these narratives, seizing control of one's life was not only regarded as possible by making one's own decisions and working hard, but was also seen as one's responsibility if the narrative being told was to transpire. The pursuit of education and training constituted one of the most frequently used strategies for mitigating uncertainty. This strategy, based on individual effort, was seen to prevent a narrowing of future options and bring into being conditions in which one's potential could be maximized.

Shannon: This course has given me a qualification to go on to do further training so that's why I really want to do the training, to get further on in life instead of stopping here.

Shelley: What do you think would happen if you stopped?

Shannon: Honestly I think if I stopped where I am now I could go into a job. I
           could get a job but it wouldn't be what I want to do and it wouldn't be
           very high paid. I could stop now and go into auxiliary nursing. At the
           end of the day though it's really being a slave to other people and
           beneath people like the matron. I want to be in nursing rather than in
           the lower, not class, I don't mean anything like that. It's just a lower job
           where you can't do as much as the nurses do. *(Shannon, eighteen years
           old, completing a GNVQ at Pearson College)*

Shelley: What do you think would happen to you if you didn't continue with
           your education from this point on?

Sarah: I think there would be less chance of me doing what I want to do. I
           don't think that I would get a proper job like a lawyer or something
           like that. I think I'd just ... I might be able to ... well I don't know if I
           could get a job which means I wouldn't get any money and I'd
           probably just end up living at home. *(Sarah, sixteen years old, completing
           lower sixth form at Greenwood School)*

While the future presented an element of the unknown, proliferation of
choice provided a source of confidence that the future, although in some
ways out of one's control, could still be successfully shaped according to
what one wanted. Educational options, for example, included a variety of
different routes to gaining qualifications, and this gave some assurance
that if one route became obstructed then another way forward would be
possible. Therefore, the notion of having choices available enters into a
map of the future defined by divergent paths upon which contingency
plans could be made:

Shelley: What if you don't achieve your goal of getting the grades to go to
           university?

Katy: If that did happen I think I would leave school and do some more A
           levels at college and then start again and hopefully do my best or if not I
           can do another course that's equivalent of A-levels and then go on to
           university. *(Katy, eighteen years old, completing lower sixth form at Ripley
           School)*

Nikky: It's like in a way all blocked together like you've got A-levels, then
           university and a job. With each thing, I know what I want from each of
           them so I just take it as it comes basically. You know if things don't go
           right then take another path and go do something else. *(Nikky, sixteen
           years old, completing lower sixth form at Greenwood School)*

Joanne: I'm going to see how this job goes because I can upgrade myself in this.
           Like if I ever wanted to do photography then I could go to college and
           I'd have a good chance at getting into photography so I can higher
           myself up in this job really. So I'm going to see how this job goes and if
           it doesn't go well and I end up leaving for some reason I can go back to
           college and train for something different. *(Joanne, nineteen years old,
           participant in a YouthWorks program)*

The construction of a narrative about the autonomous self functions throughout these discussions to mitigate uncertainty with the effect of re-inforcing that particular relation to the self. The uncertainty that entered into these narratives was also accompanied by an understanding that choices do exist; therefore, if one course of action were to become thwarted, then the individual should be able to choose another path. Choice becomes normative in the sense that everyone is free to choose and so to do other-wise constitutes a personal failing. In the next section, it is apparent that the narrative also functions to support this relation to the self as an essen-tial interiority.

AUTHENTICITY

In many of the accounts produced by the young women about their de-cisions and life plans, the structuring of the narrative was held consistent by the principle of authenticity, which acted as a moral thread running throughout their accounts. The value of being true to oneself provided an underlying resource that could be drawn upon when real or potential con-flicts and contradictions needed to be resolved. Indeed, the notion of there being an authentic self was employed as a strategy for confronting situ-ations in which a choice had to be made in order to resolve a dilemma. Giddens links the ideal of authenticity to the project of the self by sug-gesting that in late modernity the goal of self-actualization depends upon being able to transcend barriers to acting authentically. Self-knowledge, therefore, is the key to disentangling the true from the false self:

To be true to oneself means finding oneself, but since this is an active process of self-construction it has to be informed by overall goals—those of becoming free from dependencies and achieving fulfilment. Fulfilment is in some part a moral phenomenon, because it means fostering a sense that one is a "good," a "worthy person." (Giddens 1991, 79)

In the interviews, to speak and act from a position of authenticity was perceived as a way of safeguarding the "real self" from external pressures. A series of vignettes about young women facing crucial decisions were used as a way of exploring the perceptions of how choices and conflicting demands should be navigated. In these vignettes, tension is created by the location of the central character at the heart of a problem in which there is no clearly defined "right" decision, but a dilemma that definitely cannot be disregarded. In response to this ambiguity, the notion of authenticity was invoked as a way in which to ground and justify decisions.[10] This au-thenticity is about inhabiting one's self in such a way that allows for indi-vidualized action and negotiation of dilemmas. Although this particular vignette is in substance about one's relation to others, it was also read as implicitly being about one's relation to oneself. In the following responses, an emphasis is placed on relying upon one's "real self"—that beneath the person Catherine is trying to be there is in fact an authenticity constituting her essential interiority:

Alice: She should be herself because it will just carry on forever and she'll forget who her *actual self is.* If she stood up to them and was herself then they'd admire her more in the end anyway for having her own opinion. *(Alice, seventeen years old, completing lower sixth form at Greenwood School)*

Lynn: I think she should *just be herself.* Try to as much as she can to be herself because there's no point hiding behind a mask because you just get confused about your feelings completely. It's like being two different people really. *(Lynn, eighteen years old, completing a GNVQ at Pearson College)*

Lianne: Instead of trying to fit in and be like everyone else she should be herself because then no one is going to know you for *the real you* and they're just going to think that you are fake and stupid. *(Lianne, sixteen years old, inquiring about training programs at the career guidance center)*

Here, authenticity provided a moral grounding for the project of the self. For Giddens, the grounding of the project of the self in a morality of authenticity contains the potential for a remoralizing of day-to-day life. Reflexive identities, he suggests, may provide the basis for the development of life politics centered on the rights of self-actualization and issues pertaining to self-identity (Giddens 1991, 226). Questions about the political efficacy of these narratives certainly arise in relation to the project of feminism. The suggestion that a politics of self-actualization can arise out of the project of the self is further explored in chapter 7, in relation to the nonidentification of young women with second-wave feminism and the possibility that self-actualization can be conceived as politically effectual.

DETRADITIONALIZED NARRATIVES?

To what extent are these narratives indicative of the processes of detraditionalization that theorists of reflexive modernization claim result in individualized biographies? Returning to the three primary elements of narrative—content, form, and function—how can these narratives be assessed? The content of the narratives reveals what issues were of central relevance to their identity, how the young women felt about their choices, and how these choices are implicated in the process of building a particular self-identity. For them, the act of making choices initiated a particular trajectory for which they felt individually responsible. Indeed, a self defined by self-efficacy, individualized effort, and moral accountability emerged in these narratives, and the act of choosing was structured within the narrative trajectory by continuity and coherence with the effect of maintaining this particular relation to the self.

The form the narratives took reflected how choices were interpreted in view of both the kind of self these young women were constructing and the influence of ascribed statuses. An analysis of the narratives shows that these young women understood their relationship to their choices in particular ways. That is to say, that the relationship between the self and choice is not as unitary as Giddens suggests. Not everyone understands his or her relationship to choice in the same way. For some, choice was less relevant due to a sense of life events being inevitable. For others, choice was interpreted as extraordinary, inconsistent, or inherently limited. These differences arise in a process in which external references work to influence an understanding of specific life events and shape the kind of story that can be told. Significantly, the meaning of choice emerged in a relation to ascribed trajectories such that there was a tension between the choices one has, the choices one would like to have, and the choices that one is meant to have—a relation circumscribed by the effects of social relations such as gender, ethnicity, class, and race.

It has been argued here that these narratives reveal that choice is central to the emergence of a particular understanding of the self, but if we were to ask questions about origins of such a self-understanding or how this particular relation emerges, as opposed to other possible ones, then Giddens's framework becomes problematic. These narratives reveal that in constructing a story about their choices, the young women developed a particular relation to the self. The telling of these narratives functions to create and preserve this relation by acting as a device through which these young women can understand their experiences and order them in particular ways. As argued in chapter 2, this kind of subject is consistent with the instrumental, self-authoring subject implied in theories of reflexive modernization, but is the autonomous, choosing self characterized by an essential and authentic interiority itself the origin of this particular self-understanding? Clearly, this suggestion is problematic in this analysis, where it is evident that the young women's ideas of the kind of person they are is organized to a certain extent by external relations and processes within which they are embedded.

Giddens's theory of the subject as the reflexive self-constituting individual is grounded in the Enlightenment tradition of constructing the modern world as ultimately knowable and therefore manageable, but theorizing a cognitive and rational basis for subjectivity has been thoroughly attacked by both post-humanist and feminist critiques. The central premise upon which feminist critiques of the liberal-humanist tradition are based is the assumption that subjectivity is the coherent and authentic source of meaning. This individual is fundamentally a unified and knowing subject with a fixed inner essence—rational consciousness. Feminist critiques of this construction have shown that theories of subjectivity within the liberal humanist tradition have been gender-blind; therefore, the Cartesian subject is not only a masculine construct, but one that represents the historically privileged position occupied by men (Bordo 1993, 215–44; Flax 1990; Weedon 1997). The feminine has been either: an impossible representation as argued by Irigaray, "the sex which is not one"; or, as argued by Beauvoir, the feminine has been masculinity's "Other," the term against which masculine identity has differentiated itself (Butler 1990, 11).

How might the construction of an autonomous, coherent, and self-authoring self be interpreted, while avoiding the problems of positing a cognitive basis of the self? The discussion in chapter 2 of Rose's assertion that "selves are invented" requires that an analysis of the narratives told by these young women proceed from a different set of questions (Rose 1998). When these narratives are read as being indicative of the late modern regime of the self, what is it that they reveal about that regime? The content, form, and function of the narratives produced are consistent with Rose's argument that the contemporary self is constituted as "coherent, bounded, individualised, intentional, the locus of thought, action and belief, the origin of its own actions, the beneficiary of a unique biography" (1998, 3). Rejecting a humanist theory of the subject means that interpreting this relation to the self involves locating the origins of this understanding, not within the individual, but within technologies of the self—the choices that these young women spoke about are embedded in multiple sets of relations and practices.[11]

This embeddedness constitutes the conditions for a particular understanding of the self that Giddens does not fully address. An interpretation of these young women's subjectification involves examining how they have come to relate to themselves and others as subjects of certain types, particularly here in relation to how their choices are organized within schools, guidance centers, youth programs, and so forth. The type of self that is invented in these narratives arises out of the operations of problematizations, technologies, and authorities that organize the practices within which young women's choices are embedded. These result in specific ideals of personhood that are linked into a wider social, moral, and political context.

PROBLEMATIZATIONS

The problematization of conduct serves as a point of reference for the type of person one should be and is thereby central to shaping the relation to the self as being a certain type of person. Rose (1998) argues that it is in mundane practices where conduct becomes problematic to others and the self, and through these problematizations that understandings of what constitutes normality arises in relation to that which is deemed undesirable and unacceptable. Within the narratives produced by these young women, the problem of not being in control of one's life was a recurrent theme. The relationship to choice was always constructed in relation to an understanding of what actions and situations would be undesirable. This reflects the endorsement of particular values that indicate what constitutes a proper goal or course of action. Central to understandings of the undesirable was the emphasis placed on an imperative to succeed where success is about the acquisition of material wealth or status—a very specific definition of success:

Brenda: I'd want to do something to further my qualifications. A lot of my friends don't do anything. They just sit around every day and do nothing and I don't want to be like that. I want to have something. I want to have a nice house, nice car and things like that. *(Brenda, nineteen years old, inquiring about training programs at the career guidance center)*

Jessica: I'm a waitress and a cook at Little Chef but it doesn't interest me. I couldn't do it full time. I do it full time for about 9 weeks of the summer and it's awful. It's too hot and you feel everyone in the whole place is looking down on you because the whole place is full of travelling business men and they treat you like you've got no brains and you're stupid. I couldn't do it. At the end of summer I'm so glad it's finished. I couldn't do it full time. Most of my friends didn't do A-levels. Most of my friends went straight into jobs at 16 so they've been working for 3 years and I'm still the only one who's been staying in doing homework but I'm glad though because my Dad always says to me, "One day you'll be earning more than them," because they're coming home now with what I would working full time at Little Chef. So he says persevere and you'll get there in the end but it just feels like it's going on forever and I'm not even finished yet. *(Jessica, nineteen years old, completing a GNVQ at Pearson College)*

The self-narratives of Brenda and Jessica problematize the conduct of those who do not seek to achieve and, therefore, function normatively to endorse a particular self-understanding. Achievement here is narrowly defined and its definition taken for granted. Indeed, one could imagine achievement being defined in many other ways, according to a different set of values, which would open up other possible ways of being.

TECHNOLOGIES

Technologies refer to the means by which conduct is shaped in desired directions or, as Rose states, any "hybrid assemblages of knowledges, instruments, persons, systems of judgement, buildings and spaces, underpinned at the programmatic level by certain presuppositions about, and objectives for, human beings" (1996b, 132).[12] The choices of these young women are embedded within such technologies, including media constructions of single mothers, state-funded training programs, the family, schools, career advice programs, youth skills programs, gender relations, age relations, race relations, and various relations organized by ethnic traditions. As made apparent here, the narratives were produced particularly in relation to decisions regarding further education or training. When the young women spoke about having to decide which university they will attend or what kind of job they want to get, these choices were located within specific technologies that work to govern conduct. The sites where these young women were interviewed are constituted by a set of relations and practices that are explicitly oriented toward the organization of young women's choices. Central to this organization is the responsibility of individuals to engage with their life choices, particularly with regard to the planning of career and education goals:

The school doesn't exert pressure but they make it clear to you that you're going to have to fill in application forms and it gets quite confusing. I suppose I do have the summer to think about it but it is a worry always in the back of your mind—that you're going to have to make that decision. I might go and see the careers advisor or someone who is neutral and can give me their opinion of where it would be best to go. (*Anna, eighteen years old, completing lower sixth form at Ripley School*)

A consideration of such technologies indicates that the navigation of choice is a process in which the self is embedded and not simply free floating or self-referential.

AUTHORITIES

A variety of authorities are implicated in the governance of a young woman's relation to the self. These include schoolteachers, youth care workers, social workers, mothers, fathers, and family members. As argued in chapter 2, authorities come to govern the self under construction through a so-called enfolding into the self. Katy, an eighteen-year-old Asian woman, for example, talks about the pressure she is feeling about what to do after A-levels, where that pressure is partly constituted by the folding into the self of her mother's expectations about what she should be doing:

Shelley: Do you think you'll experience any pressure when you decide after
          completing your A-levels what to do next?

Katy: Yeah from my Mum. She wants me to do a degree.

Shelley: Does she feel pretty strongly about that?

Katy: Yeah.

Shelley: But you want the same thing?

Katy: Yeah but I feel more pressure because of her. In the end it boils down to that picture on the wall with degree. She just wants to be in that picture.

Shelley: How do you feel about that?

Katy: It's hard. My sister found it hard too because she had to go through the same thing because she had my Mum saying, "You've got to show them all you can do it" and I feel that's come to me now.

Shelley: How do you think you'll deal with that pressure?

Katy: I'm not sure yet. I think she's supportive of what I want to choose but I know that in her heart she wants me to do a degree so I'm going to try my hardest to achieve what I can. *(Katy, eighteen years old, completing lower sixth form at Ripley School)*

A number of different authorities worked to inform the choices these young women talked about. The fact that most of them identified educational and career choices as the most important decisions they were having to make in their lives is itself indicative of one of the ways their lives are governed by authorities. Sites such as schools, career guidance centers, training programs, work environments, youth outreach programs, and the family are assembled to meet the objective of organizing the lives of young women in particular ways to produce specific outcomes. However, it is vital to acknowledge the specificity of the narratives produced in the interviews. Technologies of the self and the forms of personhood they seek to inscribe are always heterogeneous producing fields through which we come to accord meanings to the self that are multiple and often incongruous.[13]

TELEOLOGIES

Teleologies are the specific ideals or models of personhood that are deployed through specific practices and articulated in relation to particular problems and solutions concerning human conduct (Rose 1996b, 133). The dominant ideal in these narratives is the autonomous, self-authoring self with an authentic interiority. However, the self is never unitary, but simultaneously a point of convergence of multiple technologies, which implies that this ideal existed in a relation of tension with other ideals inscribed in other practices and relations in which these young women were located. This autonomous self came into conflict with other ideals such as motherhood because it was perceived that the demands of motherhood would be inconsistent with an independent self. This same dynamic was evident in the narratives of some of the young women who had experienced an unwanted pregnancy, where that event was seen as something that had to be immediately reconciled with their desire to remain autonomous. Another example is the conflict between the ideal of marrying young held for Asian women and their ideal of pursuing independence. It is important to recognize that ideals are multiple, and not only do these operate in relation to shifting understandings of what kind of person one is, but that the ideal to which the self is oriented may shift over time and across different spaces.

STRATEGIES

These problematizations, technologies, authorities, and teleologies are linked into a wider moral, social, and political context. One of the consequences of developing a relation to the self as sovereign and free to choose is that individuals govern themselves as such subjects. As subjectivity is dependent upon the categories and meanings available within language, we are neither the authors of the ways in which we understand ourselves nor are we unified, rational beings. However, in taking up a position provided by language, individuals experience their subjectivity as though it were under their control. The experience is of being the source, rather than the effect of language (Weedon 1997, 31). This is fundamentally a misrecognition because the sovereign self is an illusion.

Within such a relation, the individual locates the self as the origin of actions, desires, and motivations, all of which contribute to one's own success or failure. To achieve or, on the other hand, to fail, is accounted for by individual effort, drive, and commitment—not hierarchical social relations or unequal access to resources, for instance. Practicing or rehearsing self-discipline assumes a central role in bringing about one's choices. Furthermore, the self is governed by an ethic of authenticity where constructing oneself as autonomous is to position oneself within a moral discourse. This was evident in discussions where strategies for dealing with future uncertainties were essentially constituted as being a matter of individual strength and conviction. The implication of this relation to the self is that both success and failure are individualized:

Shelley: Are you worried about the future at all?

Caroline: About not meeting what I want—not achieving what I want. Not getting the grades I want. And at university will I do well or … ? I'll be living by myself and I worry about not being disciplined. *(Caroline, nineteen years old, completing a GNVQ at Pearson College)*

CONCLUSION

In negotiating the act of making decisions about the future and reflecting on the choices available, these young women enunciated an understanding of self-identity. This chapter has argued that in the act of making choices, a particular relation to self emerges. The narratives constructed by the young women in relation to their understanding of their life trajectories reveal a self that is a sovereign, self-authoring, independent person who is responsible for making choices that retain a relation of being truthful to oneself. This relation is about both narratives defined from within by internal consistency and also about the embeddedness of the individual within conditions that influence an understanding of the kind of person one is and/or ought to be.

Therefore, self-identity as revealed in these narratives was to a large degree about "choosing a self" from a range of options on offer, but the identities produced were not the product of a free-floating, internally referential narrative. Here, Giddens's assumptions about the subject are inadequate because he undertheorizes the effect of the embeddedness of the narratives. It is useful, therefore, to address the "self as chosen" as a particular form of subjectification situated in practices that enjoin, inscribe, and incite a certain relation to oneself (Rose 1998, 181).

The choices that are made available and the ways they are experienced are always located within specific practices like schools, career guidance centers, and training programs. These are contexts where relations based on ascribed characteristics such as gender and ethnicity work to define the parameters of the trajectory that one "ought" to be on. Within these sites, conduct is problematized in ways that constitute and reinforce an understanding of oneself as being a certain type of person. This understanding is the result of various technologies through which a relation to the self is constituted and conduct governed. Regimes of subjectification work to give meaning to what we think we should be—we then become that kind of subject. Further conduct is oriented toward this understanding and also becomes the basis for rejecting authorities that seek to inscribe the self in different ways.

In these narratives, the construction of the self as free and independent is a particular relation to the self that came into conflict with technologies seeking to construct young women in a different way. For example, the construction of young mothers as a burden to the system, of women being best suited for secretarial work, or the idea that getting married and having children should be the priority for women, all indicated the existence of other trajectories that could inform the young women's lives, but these options were evaluated negatively in view of the relation to the self as autonomous. The implication of understanding the self as having an interiority and a "truth" also meant that choices could be negotiated on a moral basis. This negotiation has multiple implications. One of the positive effects of this relation to the self is that it allows young women to actively pursue their own goals and ideals, thereby providing conditions that support young women's agency. However, one of the negative effects is that uncertainty about the future becomes individualized, along with the blame for those who fail to make the right choices. The actual embeddedness—that is, the web of relations that contains one's choices—is thereby effaced by the "choosing self."

In summary, the relation to the self that is established in these narratives is historically contingent and situated in the local specificity of the everyday, where the autonomous self emerged as the dominant relation to the self.[14] The embeddedness that a "regime of subjectification" implies challenges the autonomy of the self-constituting subject who constructs an internally referential narrative. These ideas are explored in the next chapter, where the relation between the self and body is examined. The aim is to engage with some of the assumptions underlying the self-constituting subject to understand how meanings regarding the self and body emerge. It is argued that theories of reflexive modernization offer a limited analysis of the mind and body relation because in this approach reflexivity privileges the mind over the body, where the body, as an inscribed surface, is chosen to match the self. Limitations of attempts to transcend a mind/body dualism are discussed, and it is suggested that the problems underlying this approach are best addressed by returning to the notion of the subject as embedded in practices where the body is an event, the meaning of which is not reducible to a single realm of representation.

NOTES

1. This analysis method is influenced by the discussion of narrative analysis in Coffey and Atkinson (1996, 54–82).

2. To think of narratives as embedded in social relations relates to the positioning of the individual within ascribed statuses that, according to reflexive modernization, diminish in influence in late modernity.

3. For instance, narratives can be cautionary tales that perform moral functions (see Coffey and Atkinson 1996, 63).

4. Ascribed trajectories and statuses are used in this analysis to refer to the positioning of the individual within patterns of social relations. Such relations are organized, for instance, by gender, race, age, social class, and ethnicity. Because these relations exist as somewhat stable patterns, they preexist the individual who comes to be positioned within them. As such, they are not chosen. Bradley (1996, 212) makes the useful point that we may be active agents in the construction of our identities, but some aspects of our selves cannot be chosen (i.e., we do not choose to be White, working class, or women, etc.).

5. Rose (1996a, 1996b, 1998) describes regimes of subjectification as being concerned with the relations that human beings have established with themselves—relations in which they come to understand and see themselves as selves of a particular type.

6. Experience is important because, as Scott (1992) argues, it is through experience that the individual is constituted in specific ways. The production of the sub-

ject through experience is discussed further in chapter 5 with regard to how experience works to effect the relation between self and other.

7. Twenty of the thirty-three young women—all of those interviewed from the private and comprehensive schools—were anticipating that they would be going to a university. With the exception of one young woman who was going to take a year off and work before deciding on whether to go to a university, all of those who were completing a GNVQ planned to attend a university. Of the young women who were interviewed at the career guidance center, three expected to be on a training scheme in a year's time, five expected to be working in jobs that met with their interests, and one hoped to be working and taking some evening courses to improve her qualifications. The young women involved in the youth outreach program were less certain about what lay ahead for them. For Louise, the goal of getting her own home and a job were paramount, as achieving this would contribute to regaining custody of her daughter, but she said it all hinged on overcoming heroin addiction. AJ, who was just starting to develop self-confidence and gain some practical skills in office work, still felt too unsure of what was to happen next in her life to speculate, while Joanne hoped that she could continue to work part-time at the photography studio.

8. The term "colonization" has problematic connotations and in this respect is an undesirable term to employ, but it is argued in this study that it was consistent with the kind of relation to the self constructed throughout the interviews (i.e., a self that is able to exercise control over future events). As such, it can be considered constitutive of a particular regime of the self. I am indebted to Sasha Roseneil for pointing out the problematic nature of the term.

9. College can provide an alternative to high school. College courses may be used to gain entry into university.

10. The vignette reads as follows:

Catherine is one of the best students in her class. She is generally very self confident in school and around her friends but often in social situations, especially when boys are around, she feels awkward. To fit in she tries to be like everyone else. She pretends to agree with everything they say even when they say unkind things about people she knows. Every time this happens she feels disappointed in herself afterwards for not just being herself. She feels bad for giving into pressure to be someone who she isn't but it just keeps happening. What should she do?

11. This approach draws heavily on Foucault's theorization of specific techniques that human beings use to understand themselves. Technologies of the self "permit individuals to effect by their own means or with the help of others a certain number of operations on their own bodies and souls, thoughts, conduct, and way of being, so as to transform themselves in order to attain a certain state of happiness, purity, wisdom, perfection, or immortality" (Foucault 1988, 18).

12. Rose notes that technologies can be of two types: disciplinary or pastoral. Disciplinary techniques are those in which authority seeks to normalize, while pastoral techniques are based upon a relation of guidance between an authority and those governed. Many of the sites in which young women are located contain both.

13. This means that other constructions are possible in other sites. Constructions are spatially and temporally specific. For example, if the interviews had been conducted in a nightclub or a shopping mall, other sources of authorities, problematizations, and technologies may have effected a different relation to the self.

14. The possibility for alternate forms of subjecthood exists because of the heterogeneity and multiplicity of practices that constitute the social. There is a range of technologies in operation at any given time; however, in these interviews, the autonomous self emerged as an expression of the dominant relation to the self. Other relations to the self may emerge in other contexts.

Chapter 4

The Event of Embodied Identity

> I always change my mind about how I want to look depending on
> what I'm wearing and that sort of thing. I wish I had three different
> bodies I could change into. Sometimes it gets you down. You get de-
> pressed about yourself but in general it's just something you have to
> live with and everyone's in the same boat. It's not that much of a major
> problem.
>
> Emilia, seventeen years old, mixed-sex comprehensive school

Emilia's explanation of the relationship between her sense of self and her
body exhibits several features that may provide the basis for characterizing her account as indicative of the way the body, in postmodernity, is increasingly lived as a "project." There is the suggestion of fluidity and
indeterminacy; the centrality of image and style to the experience of the
body; and the idea of different versions of the self corresponding to different bodies. However, this movement toward a postmodern relation to the
body is qualified by the admission that, in fact, the body cannot simply be
altered or transformed to converge with particular versions of the self as it
is, nor with the self that Emilia might like to become. Recognition of the
boundaries of embodiment, accompanied by the experience of the body as
unsatisfactory and in need of modification, is also evident. The rendering
of this experience as normal, however, operates as a strategy of resisting
and evading those very forces that seek to normalize and discipline.

The nuances contained within this short excerpt illustrate the complex
relationship between identity and embodiment—a problem that this
chapter engages with via the embodied experiences of young women.
Discussions with these young women raised questions about what bodies
mean to those who live with them, the processes through which under-

standings about self and body arise, and how these may transform through embodied practices. These questions are central to understanding women's agency. The aim of this chapter, therefore, is to elaborate a strategy for engaging with these issues through interrogating the self/body relation.

The point of departure for this analysis is what Giddens (1991) has argued is becoming the prevalent relation between bodies and selves—that is, the body as part of the reflexive project of the self. The limits of Giddens's approach are considered, placing particular emphasis on the mind/body dualism implicit in his theory of identity formation, where the mind is privileged over a body that, by its denaturalization in late modern conditions, he suggests becomes an object of choice. The problem of this dualism and its implications, which are of particular relevance to feminism, are critiqued within the larger context of how bodies are inherently implicated in the ongoing process of the constitution of self-identity yet never wholly contained within the realm of representation. It is argued that the body serves not simply as a natural foundation or passive surface upon which meanings are inscribed by systems of signification, but that there is an irreducibility between the subject and object. To understand the ways in which young women actively live their embodied identities, therefore, we need to develop an approach that can envision a body beyond the binary of materiality and representation—the body not as an object, but as an event. As such, it is argued that the recent turn in feminist philosophies of the body from a Cartesian framework to one more clearly influenced by Spinoza is a useful strategy and one that should be pursued (Buchanan 1997; Colebrook 2000; Gatens 1996, 2000).[1]

THE BODY AS PROJECT—REFLEXIVITY AND CHOICE

In Giddens's theory of structuration, the body is of central importance to his theorization of the relationship between agency and social structures because the regularized control and reflexive monitoring of the body by the knowledgeable agent is a necessary condition for action. This reflexive control of the body within predictable routines is intrinsic to the maintenance of ontological security (Giddens 1984, 66). Beyond this fundamental relationship between the reflexive monitoring of the body and action, however, Giddens suggests that within conditions of late modernity, reflexivity is accelerated such that "the body, like the self, becomes a site of interaction, appropriation and reappropriation, linking reflexively organised processes and systematically ordered expert knowledge." One effect of accelerated reflexivity is that the body, once a given aspect of nature, becomes a project increasingly open to human intervention and, like nature, is colonized and made subject to revision (Giddens 1991, 218). The blurring of the boundary between what is natural or given and what is open to choice and reorganization means that the self can be freed from bodily determination. The size, shape, and appearance of the body become part of an expressive exterior of the self that is constantly monitored and managed (Shilling 1993). Through the development of technologies and techniques such as genetic engineering, reproductive technologies, plastic surgery, and health and diet regimes, bodies not only become objects for human management and reconfiguration but increasingly central to one's identity.

Like other aspects of identity, the body becomes the responsibility of the individual who may cultivate and actively restructure the corporeal through the pursuit of specific body regimes chosen from a diverse range of lifestyle options. These choices are made apparent, for example, in guidebooks and practical manuals that give advice on a wide set of concerns ranging from health and exercise programs to lovemaking techniques. The link made in Giddens's work between the self, the body, and image is often identified as a central feature of the consumer culture said to be coterminous with late/postmodernity. Experiences of the self and body are mediated by the constant projection by the mass media of a proliferation of lifestyle images and options, all of which may be incorporated into one's own project.

MINDS WITHOUT BODIES?

Giddens's analysis of the body and self-relationship is open to three main criticisms: the conceptualization of the mind and body relationship as a binary, a privileging of mind over body, and a blindness to the gendered nature of this binary. The mind/body dualism places a significant limit on understanding "how people's experiences of, and responses to, social structures are shaped by their *sensory* and *sensual* selves" (Shilling and Mellor 1996, 2). Indeed, this binary limits the possibility of a deeper consideration of how it is that the body is implicated in the formation of identity. According to Shilling and Mellor:

People comprise both minds and bodies in Giddens' analysis of modernity, but are *essentially* minds for most of their lives and tend only to be shaped by their sensual responses when there is a breakdown in their reflexive attempts to understand or engage with the world. (Shilling and Mellor 1996, 2)

Through a rational and reflexive engagement with the choices and options on offer, the body becomes the material upon which the mind acts. Through reflexivity, the mind creates self-identity with the then reworked body to conform with this reflexively ordered narrative, but by effectively placing the body outside the actor, the actor becomes fundamentally a thinking and choosing agent, not a feeling and being agent (Turner 1992, 87). This overemphasis on processes of reflexivity produces a social actor whose mind takes over the body—a privileging that leads to a view of the social actor as disembodied (Shilling and Mellor 1996, 4). The individual is a reflexive but not embodied self—a disembodied consciousness (Turner 1992).

The critique of a Cartesian approach to the mind/body relationship is a particularly well-established problematic for feminism. Indeed, a critique of this binary has been central to a feminist challenge to Western metaphysics, the foundation of which is the equivalence of the mind with the masculine and the privileging of the mind over the body—the devalued realm associated with the feminine (Bordo 1986; Braidotti 1994; Butler 1990; Flax 1992; Hekman 1990; Nicholson 1990).[2] Theories such as Giddens's risk reproducing the disembedded and disembodied subject of masculine thought along with constitutive assumptions of objectivity, universality, and rationality. This founding system of binaries has served to negate the feminine and locate women outside the realm of the subject. As a consequence, the feminine (and the female body) has historically been constituted as that which must be defined, directed, and controlled through the application of disembodied, objective, masculine knowledge. Bordo explains:

The constant element throughout historical variation is the *construction* of the body as something apart from the true self (whether conceived as soul, mind, spirit, will, creativity, freedom ...) and as undermining the best efforts of that self. That which is not-body is the highest, the best, the noblest, the closest to God; that which is body is the albatross, the heavy drag on self realization ... *the body* is the negative term, and if woman *is* body, then women *are* that negativity, whatever it may be: distraction from knowledge, seduction away from God, capitulation to sexual desire, violence or aggression, failure of will, even death. (Bordo 1993, 5, emphasis in original)

Giddens does not address the specificity of the relationship between the body and gender, acknowledge that the mind/body relation is inextricably gendered, or recognize that positing opportunities for freeing the body from the constraints of modernity has gendered implications. Indeed, women, who have always been more embodied than men because of the association of the feminine with the body, have long been aware of the form and appearance of their bodies and the extent to which they are responsible for creating that surface in accordance with cultural ideals and images "whose content is far from arbitrary, but is instead suffused with the dominance of gendered, racial, class, and other cultural iconography" (Bordo 1993, 250). These issues have prompted questions about how bodies come to acquire meaning in the social world and, more specifically for feminism, how phallocentric constructions of femininity may be resisted and/or transformed.

The sociology of the body has been primarily concerned with the question of what bodies mean—that is, how does the body become meaningful within the realm of social relations? Answers to this question have relied primarily upon social constructionist strategies.[3] Many feminist critiques of the processes by which women's bodies acquire their meaning share the assumptions of this approach. Constructionist approaches have leant themselves well to feminist projects because they undermine the taken-for-granted naturalness of the body—a body that has served as a justification for natural difference between the sexes and, thereby, the naturalization of a system of structured gender inequality. Deconstructing binaries such as mind/body, subject/object, reason/emotion, and culture/nature has effectively led to an understanding of how representations work to naturalize that which is socially constructed and deeply political. This critical perspective has been applied to representations of the female body to show that the body we experience and conceptualize is always mediated by constructs, associations, and images that work to enjoin a particular relation between the self and the body. The impact of the cultural upon the material is such that for "women, associated with the body and largely confined to a life centred *on* the body (both the beautification of one's own body and the reproduction, care, and maintenance of the bodies of others), culture's grip on the body is a constant, intimate fact of everyday life" (Bordo 1993, 17). But if culture is gripping women's bodies, then how tight is this grip and what does this mean for women's agency?

WOMEN, BODIES, AGENCY

Feminism has posed that the body is a medium through which oppressive cultural norms of femininity are expressed.[4] Employing constructionist strategies to critically engage with the question of how bodies come to acquire particular meanings has been effective for feminism; however, this has often been at the expense of recognizing women's agency. Too often, women are cast as cultural dupes and victims of cultural constructions of femininity.[5] Bordo (1993, 166) attempts to refigure women as not simply passive victims but as active producers of the body through their pursuit of continually shifting ideals. However, in her analysis, "female bodies become docile bodies ... whose forces and energies are habituated to external regulation, subjection, transformation, 'improvement'" via the "exacting and normalising disciplines of diet, makeup, and dress." The focus in this analysis is on the ways in which women come to discipline and survey their own bodies by engaging in practices that produce their own docile bodies according to the dictates of idealized discursive constructions of feminine embodiment. Thus, the dominant relation women are posited to have with their bodies is one that is discursively mediated and, it would seem, significantly overdetermined, in which women live with a constant sense of the body as being in need of improvement.

When the young women interviewed in this project were confronted with the question of whether or not they ever felt pressure to change an aspect of themselves in general, one of the most frequent responses involved the issue of bodily appearance. Their desires to transform an aspect of their body revealed a deep awareness of their own embodiment and the ways in which the body was defined as a problematic part of the self. These young women acknowledged that they did experience the normalizing force of idealized body images:

Shelley: Do you ever feel pressure to change aspects of yourself?

Brenda: Pressure to lose weight. That's what I really need to do because before I had the baby I was only 8 and a half stone and now I've gone to eleven stone. I feel pressure by people being able to walk around with skimpy tops on and little trousers and I can't do that like I'd like to do it. That's the only pressure really because of role models and what they look like. (*Brenda, nineteen years old, career guidance center*)

Georgia: Everything. Really badly so. I'm really insecure about everything. Everyone, like my Mum, my Dad, my boyfriend—they always say, "why don't you believe in yourself?" I'm really paranoid so much about my weight. I know I'm not fat when I see other people who are but I know I've got lumps and bumps that I'd rather weren't there. (*Georgia, eighteen years old, further-education college*)

The young women were asked to identify what they believed to be the sources of this problematization of the body and to account for why they thought the way they did about their own body. Social pressures from peers, parents, and society in general played a part in their experience, but a predominant force that they felt undermined their confidence and ability to feel good about themselves was the media and the ways in which media representations organized their own, as well as others', ideas about how their bodies should look. It could be said here that their bodies are problematized through the normative effects of the discursive constructions of femininity or the internalization of body images constituted through phallocentric representational economies—assumptions that underlie many feminist analyses relying on the body as materiality inscribed by or constituted through representation:

Lianne: It's just about the way you look like when you look in magazines. It really annoys me actually when there's all these thin people and if lads are watching a film … I've got loads of boy mates and … it's like they say, "Oh look at her. She's got a really nice body!" It just makes me think, "Well they're not saying that about me because I don't look like that." I'm not saying that I'm fat and stuff but it's just the way you're expected to look in their eyes. *(Lianne, sixteen years old, career guidance center)*

Mel: There's lots of pressure from magazines. Everybody reads magazines which might say something and it comes across as the best way to do things and a lot of magazines when they have clothes and all these different fashions you think to yourself, "If only I could own that." There's a kind of pressure there to keep up with the fashions or to be the ideal person. You're meant to be really skinny and there's a lot of pressure for teenagers to look like supermodels. *(Mel, sixteen years old, all-girl private school)*

These young women demonstrate a clear awareness of the mediation of their own relationship to their bodies and to others by media imagery, and they identify the normative nature of this mediation. However, the complexity of embodied identity transcends this analysis. While representations of ideal femininity affected the embodied selves of these young women, it became apparent through the course of the interviews that to rely on a feminist critique of representation that constitutes the body as wholly discursive was inadequate. When the relation of women to their bodies is construed as disordered because of the disciplinary effects of representation,[6] women are cast as the victims of representation: "trapped in embodiment through stereotypical and alienating images" (Bray and Colebrook 1998, 35). Feminist critiques of representation, thought, and image have been vital for bringing materiality, via sexual difference, back into the project of theorizing female subjectivity and these critiques continue to be of great importance; however, such attempts to do so have often been complicit in reproducing the materiality/representation binary they set out to challenge in their antirepresentational critiques. Where some feminist strategies emphasize the corporeal origins of femininity and sexual difference (Braidotti 1991, 1994; Irigaray 1985),[7] others focus on the discursive (Butler 1993),[8] but both critiques of representation are haunted to some extent by the maintenance of the mind/body dualism where representation is conceived as a negation of corporeality.[9]

In the first strategy for theorizing corporeality, representation is critiqued as a space organized entirely by phallocentric logic. The female body (and subjectivity), therefore, is distorted, objectified, and silenced by a repressive and monolithic realm governed by the masculine (Braidotti 1991, 1994; Irigaray 1985). Here, representation is founded upon the negation of the originary maternal/pre-Oedipal/preconscious in order to produce a relation of difference around which identity is organized. The problem of phallologocentrism (Braidotti 1994) suggests that corporeality, materiality, and sexual difference are radically anterior to thought, that women can only ever be outside of representation, and that within current representational practices women's bodies can only be negated. Women will, therefore, remain trapped by distorted images until a more gynocentric form of representation is developed allowing women to see themselves as autonomous subjects (Bray and Colebrook 1998). The solution, which is not without its own set of problems, seems to reside in an authentic female body that evades the negation of phallocentric signification.

This strategy tends to reinforce the mind/body dualism of Cartesian thought because women are explicitly, even authentically, positioned as *bodies*. While men are explicitly located within the realm of thought, language, signification, logic, and so forth, female bodies are posed as representation's transgressive Other. Ultimately, to pursue this strategy requires feminism to produce or retrieve this pre-representational body in an illusory search for an uncontaminated origin. If female bodies are beyond representation, then any strategy that adopts this view will preclude examination of the specific practical, historical, and cultural techniques that regulate and produce, yet never fully determine, specific bodies. Furthermore, "as long as corporeality, materiality and authentic sexual difference are understood as radically anterior to thought, or negated by representation, feminist critique will only be a reaction against dualism" rather than a project that might embrace more affirmative strategies and acknowledgment of female embodiment (Bray and Colebrook 1998, 38).

A second strategy for bringing materiality back into feminist analyses of the subject has been to explore and demystify the ways in which practices of signification claim to *represent* bodies when in actuality these very practices work to constitute them. This argument is exemplified in Butler's work, where a challenge is made against the distinction between materiality and discourse (Butler 1993). Butler asks why the materiality of sex is understood as the irreducible site upon which culture constructs gender but is not itself understood as a construction (Butler 1993, 28). Here, the irreducibility of sexual difference (i.e., materiality) posited in the above approach is refigured as a necessary condition for the very construction of materiality. The very distinction or exclusion of materiality from linguistic construction provides the condition for its construction—a constitutive exclusion. Sexual difference (the material body) is an effect of signification made to appear through language. The ontological status given to the body, therefore, is a constitutive effect of power and not a primary given (Butler 1993, 35). Within phallocentric economies, intelligibility, or what can be spoken, requires a constitutive outside—an exclusion that in this case is materiality.

While Butler does not posit an authentic, originary body that is negated by phallocentric representations, she still relies on the idea of the body being a "constitutive outside"—thus sustaining a binary relation between representation and materiality. All systems of signification, she maintains, are not self-contained or self-sufficient, but effect an exteriority that they purport to represent. A primary advantage of this argument is that it circumvents biological determinism or essentialism, but Butler's work, although able to offer valuable insights into the workings of signification and materiality, can be criticized for still retaining a dualism of discourse and matter, where matter is posited as radically anterior. Within the terms of her argument, representation remains a negation of matter, and matter is posed as an outside upon which the production of meaning depends. (Bray and Colebrook 1998, 44). Thus, a distinction is drawn between the discursive and the constitutive outside, producing a duality between signification and matter. Colebrook (2000, 78) asks, "The body is, it is true, only *thought* after the event of discourse. But does this render the body itself an *effect* of discourse?"[10]

In summary, both of the strategies discussed above interpret representation as a negation, where meaning is made possible through that which is outside, repressed, or excluded—thereby relying on a binary relation. The body (sexual difference) conceptualized in these approaches is either an effect of representation or produces specific modes of subjectivity or thought. Signification either produces sexual difference or sexual difference produces signification. Either way, a mind/body dualism remains, and the body is made subordinate to the mind as an object of culture. One of the most serious limitations of privileging the realm of representation as the origin of corporeal meanings is that the underlying assumptions dissolve the active role of the subject in generating the meanings attached to their own embodied identity. In many feminist arguments, phallocentric representations *cause* women's self-images, particularly those generated in the mass media and advertising. Ultimately, this pathologizes women's reading practices by suggesting a simplistic ingestion of imagery and a resultant incorporation of these meanings into the self and onto the surface of the body (Bray and Colebrook 1998).[11] In short, women's own understanding of their embodied selves is reduced to an effect of image consumption, while the processes and practices through which the self and the body become meaningful are left untheorized.

The problem remains of how to undertake an analysis of female embodiment and subjectivity that can transcend a mind/body dualism and acknowledge an irreducibility between mind and body, subject and object, culture and nature, and so forth. According to McNay:

As the point of overlap between the physical, the symbolic and the sociological, the body is a dynamic, mutable frontier. The body is the threshold through which the subject's lived experience of the world is incorporated and realised and, as such, is neither pure object nor pure subject. It is neither pure object since it is the place of one's engagement with the world. Nor is it pure subject in that there is always a material residue that resists incorporation into dominant symbolic schema. (McNay 1999, 98)

An analytical approach that can incorporate this point would question the idea of the body as an effect of image consumption, proposing instead the body as constituted by more than the capacity to be a sign or image via the internalization of distorted media representations. In short, according to Bray and Colebrook (1998), it is more than a semiotic problem; instead, the body is a site of practices, comportments, and contested articulations:

The body is not a prior fullness, anteriority, or plenitude that is subsequently identified and organised through restricting representations. Representations are not negations imposed on otherwise fluid bodies. Body images are not stereotypes that produce human beings as complicit subjects. On the contrary, images, representations, and significations (as well as bodies) are aspects of ongoing practices of negotiation, reformation, and encounter. Neither the body nor the feminine can be located as the innocent other of (patriarchal) representation. (Bray and Colebrook 1998, 38–39)

A problematization of representation is required, by "regarding the body as the threshold or borderline concept that hovers perilously and undecidably at the pivotal point of binary pairs" (Grosz 1994, 23). This strategy is further explored in relation to how transformation in the meaning of embodiment can be effected through an engagement in processes and practices in which both the subject and object are implicated. This first involves a critique of reading practices as *the* site where women's bodies are inscribed by culture (i.e., idealized images of femininity). It is argued that to locate young women's discernment of their own embodiment as purely an object of cultural inscription is to undertake an insufficient analysis.

RESISTANCE AND REPRESENTATION

In the interviews with young women, the relationship between self-identity and body transcended the meanings inscribed on the surface of the body. While cultural representations of women's bodies may work toward discursively constructing bodies in particular ways, such texts encountered by the young women suggested that they engage with these images and their own bodies in critical and subversive ways. As stated earlier, media projections of thin, fashionable, and glamorous women were often cited as contributing to the dissatisfaction they felt with their own bodies. However, most of the young women were able to negotiate these discursive constructions and their effects in a way that allowed for strategies of resistance, thus lending support to the suggestion that the relationship between self and body is about a process more complex than one that involves the inscription of the text upon the surface of the body:

Shelley: So the main pressure you feel is from magazines?

Lynne: Yeah magazines definitely because it's all too easy to look at a magazine and think how happy people's lives are then you look at your life and think you're not that happy. Or you think about how those people look and how they've got this extensive wardrobe and go on nice holidays.

Shelley: When you see that do you think your life should be more like that?

Lynne: Yeah until I start thinking about it then I think, "Oh hold on a minute!" But I think it's definitely a massive influence on people—the media.

Shelley: How do you resist that pressure?

Lynne: Basically I just get a grip on reality because there's no way you're going to be as happy as these people in the magazines with beautiful figures and nice clothes and loads of money. For happiness you need to look at your own self-concept and the people that are around you. *(Lynne, eighteen years old, further-education college)*

Sarah: There's always like skinny people walking around and well dressed people which the media has taken too far because people aren't like that in real life. There's no point in changing to be like them because nobody is like them apart from in the media. It's not really reality.

Shelley: Do you do anything to resist that pressure?

Sarah: Like with programs like *Baywatch*. I just don't watch them. They don't interest me. There's no point. I used to read magazines when I was younger but now I don't have time to read them anymore. There's no point. *(Sarah, sixteen years old, all-girl private school)*

While experiences in daily life are mediated by an abundance of images, it is also a context in which young women engage with those images, their own embodiment, and their positionings within systems of representation in a resistant fashion. In the following example, Lianne is able to recount the experience of being positioned in relation to the slender ideal of female embodiment and how it feels to take up that position. The effect of this positioning is normative because she feels she ought to take responsibility for transforming her body in relation to idealized constructions of femininity. Having self-consciously performed this mental operation, however, she subverts a cause-and-effect relationship between the text and her body by returning to the unproblematic relationship she had established between her body and her self prior to encountering the text:

Sometimes I think I've got to lose weight then I think "No" because I'd be doing it for someone else and not for me because I don't really want to and I'm happy with myself anyway. *(Lianne, sixteen years old, career guidance center)*

One other strategy developed by these young women in dealing with the pressure to make their bodies conform to images of ideal femininity was to normalize a pathological relationship to their bodies. The discomfort produced by their desire for what they did not have was dissolved by placing all women within this position. Indeed, having a problem with the way one looks was interpreted as quite a normal relationship, thereby lessening the impact of the disciplining and normalizing function of media imagery. Rather than feeling as though one's body was abnormal and in need of transformation, *that very feeling* was normalized. Through this maneuver, their accounts of what actually constituted normality undermined what cultural influences dictated as being normal, thereby counteracting the disciplinary capacity of these representations:

Lauren: There's social pressures that you obviously get as a girl. You know you've got Kate Moss and people like that. There's just that normal type of pressure that you get growing up as a young woman—feeling like you should be 3 stone lighter and things like that. *(Lauren, nineteen years old, career guidance center)*

Sarah: If someone said I could change my body I'd probably want to be taller and slimmer and have a prettier face but that's just what everyone would say. *(Sarah, sixteen years old, all-girl private school)*

All of these comments subvert the normalizing and homogenizing effects of images and representation. Even though a desire to transform the body is expressed by these young women, this desire does not then translate into a need to actually undertake action to adapt or discipline the body accordingly. The body is not merely an object that becomes the focus of a lifestyle project. These comments suggest that representations of idealized femininity, which work at the level of appearance, do not fully determine a self that is able to engage with the body and these representations as a site of resistance. Therefore, consideration must be given to what embodied agency means. If bodies, as Giddens (1991) argues, are becoming less of a given by nature and more the product of choice, then what does a chosen intervention into the physical mean? One of the ways to explore this question is through an analysis of cosmetic surgery as the epitome of human intervention into the materiality of the self.

BODY PRACTICES: DOING VERSUS LOOKING

Cosmetic surgery is often cited as the exemplar of body project practices and in the postmodern world a practice whose prevalence is on the increase (Bordo 1993; Shilling 1993).[12] What does the increased popularity and acceptance of this technology reveal about the ways in which women live their bodies? What issues are raised for women's embodied agency by these practices? In her analysis of women who undergo cosmetic surgery, Davis (1995) emphasizes that women's agency must be central to any account of the relationship between identity and the decision to alter one's body. To disavow women agency would mean that, "cosmetic surgery becomes a strangely disembodied phenomenon, devoid of women's experiences, feelings, and practical activities with regard to their bodies" (Davis 1995, 57). Furthermore, an argument that treats women who have their bodies surgically altered as compliant to a system that serves men's interests and reproduces the conditions of their own oppression, relies on a faulty conception of agency—that women could not possibly make an active and knowledgeable choice.[13] These practices, Davis concludes, are not about women wanting to become physically beautiful, but about women renegotiating their relationship to their bodies and, through the body, the world around them. In short, it is about embodied subjectivity where the body is situated in culture rather than determined by it (Davis 1995, 169). Her study provides insight into how women live their bodies and suggests that subjectivity and the material body are aspects of the self that are irreducibly linked such that bodies are never just objects but part of a process of negotiating and renegotiating self-identity.

The complexity of the relationship between self and body was explored with the young women in this study by asking them how they would respond to a scenario in which a decision to undergo cosmetic surgery was being negotiated.[14] Responses were equally split between those who advocated surgery, those who advised against it, and those who were ambivalent—that is, those whose answers (whether approving or disapproving) were reached only after a lengthy and often contradictory process of analyzing the complex set of considerations implicit in the scenario. The following response from Anna is notable because it was one of the few that so outwardly condemned the practice by embedding it within a larger social context:

Well I see why people do it but I think what's sad and what needs surgically removing is the fact that they have to do it in the first place. The fact that society is so driven by the way that people look and behaving towards people because of the way that they look that they feel the need, in order to feel good about themselves to change the way they look … It's just a way of avoiding the bigger issue of how society treats people in the first place. *(Anna, eighteen years old, mixed-sex comprehensive school)*

While Anna reconstitutes the scenario as a dilemma whose solution is rooted in the transformation of societal values, most of the young women considered the dilemma as being inherently about constructing an identity. Here, emphasis was not placed on dominant ideals but on individualized intentions, needs, and desires. A prevailing response involved the assessment of the surgery in terms of whether it could boost one's confidence, but significantly, this confidence was perceived as something that resides beyond the surface of the body and, therefore, escapes it. It is significant that in the narratives about the self discussed in chapter 3, these young women invoked confidence as a value of central importance. When applied to the body, the suggestion that the surface of the body could be so readily altered to fit with a narrative about confidence did not follow. For example, both of the young women quoted below felt that confidence is not just about how one's body looks:

Mel: I don't think I could do it myself ... but I think a lot of people now seem to be doing it so people think, "Oh I could do with this changing or that changing" and really they're just changing their outside appearance and when they've had it done I think in the long run they won't feel the confidence inside. It'll still be lacking. *(Mel, sixteen years old, all-girl private school)*

Shelley: Do you think if you feel that there is a part of the way you look that is affecting your confidence that changing that body part will help you feel more confident?

Alice: Probably would do for awhile but then you'd find something else that you want to change and it would be never ending. And you'd think I won't look good until I get this done and it would just go on forever. *(Alice, sixteen years old, all-girl private school)*

These responses suggest that the surface of the body is not simply reducible to the self or vice versa. Changing the surface appearance of the body does not correspond to a transformation of the self in and of itself. Thus, the young women spoke about their bodies and self-identities in ways that challenge the idea that a body can be chosen or transformed through interventions enacted upon its surface. This draws into question Giddens's suggestion that the body is increasingly a "project" (an object) that is made and remade according to the definition of the narrative of self that is under construction. Neither the self nor the body can be chosen because they are very often lived as though they are already there. The body is already the self. The self is already the body. The way these young women spoke about their embodied selves gives cause to question if there is a separation—a mind/body split:

Lianne: I think everyone can learn to live with something they don't like because everyone has a flaw. But having surgery, that's just being thick— *having a nose that's not you*. It's just part of her and she's got to learn to live with it. *(Lianne, sixteen years old, career guidance center)*

Lucy: I don't think it's ... well it's not that it isn't right but I don't think it's something I would do. *This is my face. (Lucy, sixteen years old all-girl private school)*

Nicola: I don't think that she should have the surgery because *this is the way she was made* and she's got to learn to get confidence in herself otherwise no one will have confidence in her. *(Nicola, seventeen years old, all-girl private school)*

Sarah: People should just *realise that you are what you are* kind of thing. There's no point trying to change it because it might not fit with what you are. It won't help. *(Sarah, sixteen years old, all-girl private school)*

The suggestion that embodied selves exceed a culturally inscribed surface is also apparent in instances where the solution to the cosmetic surgery dilemma was resolved by the conclusion that the surgery should be chosen. Still, in these cases, altering the body was about more than a modification of surface appearance. Instead, it was suggested that undergoing cosmetic surgery was about transforming the way the body was lived—not how it looked. In most cases, the underlying concern was about confidence and how changing one's body would allow the self to enter into situations with an increased sense of efficacy. Even when a pronounced sense of ambivalence was expressed, it was held that if cosmetic surgery allowed the young woman in question to live her embodied self differently, then it would be an acceptable choice for her to make:

Lynne: I think that she should have it because I think the only reason she is disappointed in herself for wanting to have the surgery is because of her friend's opinions but like if she's got a lack of self confidence then if she has the surgery then psychologically she'll be able to feel good about herself, so whatever she wants to do. *That's going to affect her whole life isn't it?*

Shelley: What do you think about her friends telling her that she should just be self confident anyway?

Lynne: Yeah I can see the point because I say that to people but you keep on telling people that, giving them compliments and if they don't end up feeling a bit happier then that's what they need to do. *I mean I don't agree with cosmetic surgery for stupid reasons* but if that's what she wants then she should do it. *(Lynne, eighteen years old, further-education college)*

Lynne makes clear the point that a uniform position for or against cosmetic surgery is too simplistic and that one's evaluation must take into account more than just appearance for its own sake. She states that there are "stupid reasons" for undergoing surgery, but if the decision is about feeling good about oneself—a feeling that would have ramifications for the wholeness of her life—then it would be okay.

The idea that the relation to the body is about the way the body is lived is also apparent in the young women's responses to the questions pertaining to their own desires to change their bodies if they could. The desired modifications were about transforming the ways that the embodied self lived relations within which the individual is embedded. These responses suggest an experiential basis for the relation between self and body that goes beyond the body's surface appearance. For example, many of the young women stated that the changes they would like to make would result in them having more impact or an enhanced sense of agency. The emphasis is not on "looking," but on "doing":

Shelley: What is the relationship between confidence and being thinner?

Caroline: I think because you feel better about yourself. I mean I only have to exercise a couple of days and I feel better within myself. *It's not about my body having changed* but you feel different because you've done something instead of lying in bed and eating a lot of sweets.

Shelley: So it isn't about the way your body looks?

Caroline: Yeah, yeah. *(Caroline, nineteen years old, further-education college)*

Shelley: If you were taller, how do you think that would affect who you are or how you feel about yourself?

Prea: I think it would help my confidence. I don't know why it would. I just feel it would because like with some people I meet, like with the guys I meet they're always a lot more taller and I feel that if I were taller I could, I don't know, *be more in control. (Prea, nineteen years old, further-education college)*

As discussed earlier, the desire for control[15] expressed here could be evidence of the "discipline and normalisation of the female body" and an "amazingly durable and flexible strategy of social control" in which "preoccupation with appearance" still affects women far more powerfully than men (Bordo 1993, 166). Certainly, for some of the young women in this study, dissatisfaction with the body was experienced as a need to be more self-disciplined and individually responsible for its size and shape. This indicates, therefore, that bodily discipline can be about the development of a relation to the body in which agency becomes constrained through repetitive and obsessive practices, such as dieting and exercise. But it is important to avoid the total conflation of desire for confidence with a disciplinary form of control. For some of the young women, an expression of desire for control translated into a desire for bodily transformation that would have the effect of empowerment:

Lynne: I'd be taller. I don't know why … no I don't think it is because I actually want to be taller. I think it's just that I want to be taller in my personality than I am and with a bit more weight on me. I know it sounds strange but if I were taller, I'd be cautious towards people and their ulterior motives. *(Lynne, eighteen years old, further-education college)*

Prea: I'm sure that I'm meant to be taller than I am. I mean I would like to be taller but I know that's one thing I can't change so I'm not even going to worry about it but I would like to be taller. You know so that I could make myself be heard and seen. *(Prea, eighteen years old, further-education college)*

These expressions of a desire to change the body suggest that the meanings of body modification can transcend their implementation as disciplinary technologies. As Davis (1995) suggests, offering the opportunity to renegotiate embodiment—cosmetic surgery, for example—can be one of the many technologies employed in self-formation and transformation. It can be part of an active strategy undertaken in a context where embodied identity is "the outcome of an individual's interaction with her body and through her body with the world around her" (Davis 1995, 169). The experience of the body is about ongoing, multiple processes and not just surface appearance. By theorizing bodies and selves as processes, we can begin to understand how each is implicated in the other, and this is particularly significant if we are to understand that the critical task of engagement is not to ask what bodies mean, but what they can do.[16] In asking this question, we can begin to explore how embodied selves are processes that give rise to new understandings, experiences, and significances that operate beyond the effects of representational practices.

As the following comments by Shannon demonstrate, the ways in which the relationship to the body may transform or how one feels about it may change are brought about not through actually altering the body's surface or the surface inscription of meanings, but through an embodied process involving particular experiences and engagements in certain practices that allow the body to make new, transformative connections:

When I was younger I really wanted to be slimmer but as I've got older I've come to terms with myself as a person and I'm not striving to be somebody that I'm not whereas a couple of years ago I was striving to be that slim person in the magazine. The thing that stopped me was friends talking it through, growing up and realizing that it is the media—looking around you and thinking, "Well there are people like that but not everybody" and in college everyone is their own personality. You dress the way you want to. No one criticizes what you say. You've got your own opinions that you can say. Not like at school where your teachers say, "No that's wrong" and where you're not allowed to speak. You can speak out more and be the person you are really rather than the person you were trying to be. I did want to be slim because of the media but now I don't want to be so I really can think about me as a person and my body as being what I am. *(Shannon, eighteen years old, further-education college)*

Shannon's relation to her body is partially affected by fashion magazine images, which she admits used to intensely mediate this relationship. However, the body is never purely an object inscribed by cultural texts "in that there is always a material residue that resists incorporation into dominant symbolic schema" (McNay 1999, 98). Shannon's embodied self moves from the inscription of culture via her reading practices, toward new meanings which emerge from her active involvement in practices such as talking with friends and going away to college where she begins to live her body in a different way as a result of being able to speak and be heard. She is signaling a production of embodiment that is neither purely subject (self) nor purely object (body). She moves from experiencing her body as an object to a relation in which body is lived in terms of what it can do. To understand this production demands the rethinking of an ontology founded on binaries.

If the accounts of the relation between self and body rendered in the narratives of the young women in this study are to be more fully understood, then the starting point for such an analysis must break free from the constraining influence of the mind/body dualism and the Cartesian tradition. As argued here, this is a problem that continues to disturb many of the attempts made by feminists to think about embodied identity in a critical yet nondeterministic way, and in a way that grants women agency. One possibility for a feminist reconfiguration of these problems is to begin from a radically altered ontological position. The deployment of such an ontology would deliver a strategy for exploring the mind and body, representation and materiality, narrativity and corporeality in nondichotomous and nonreductive ways. Models and metaphors are required that implicate the subject in the object and lend insight into the constitutive articulation between the inside and the outside of the body (Grosz 1994, 23). A potential source of such metaphors is the work of Deleuze and Guattari (1987). Grosz argues for the efficacy of their philosophical framework because in their work

Subject and object can no longer be understood as discrete entities or binary opposites. Things, material or psychical, can no longer be seen in terms of rigid boundaries, clear demarcations; nor, on an opposite track, can they be seen as inherently united, singular or holistic. Subject and object are series of flows, energies, movements, strata, segments, organs, intensities—fragments capable of being linked together or severed in potentially infinite ways other than those which congeal them into identities. Production consists of those processes which create linkages between fragments. (Grosz 1994, 167)

Within this framework, the subject, the social order, and even the natural world are reconfigured as microprocesses; a myriad of intensities and flows with unaligned or unalignable components that refuse to conform to the requirements of order or organization. Bodies then can be thought of not as *objects* upon which culture writes meanings, but as *events* that are continually in the process of becoming—as multiplicities or assemblages that are never just found but are made and remade. This is a fluid process of transformation that Shannon, in the example above, explains—a process of connections, extensions, and reformations—a process of becoming.[17] The body is reconstituted as an active, productive force and not an effect produced through the repression of some essential origin. The body is productive because it connects. Indeed, one of the advantages of this approach is that it allows the female body to be thought of in affirmative terms, or as an active and positive event rather than as a negated origin, a lack, or the disqualified other of phallocentric representations.

Theorizing human action as productive in this way also endorses women's embodied agency because questions regarding the body shift from asking, What do bodies mean? to What can bodies do?[18] This is a particularly useful counter to feminist evaluations of body practices in terms of whether they are either liberatory or repressive. The framing of such questions relies on "the possibility of a free consciousness that could precede, and be revealed beneath, representations" (Bray and Colebrook

1998, 57). But if action is seen as positive or productive, then evaluations of that action can be made on the basis of "its force within a network of other acts and practices, and not in reference to a putative origin" (Bray and Colebrook 1998, 57). Instead, understanding the body means examining what things it performs, what transformations and becomings it undergoes, the connections that it forms, and the capacities that it can proliferate (Grosz 1994, 165).

Theorizing from this position allows the body to be seen as more than a limit and suggests that the body itself might have effects and modes of being that are not reducible to its status as image (Bray and Colebrook 1998, 41). Representation does work in some way to constitute the body, but it is only *one event* among others and, as such, is not determinate.

"The body is a negotiation with images, but is also a negotiation with pleasure, pains, other bodies, space, visibility, and medical practice; *no single event in this field can act as a general ground for determining the status of the body*" (Bray and Colebrook 1998, 43, emphasis added).

CONCLUSION

The aim of this argument has been to critically engage with theorizing the self/body relation, particularly the privileging of discourse in the constitution of the body which results in the disappearance of the material body behind layers of representation, becoming only what can be "spoken or readily put into words" rather than a lived body (Radley 1995, 7). Consequently, the body tends to be conceptualized as an inert mass controlled by the mind via discursive mediation, where the mind is seemingly abstracted from an active human body (Shilling 1997, 79). Bodies cannot simply be treated as though they are the natural foundation upon which culture overlays a disciplinary system of meanings. Their existence is not purely as a prior surface or blank page passively awaiting culture's inscription. As Radley explains, various forms of social constructionism

Capture the body only insofar as they show how its functions, its movements, its "inner" and "outer" workings, have been shaped by social structures and discourse. From the latter perspective, the sign (text) separates itself from the spectacle which it represents, objectifying and separating out the body as "not-mind." The de-realisation of the body-subject through representation leaves it (as flesh) marginalised. The consequence of this situation is that, within discourse, the lived body is rendered knowable only through the constructions that are its multiple realities, but its existence as a lived entity is effectively denied. (Radley 1995, 7)

If the relationship between self-identity and the body is one in which both are increasingly indeterminate and open to choice, then it becomes important to interrogate not only processes of subjectification and embodiment, but also what *choice* means. Such a position challenges Giddens's theorization of an instrumental relation to the body where the body is brought into the self-reflexive biographical project as an object of choice. It has been argued here that engaging critically with the notion of choice requires an understanding of why the mind/body binary must be replaced with alternative modes of thinking about embodied selves. This is particularly crucial for feminist projects, since attempts to bring materiality back into the terms of subjectivity analysis have constituted a significant part of feminist critiques of metaphysics. It is argued here that feminist critiques, while effectively engaging with representation, remain constrained in their theorizing of women's embodied agency by positioning the body as being either misrepresented or unrepresentable. Critiques of representation too often remain within a binary logic and consequently fail to acknowledge that the embodied self exceeds representation. To think outside or beyond representation is a problem that underlies the more general question of what it means to live the body. It has been demonstrated here, through engaging with young women's accounts of their embodiment, that this demands the initiation of a different ontological strategy—one that can accommodate the possibility of thinking beyond a division between materiality and representation. The movement advocated here is toward a way of thinking, not about what the body means, but what it becomes through a multiplicity of continuous connections with other bodies.[19]

This does not argue that textuality cannot be implicated in the relation between self and body, but that it does not provide a wholly sufficient strategy because the self/body relation is lived via its immersion in a multiplicity of sites, knowledges, and practices. It has been proposed here and illustrated empirically that a strategy defined by the refusal of dichotomies can lead to an understanding of embodied subjectivity as a site of social, political, cultural, and geographical inscriptions, productions, and constitution (Grosz 1994, 23). Women's bodies are more than just the product of image consumption, and therefore relying on one particular practice in advance as an explanation for women's relation to their bodies in general is insufficient. Indeed, a Deleuzian ontology defies the application of singular explanations or accounts and collapses the humanist privileging of mind over body. A refusal of a single explanation or a point of causal origin is made in favor of locating the body, as an event, within the context of a multiplicity of practices and regimes; a network of activities through which a body becomes. These practices and connections work to form the event of the body. Analysis of bodily practices, therefore, requires an examination of the specific historical and political locations within which they occur, while also recognizing unintended effects and the impossibility of predicting in advance the nature of or distribution of alignments. This discussion implies that attempts to theorize embodied identity do away with notions of an authentic female body or identity and the rhetoric of alienation that accompanies many feminist antirepresentational critiques. Being cannot be reduced to an effect of the consumption of images, but instead is the result of various forms of self-inventions that occur within embodied practices, which also are not effects of representation but sites of production.

We can achieve a more complex and thorough understanding of the relation between identity and body by deploying this way of thinking about embodied identity than by relying on Giddens's instrumental relation to the body as something that is brought into the self-reflexive biography project as an object of choice. Because media stereotypes do not produce human beings as complicit subjects, the body is never just an effect of reflexive engagement with images of lifestyle and shifting representations of possible selves that one may become (Bray and Colebrook 1998, 38). Textuality can be implicated in the relation between self and body, but it is never a sufficient explanation for how women live their bodies. The self/body configuration is lived via its immersion in a multiplicity of sites, knowledges, and practices; therefore, understanding the choices women make in "doing" an embodied identity requires a move beyond reductionist accounts.

In the next chapter, the theme of the choosing subject continues to be explored by considering how having choices in one's life implies that there could be limits to these choices. This discussion is oriented toward understanding how theories of reflexive modernization fail to theorize social inequality and the differential relation individuals have to choice. As argued in chapter 3, choice must be understood as embedded within particular relations and practices. The "choosing," autonomous self and its limitations are analyzed, drawing upon the notion of difference and the self/other relation. It is argued that the self does not choose experiences that then constitute it, but that the self is constituted through experiences, the meanings of which are organized through the relational operation of identity and difference. Subjectivity, therefore, is a site where the understandings of self and other are produced within specific locations where identities are always multiple and open to revision through participation in localized practices that can effect a shift in identifications.

NOTES

1. Buchanan (1997, 76) summarizes Spinoza's rejection of Cartesian dualism for a mind/body parallel via Deleuze (1988, 18): "an action in the mind is necessarily an action in the body as well, and what is a passion in the body is necessarily a passion in the mind."

2. Many feminist epistemologies challenge norms of disembodied reason and objectivity by asserting the centrality of the body's role in the production and eval-

uation of knowledge (see Bordo 1986; Grosz 1993). Haraway (1988, 589) makes a similar point about the impossibility of knowledge production from a position of objectivity in arguing for "politics and epistemologies of location, positioning, and situating, where partiality and not universality is the condition for being heard to make rational knowledge claims." This argument relies upon "the view from a body, always a complex, contradictory, structuring, and structured body, versus the view from above, from nowhere, from simplicity" (Haraway 1988, 589).

3. In constructionist theories, the body is conceived in various ways. For example: the body as an object of control and scrutiny, governed through relations of power and knowledge (Foucault 1977, 1979); the body as a medium through which meanings are transmitted and social categories reproduced (Bourdieu 1984); and/or physical existence, as influenced by semiotics, is overruled by the primacy of discourse and language (Barthes 1972). For a discussion of constructionist theories, see Radley (1995).

4. For feminist critiques of beauty practices as a system of domination through which women are oppressed, see Bovey (1991), Brownmiller (1985), Chapkis (1986), and Wolf (1990).

5. Dorothy Smith (1990) makes the useful argument that women actively produce their bodies in relation to textual constructions. As such, femininity is a practice of everyday life.

6. For feminist critiques of representation, eating disorders are often of central importance because they implicitly demonstrate a negation or repression of the body "according to a limited, reified, or dominant body image" (Bray and Colebrook 1993, 41). For studies of eating disorders, see Bruch (1979), Chernin (1983), MacSween (1993), and Orbach (1986).

7. In this argument, sexual difference is treated as ontological and constitutive of the subject, and as a condition for representation.

8. In this strategy, sexual difference is theorized as an effect of representation. For instance, Butler (1993) argues that materiality cannot be located as an exterior to representation or as a pure outside to discourse; therefore, sex is an effect of gender (see critiques in Bray and Colebrook 1998 and Colebrook 2000).

9. This argument is developed effectively in Bray and Colebrook (1998), from which the following analysis substantially draws.

10. Colebrook (2000, 78) makes the important point that Butler conflates "the *being* of a thing with the mode in which that thing is known."

11. See Probyn's (1987) analysis of anorexia. She makes the important point that the subject of anorexia is located at the intersection of multiple and intersecting discourses; thus, her argument challenges reductionist analyses of the relationship between eating disorders and representations.

12. The relationship between technologies and body transformation has become a growing object of study for the social sciences, often throwing into question the distinction between subject and object. For discussions of the implementation of technologies for the modification of bodies and the implications of these practices, see Balsamo (1995), Featherstone and Burrows (1995), and Wendell (1996).

13. Davis draws on the work of Bartky (1990), Smith (1990), and Young (1990) to construct a theory of female agency in relation to the practices of cosmetic surgery. This approach avoids reducing women's actions to the effects of male oppression or phallocentric discourses.

14. The scenario presented was:

> Anne has always been self conscious about the size and shape of her nose. Her best friend says that she should just try to feel good about herself rather than focusing on what she doesn't like about herself. Recently, Anne's Aunt gave her some money to put towards visiting her cousins in Australia. She is really excited about having the opportunity to travel but she recently has considered using the money for cosmetic surgery instead so that she can finally feel more self confident and better about herself. She thinks that a trip will only last for 1 month but a nose job is forever. On the other hand she is disappointed in herself for wanting to have the surgery. What should she do?

15. In some feminist critiques of women's relationships with their bodies, the notion of control is seen to represent the logic of the masculine, while the disorderly feminine body becomes the object of regulation (MacCannell and MacCannell 1987; Székely 1988; Turner 1996, 126–42).

16. Buchanan (1997, 75) articulates this point in his argument that the body must be reconfigured as a sum of its capacities.

17. For a discussion of inventing and becoming a new self through a capacity to connect with other bodies, see Bray and Colebrook (1998), Buchanan (1997), and Grosz (1994, 173).

18. Drawing upon the work of Deleuze, Buchanan (1997) argues that a body can do what is articulated in terms of its affects. Affects refer to the capacity of the body to form specific relations, where relations refer to the virtual (potential) links between bodies that can be formed.

19. In this way of thinking, bodies are not just restricted to other humans or organic entities, but also opened out to the possibilities of connections with the inorganic.

Chapter 5

Relations of Difference and the Reflexive Self

We are eye witnesses to a social transformation within modernity, in the course of which people will be set free from social forms of industrial society—class, stratification, family, gender status of men and women—just as during the course of the Reformation people were "released" from the secular rule of the Church into society.

Ulrich Beck, *The Risk Society*

Detraditionalisation involves a shift of authority: from "without" to "within." It entails the decline of the pre-given or natural orders of things. Individual subjects are themselves called upon to exercise authority in the face of disorder and contingency which is thereby generated. "Voice" is displaced from established sources, coming to rest with the individual.

Paul Heelas, *Detraditionalization*

By suggesting that individuals have increasingly come to be the source of their own identities, proponents of reflexive modernization have provocatively engaged with matters that have been central to the project of sociology—namely, theorizing the nature of social divisions and inequality. Indeed, the study of social relations and their organization into stratified social structures has been a primary focus of sociology. Social divisions organized through the categories of race, class, gender, and ethnicity have been considered to be at the very heart of the social order and central to the formations of identity and the production of differential social outcomes for individuals and groups (Anthias 1999, 162). To suggest that their influence is diminishing, as have theorists of reflexive modernization, is to come into confrontation with many sociological assumptions.

Criticism has been leveled at theories of reflexive modernization for inadequately addressing how social inequality, which works to define life chances, ultimately impacts upon the formation of identities and of possible answers to the question, Who am I? (Anthias 1999; Bradley 1996; May and Cooper 1995). The do-it-yourself biography of reflexive modernization is not classed or gendered, for example. The problematic tendency in theories of reflexive modernization is toward an almost complete detachment of identity from institutional contexts, resulting in an insufficient amount of attention being given to ways in which identity is linked to sets of lived relationships that involve "differential access to power and resources and are, therefore, not only aspects of social differentiation but also of social inequality" (Bradley 1996, 203). Within these critiques, the notion of difference is seen to underlie the organization of social relations into hierarchies of power and exclusion. According to Anthias:

Gender, ethnicity, "race" and class are pivotal forms of differentiation and stratification of human populations in the modern era. They may be seen as crosscutting and mutually interacting discourses, practices and intersubjectivities that coalesce and articulate at particular conjunctures to produce differentiated and stratified social outcomes. (Anthias 1999, 176)

In view of this analysis of the operation of difference, it is not surprising that theories emphasizing individual choice in the production of identity are often accused of neglecting to give more careful consideration to the ways in which social relations characteristic of modernity continue to structure and limit those choices. Bradley (1996, 203) argues that recent processes of cultural change have eroded and destabilized long-standing relationships to create a more fragmented and individualized society. However, she maintains that this is not to say identities have broken free of structured relations of difference and inequality. She stresses that identities in late modernity are still embedded within lived relations that put constraints upon one's possible range of identifications. In short, the suggestion made by proponents of reflexive modernization that individuals are being freed from social forms of industrial society and that identities as a result are becoming less constrained requires a consideration of the multiple ways in which identifications are made[1] and how they articulate with life choices and life chances.

The aim of this chapter is to explore how difference is implicated in the construction of identities and how the term itself has been used in the project of theorizing identity in late or postmodern social conditions. The uses of difference are explored through the analysis of how young women's identities and their choices about who they would like to be are shaped by discursive constructs (particularly class, ethnicity, and gender), and how these discourses impact upon the process of making identifications. This analysis considers the relation between identity and difference in order to address the ways in which notions of difference enter into the narratives of the self that are produced by the young women in this study and into the narratives produced by the practitioners who work at the sites where the young women were interviewed. The objective is to understand how difference works to organize an understanding of the choices available to young women and how the operation of difference informed the process of negotiating the experience of those choices from different subject positions.

Here, the concern is twofold. First, this analysis is about the young women's understanding of the self that emerged through their positioning within relations of sameness and difference. Second, it is concerned with the organization of the interview sites through mutually interacting discourses, practices, and intersubjectivities, which articulate within technologies of the self. In other words, the means by which the organization of practices, knowledges, authorities, and relations within schools, career guidance centers, youth programs, and so on, effect a relation to the self. This theoretical and analytical problem requires an unraveling of the multiple dimensions contained within the concept of difference. These dimensions include difference as destabilization, as a relational operation, and as experiential specificity and diversity.

DIMENSIONS OF DIFFERENCE

In contemporary social theory, discussions of identity have become inextricably linked to the notion of difference. In postmodern theories of identity, difference has become "doxa, a magic word of theory and politics radiant with redemptive meanings" (Felski 1997, 11). While it has become *the* catchword for theorizing social identities, relations, and social division, its meanings and uses are many. For purposes of analysis, three dimensions are discussed here: difference as a process of destabilization within a particular historical context, difference as a relation through which meaning is produced, and difference as experiential diversity.[2]

Difference as Destabilization

This dimension of difference is implicit in the analysis of processes that effect the transformation of modernity to late or postmodernity, where modernity is conceptualized as a process of increasing differentiation of social spheres and the disembedding of social relations. This shift is characterized by a fragmentation[3] and destabilization of the social order into a form that is increasingly plural and fluid in nature. As the influence of social relationships that were organized around ascribed characteristics dissolves, the ways that we as individuals locate ourselves within society and the ways that we perceive others as locating us are affected (Bauman 1996a, 1996b; Beck 1992; Giddens 1991). Here, differentiation means that increased possibilities for self-definition result from the dissolution of the organizing force of sets of social relationships that traditionally fixed identity in place. Potential sources of identification multiply and the traditional parameters of identity diminish as a common point of identification. While in modernity, identity revolved around one's occupation or one's function in the public sphere or family, postmodern identities are often seen as constantly shifting and revolving around consumption, leisure, and media images (Kellner 1992; Sarup 1996). In this theorization, the unitary self of modernity has been thoroughly deconstructed, leaving behind a subject whose identity is formed "within a paradoxical space in which there are no fixed centres or margins" and where identities cannot be attached to singular, uncomplicated subject positions (Hetherington 1998, 24). Difference, rather than identity, becomes the organizing principle of postmodern identities.

For theorists of reflexive modernization, destabilization of the parameters of identity means that choice necessarily becomes a key aspect of day-to-day life. As Giddens argues, "modernity confronts the individual with a complex diversity of choices and, because it is non-foundational, at the same time offers little help as to which options should be selected" (1991, 80). These choices are not just about how to conduct one's life, but also more fundamentally about *who to be.* Late modern social conditions demand an active contribution on the part of individuals in constructing a do-it-yourself biography, where having to choose who to be from among a widening range of possibilities is not a choice in itself. Beck and Beck-Gernsheim argue:

The human being becomes ... a choice among possibilities.... Life, death, gender, corporeality, identity, religion, marriage, parenthood, social ties—all are becoming decidable down to the small print; once fragmented into options, everything must be decided. (Beck and Beck-Gernsheim 1996, 29)

In summary, reflexive modernization offers an interpretation of modernity as a process of detraditionalization, whereby social forms associated with industrial society transform in such a way that social relations and identities become more fluid, plural, and necessarily chosen by a reflexive social actor. This assessment brings into question the extent to which individuals are constrained in the self they can choose—that is, how the definitions of self in one's own subjective account are affected by their embeddedness within social relations. This question is implicitly linked to an analysis of processes by which subjective accounts of the self are accomplished. This issue involves the second meaning of difference, that is, difference as a relation through which meanings are produced.

Difference as a Relational Operation

Understanding how difference operates in association with the formation of subjectivity has been fundamental to the ontological assumptions underlying poststructuralism, particularly the deconstruction of the unified, rational, and universal subject who is the origin of the meaning of self (Weedon 1997). Within the terms of poststructuralism, meaning is understood through the method of its construction, that is, through the operation of difference (Crowley and Himmelweit 1992). The fundamental premise is that meaning is constructed through linguistic opposition rather than absolute reference (Barrett 1987, 33).

Recognition of the relational production of meaning is important to understanding the production of identities within specific contexts because difference is not just about processes that free agents from structured social relations, but also about the ways in which social relations are organized discursively through the meanings assigned to those relations. These meanings provide positions from which the individual achieves an understanding of the self in relation to others. Relational theories[4] of identity suggest that the establishment of identity rests upon the power to repress the other—or that which is positioned as different (Hall 1996, 4–5). The self/other relation through which identities are organized is a binary construction in which one term is privileged, with the value of each term reliant upon the other. Identity, then, is a negotiation of positionality located in the relation between the two terms rather than in the terms themselves. In this regard, the terms are not opposites but inevitably defined through each other (Burr 1995, 107). The implication of this relation is that in undermining the foundations upon which the unified subject depends, deconstruction has delivered a subject whose coherence relies upon that which is repressed.

Deconstruction has effectively shown that meaning is never fully present in a sign and therefore can never be secured permanently. The closure that is reached through the fixing of meaning is, therefore, necessarily achieved through the operation of power (Hall 1996). The binary of self/other within which identity resides contributes to the organization of social relations in which those who can identify with the privileged term do so at the expense of those who are marginalized. Rutherford explains:

In the hierarchical language of the West, what is alien represents otherness, the site of difference and the repository of our fears and anxieties ... difference speaks of the otherness of "race," sex and class, whose presence and politics so deeply divide our society. It is within their polarities of white/black, masculine/feminine, hetero/homosexual, where one term is always dominant and the other subordinate, that our identities are formed. Difference in this context is always perceived as the effect of the other. (Rutherford 1990, 10)

However, the repression upon which identities depend also means that sites of the marginalized other can become sites of resistance. Brah (1996, 116) states, "experience is a site of contestation; a discursive space where different *and* differential subject positions and subjectivities are inscribed, reiterated, or repudiated."

In summary, difference refers to the ways that meanings are produced in the relationship between terms, where those terms are defined in a negative relationship to each other (I am this because I am not that). The significance of this relational production of meaning is that these binaries discursively organize social relations into a hierarchical configuration, but where meaning is never secured once and for all.

Difference as Experiential Diversity

The third dimension contained within the notion of difference refers to diversity within social categories such as gender. It has been recognized within feminist theory that the category "woman" is not constituted by uniformity but by a diversity of experience and situations (Riley 1988). As such, this category is divided by multiple axes of identification, which implies that it is very difficult to assume in advance any foundation for shared identity between women (Anthias and Yuval-Davis 1990; Hooks 1991). This understanding of difference as experiential diversity has been central to the need to understand identity as a multiplicity. In terms of theorizing subjectivity, the subject is always in process and not a pre-given entity or, as Brah (1996, 116) argues, difference is about the experiencing subject. Experience is not a transparent reflection of a pre-given reality, but is itself a cultural construction—not an "unmediated guide to truth," but *a practice of making sense.* The idea of a subject to which experiences happen must be replaced with an analysis of experience as the very site of subject formation. Within processes of subject formation, meaning emerges within relations of sameness/difference and self/other so that sameness depends upon a relation to difference (it is often easier to say *what one is not,* rather than *what one is*).

The concept of difference, both as a process that gives rise to a particular set of social conditions and as a relation through which meaning is produced, has also been central to the development of a recognition that identities are located at the point of intersection between multiple ways of being or of making identifications. These ways of being are not just about being female, for example, or about being Black, but about the identities that emerge through the complex interaction of different discourses that are inscribed in the experience of everyday practices and relations. Thus, identity emerges not as a sum of its constituent parts, but as an articulation of interlocking axes of difference.[5] Within the conflicting and often contradictory intersection of discursive positions, new identities may emerge that are not just about being female, Black, or middle-class, but about how all modes of identification articulate within a particular context.

Poststructuralist theories have exposed the fact that identity, because of its link to difference, can never be reduced to a single or predictable location. The problem of doing so is illustrated by assumptions underlying identity politics—namely, that a single category of identity can provide the basis for unification around a common identity because members of this category share particular characteristics, experiences, beliefs, needs, and so on. According to Whelehan:

All political movements that focus on a particular identity (femaleness, gayness) as the basis for political action, effectively presuppose that particular properties define such groups, implying that there is an essence within identity which is fixed and can be unearthed through a discussion of an oppressed group's experience of subjectivity. (Whelehan 1995, 205)[6]

Any move toward reducing multiple aspects of one's social location to a single category produces a relation of oppression because assuming a unitary and unified experience denies that individuals are always more than just one category of identity and that these other ways of understanding the self may be equally, if not more, significant within any given situation or context. The subject must be thought of in ways that can allow for the operation of multiple identifications within specific social and historical contexts. Hall explains a discursive approach to identifications:

Identification as a construction, a process never completed—always "in process." It is not determined in the sense that it can always be "won" or "lost," sustained or abandoned. Though not without its determinate conditions of existence, including the material and symbolic resources required to sustain it, identification is in the end conditional, lodged in contingency. Once secured, it does not obliterate difference ... identification is, then, a process of articulation, a suturing over, an over-determination not a subsumption. There is always "too much" or "too little"—an over-determination or a lack, but never a proper fit, a totality. (Hall 1996, 2–3)

Reducing the multiplicity of the self to a single location constructs the self as a totality and violates the complex unity of identity that is forged out of differences by characterizing, in a totalistic fashion, one particular attributed essence—or a constellation of essences—as accounting for the complete identity of the subject (Taylor 1998, 342).[7]

STABILITY AND FLUX

Although there is never a single narrative or discursive positioning that can account for identity, this does not mean that identities, characterized by excess and fragmentation within much postmodern theorizing, escape unity and coherence. Indeed, identity is about the achievement of a sense of a coherent "I" and the experience of continuity within and across one's own embeddedness within relations of sameness and difference. Here, the recognition of the centrality of difference to identity is about the tension between the two, not the triumph of one over the other. To understand this relationship, it is useful to distinguish between two distinct yet related forms of identity that describe how relations of sameness and uniqueness are enacted: categorical and ontological identity (Taylor 1998, 345). Categorical identity is about the sameness that results from the recognition and classification of others as being the *same* as one's self in terms of social categories like gender or ethnicity. Ontological identity is about one's distinct *uniqueness*, which results from the recognition of one's individual self as being different from others.

When our identities are an expression of sameness or identification with available social categories, such as gender, they work to "stitch the subject into structure" and align subjective feelings with objective[8] places we occupy in the social world (Hall 1992, 276). When identities are about one's distinct difference, they often contradict or challenge a collective or shared social identity. This movement between categorical and ontological identification involves symbolic processes—that is, how we make sense of or give meaning to social relations and how we position ourselves within these relations through the operations of sameness and difference. Therefore, for example, gender identity is about the meanings that we attach to sexual difference and the category "woman," as well as the diversity or difference of experience that is contained within that category.

Identities are based on social categories or constructs used to define, explain, and/or justify various forms of differentiation. The meanings that are assigned to social categories work to organize relations in specific ways, but these categories are socially constructed and are therefore inherently unstable, contestable, and historically specific. On the other hand, an element of stability is introduced by the organization of lived sets of orderly social relationships by social categories that persist over time. Together, these two elements—social constructs and lived relations—can be used to understand that identities are constructed in a social world that is both unstable and continuous, fluid and structured (Bradley 1996, 7). The meanings that we attach to categories such as "woman" and the internalization or refusal of our positioning within those categories become lived out in everyday practices. Therefore, the processes involved in categorical and ontological identifications contribute to both the reproduction of existing constructions of difference and to challenges to these constructions presented by a refusal to take up or identify with particular positionings.

In summary, identity is a mode of being, a practice of making sense that is intimately connected with experience, subjectivity, and social relations (Brah 1996, 123–24). The subject in process does not escape coherence but is expressed and experienced through identity, or as Hall (1996, 5–6) states, "points of temporary attachment to the subject positions which discursive practices construct for us." The relational nature of identification depends upon the operation of sameness and difference, expressed through categorical and ontological identities. The formation of identity is a movement traced through relations of simultaneous sameness and difference. In this way, identity is a "relational multiplicity" (Brah 1996, 124) that assumes specific patterns but is never wholly a totality nor reducible to one location. Similarly, the living out of the meanings of social categories in particular ways accounts for both the stability of social categories over time and space, as well as for their repudiation and transformation. For example, the meaning and practice of gender has transformed in the past fifty years and continues to do so, but alongside remnants of sexism and patriarchal structures. The argument in development here is that proponents of reflexive modernization draw on the notion of difference as destabilization of social relations and focus upon the concomitant freeing of individual identity from social structures. However, to theorize identity, we need to engage further with the various dimensions contained within the concept. This is necessary to the analysis of subjective experience, which as the site of subject formation, is organized and made meaningful through relations of identity and difference, sameness and uniqueness.

NARRATIVES ABOUT CHOICE AND CONSTRAINT

As discussed in chapter 3, narratives of the self are given form through the ordering of experiences and events into an internally consistent trajectory. The structuring of one's narrative is influenced by the positioning of the individual within discourses that make available particular meanings and positions from which one is able to assign significance to one's experience. Contours of self-narrative are about choice, as Giddens suggests, but they are also about constraints whose influence limits and imposes meaning on those choices. The critique against theories of reflexive modernization stresses that overprivileging the extent to which choices are available to social actors who occupy stratified positions within a social order marked by social divisions leaves unanswered questions connected with the ways in which late modern identities still rely upon and reproduce relations of inequality. Having choice is to a large degree about having freedom from constraints; therefore, being able to choose a self and bring that self into being is tied to the resources—material, symbolic, cultural, and so on—that one is able to access and deploy. The young women in this study identified a range of factors that they felt limited the choices they had available to them. These discussions about the limits they experienced gave some indication of how they were positioned by others and how they positioned themselves within relations of inequality.

The sites in which the young women were interviewed reflect the kinds of social institutions established to provide services to young women and within which choices about their identities are conducted. Each site represents a specific kind of institution that operates to organize young women's lives differently according to how their needs, resources, abilities, aspirations, and so on are defined and managed. For example, attending a private all-girl school like Greenwood is a distinctly different point of location from a youth-skills program like YouthWorks, which is designed to meet the needs of those young women who have few resources or options available to them.

In certain respects, the interview sites, as social institutions, represent different objective positionings within a social order divided according to relations of race, class, disability, gender, and sexuality. These sites are also internally organized according to the definition of these relations, and these definitions, or the values assigned to these axes of difference, are used to position the young women who enter into them. Depending upon which site a young woman enters, she is positioned as "a single mother," "middle-class," "a young Asian woman," "a school leaver," "an ethnic minority," and so on. All of these positionings have implications for the choices that are available to young women within those sites. These positions affect how choices are constructed by specific institutional discourses, how these choices are managed, how the young women who enter into these institutions come to interpret their own relationship to choice, and how they then negotiate their options given the diversity of experience they bring with them to that moment of choosing.

The main discourses that arose in the interviews with both the young women and the practitioners related to class (material/cultural/social resources),[9] gender, race, ethnicity, and age. Discourses about each of these reflect the ways in which those practitioners working with young women position them around axes of difference and the ways in which young women also position themselves.

Practitioners' Constructions of Difference

Each of the practitioners described at length the kind of young woman who would be situated within that site. Their narratives reveal the dominant discourses that operate to organize an understanding of the young women for whom they provide services. One of the most prevalent ways of describing the young women was in terms of class, which was expressed in relatively abstract concepts like access to resources—with resources being broadly defined. In the following excerpt, the head of sixth form at Ripley School constructs this institution as a place of mixed class and race—relations that underpin his understanding of the school's organization. It is significant that his narrative reveals a particular construction of these relations:

The school itself is in a very middle class area as you can see by the houses in the surrounding area. There's some very nice, big houses around the park areas. It's a well sought after suburb to live in. Our traditional catchment area goes from this area here into the city centre. It goes into the city centre and into Harley and Chilton which are very much, and have been for years, decades—working class areas—cheap houses, high density and certainly over the past 25 to 30 years those areas have become more ethnic minorities. Harley in particular has a large Asian community and Chilton is an African Caribbean community so the school as such draws from this area and those two in particular. We also get a mixture of children from the Granthill area which is rather different in that it is very much white working class. Not a particularly nice type of person in actual fact. There's a certain amount of racial politics and so on that goes on in Granthill which is not particularly savoury. Fortunately we didn't get too many from there but there's usually a handful in each year but fortunately within the school there doesn't seem to be too much racial tension but I wouldn't like it if we had a larger group in from that area there with the number of children we have who are ethnic minorities. But the white children that reside in this area—the middle class white children are a little bit more liberal minded so again there's not the racial problems that might be there between the working class whites and the blacks and Asians. It makes for an interesting place but as I said fortunately we've not really had any major racial problems. Certainly not between whites and ethnic minorities. If anything, if there are any problems then it's often between African Caribbeans and the Asians for one reason or another. *(Mr. Preston, head of sixth form, Ripley School)*

Within this site, Mr. Preston constructs relations according to specific discourses—race and class being predominant. When young women enter the Ripley School, they are positioned within these discourses that not only define social relations in specific ways, but also seek to inscribe individuals in a particular manner. Mr. Preston, for instance, produced a story about Ripley as a place defined by social divisions. This is a terrain mapped by relations of difference through which the student population is divided—class, racial, and ethnic—which are then constructed in a particular way, that is, as relations that are problematic, conflictual, and in need of management.

The other research sites were similarly discursively constructed according to dynamics of social inequality. If the young women who entered the interview sites were located according to class background or in terms of their access to resources, then Greenwood School defined the upper end of the scale, with career guidance and especially the YouthWorks program fixing the limit of the other end. Having material resources was central to the way in which the head teacher of Greenwood School located the young women attending that institution:

We're not a catchment area although we of course draw from within an area where parents can drive the pupils. They are parents who have decided that they want private education for their girls. Necessarily, therefore, they are wealthier—on the whole I would say middle class to whom education is very important. I would go on to say there is also a large section of people in the school whose parents are not really interested in education at all. They are more interested in the social kudos of having their child in a private school. The parents are very concerned about making a good lifestyle for their children whether it's through education or social contacts or whatever. *(Mrs. Conway, head teacher, Greenwood School)*

In this narrative, the young women are positioned in relation to the resources they have available—wealth and cultural capital—both of which are necessary for them to attend this school, but which then serve the goal of perpetuating that privilege. This construction draws on the same discourses as the ones used by practitioners to portray both the career guidance service and the YouthWorks program, but in these particular sites, the young women were located much differently within those discourses because they were described as having restricted access to the kinds of resources essential to having life choices:

[YouthWorks] is an organisation that works with the most excluded types of young women. Young women who are excluded from standard provision really. They might be excluded because they've got a disability, it might be their colour, their sexuality, it might be the fact that they don't attend school. They are called non-attenders or they might be excluded from school rather than expelled. Generally, it's about building confidence and offering alternate choices.... They don't have similar problems but they are all excluded in some way. It might be that they've been in care all their life. We've got a young woman who is just out of prison. We've got another young woman who is using drugs and then we also quite often tend to work with young teenage women with children. Simply by having children so young, they are excluded from a lot of things. So although the problems are all different they are all excluded. *(Geri, youth worker, YouthWorks program)*

The idea that availability of resources is linked to family background was a recurring framework used to describe the nature of young women's lives. Geri, like Mrs. Conway, drew upon this relationship, but then placed this within a discourse of social exclusion. For Geri, this exclusion was also linked to a wide range of different relations: race, gender, class, disability, and sexuality. Within each of these types of relations, the young women who participated in YouthWorks were defined as marginalized.

The examples cited here indicate that class, as a social construct, is used as an interpretive device by practitioners to account for why young women end up where they do within different types of institutions. In this manner, class is used as a way of conceptualizing life chances and for explaining how young women's lives will have different outcomes.

Resources: Linking Choice and Confidence

When practitioners spoke about young women's positions within sets of social relations, it emerged that availability of choice and options about career and education goals were directly related to the nature of resources they possessed. Therefore, because the young women were positioned differently in relation to their access to resources, they were also seen as having different relations to choice. The availability of choice was constructed as a privilege that was linked not so much to "social class," but by the specific family background the young women had come from, upon which their access to resources and, therefore, their relationship to choices depended. For example, Mr. Preston spoke of the educational system as favoring the middle classes in terms of the structure of the courses that are offered to students at the age of sixteen—the system favors those who tend to take the traditional middle-class route from A-levels to university. Diane also defined the parameters of choice available to young women at career guidance as mediated by economic necessity:[10]

I think it's still the case that a lot of families—particularly those on lower incomes—have a need for that young person to work and would find it difficult to support them through college situations as a result of that … rather than a young person deciding to do a college course because they feel it's what they will enjoy— the pleasures you get from learning and developing etc. etc. A lot of that kind of privilege really has gone. *(Diane, youth counselor, career guidance center)*

The importance of having confidence and being able to do what one wanted was, as discussed in chapter 3, a central part of the narratives constructed by these young women. Confidence was expressed as an internal quality of the self that was used in the navigation of choices. Within the context of the interview sites, however, all of the practitioners linked the young women's expression of confidence—being able to assert oneself and actively make choices—to the availability of external resources demonstrating the subjective and objective dimensions of choice.[11] One of the themes that emerged in these discussions was that confidence is constructed as the product of having a particular family background and is, therefore, a resource in itself that could potentially impact upon the ways in which young women navigated the kinds of choices they encountered. Thus, the recurring topic of confidence was placed within a discourse about life chances:

If you're talking about youth work you are talking about the ability to make in-formed choices and to make positive choices in your life. Well a lot of the young women that we work with, their choices are limited by outside factors and by their own confidence. Sometimes the only choices they feel they have are self harming in various ways. It might be through drugs or it might be through actual self harm or they might feel the only option open to them is to have children. *(Geri, youth worker, YouthWorks)*

This characterization compared to the levels of confidence exercised in the other interview sites. Mr. Preston explained that in his school there was a big difference in confidence that he accounted for by drawing upon the discourse of social class. The greater amount of confidence he ascribed to middle-class youth within the context of education was attributable, he argued, to the fact that their parents understood the system and knew how to navigate it to the best advantage. In Mr. Preston's account, social class becomes objective—something that exists out there, independent of the individuals who come to occupy the positions. It is a pattern of social relations that exists over time and is deployed by him as an interpretative device that may be used to account for individual life chances and to de-scribe the reproduction of social inequality. He explained:

The dominant culture within this area is middle class and amongst the students themselves and those students from perhaps more working class backgrounds can feel a bit peripheral. Not that there is any overt snobbery or anything like that but it is a cultural difference.... The middle classes are expecting to go on to jobs of the type that their parents do or perhaps even better if they can.

At Greenwood School, Mrs. Conway also linked confidence to re-sources. With regard to the young women at the private school, she said that in general they have been so "loved and so treasured and bolstered up" that they think they can have what they want simply because they want it and not because their abilities warrant it or because they have worked for it. Therefore, not only are they used to being given what they want, but they've also been *given the confidence to expect it.* This expectation contrasts with the young women who participated in the YouthWorks pro-gram. As Geri explained, the notion of confidence has resonance for the young women she works with because the media often depicts young women as confident, self-assured, and outgoing, thereby providing a nor-mative point of reference. However, the particular group of young women at YouthWorks perceives confidence as something that belongs in the do-main of *other* young women and not theirs. They see it as something that young women in general should possess but something that they them-selves lack.

All of these examples indicate that relations of difference, notably so-cial class, are used as a framework to interpret the relationship young women have to choice, as well as how they will go about negotiating these choices. Choice is constructed as intrinsic to relations of difference within which these young women are positioned. The identities being produced by these young women are linked by the practitioners to the unequal distribution of choice—a reflection of their positionings within patterns of intersecting social relations that exist over time. In these accounts, difference translates into a condition of having, or not having, choices.

In addition to discourses about class, gender also entered into the ways the interview sites and the practices within them were constituted. One of the clearest examples of this was the way in which routes through the institutional settings were perceived as gendered, with young women more likely to pursue disciplines in social sciences and humanities. For example, Mr. Preston maintained that vocational courses were more likely to be pursued by young women than young men.[12] The GNVQ in health and social care at Pearson College was also described as traditionally female-dominated and perceived as being attractive to some young women as "anybody can be a carer because it's seen as a female thing."[13]

Young women and young men within these sites are also constructed as being different in relation to their educational, vocational, and social needs. At the career guidance center, it was claimed that at age sixteen it was more likely for young men to leave the school system, but among those young women who did, they were more likely to be looking for a long-term career path and financial independence rather than just a job to earn some money immediately. In the context of youth work, the pattern of young women's needs was contrasted with that of young men:

With young men a lot of youth care provision tends to be focused upon offending behaviour because I think that a young woman and a young man can have similar situations but what young men tend to do is go out and smash things up, steal, beat up other people. What young women tend to do is self harm like drinking or slashing themselves so there are different sorts of interventions and different sorts of work. (Geri, youth worker, YouthWorks)

One of the defining characteristics of the gender discourses drawn upon is that gender, as a social category, was incorporated into explanations as a social relation that had undergone significant historic transformation, and interestingly, was formulated as a discourse that had, through social change, become defined by increased choices and opportunities for young women. The transformation of gender as an organizing principle of women's lives provides a framework within which to understand young women's choices in the present compared to a past when women generally had to choose either domesticity or a career within a limited number of areas. Mrs. Conway, for example, who has been involved in teaching for thirty years, reflected upon the choices she had available when she was the age of the young women interviewed:

When I left school, in my particular circumstance which wasn't the same as the girls in this school—I was very much from a working class background where going on to any form of further education was considered bizarre. Girls left home only to get married. Their first job tended to be from home and they earned money for awhile and paid money into the family income then left to marry. When they left to marry, they left work and you brought up your family and then later on when your children had grown up you might just go back to do some sort of work against old age or your husband had left you or I don't know but certainly to insist on staying at school beyond the age of fifteen, as it was then, was considered odd unless you went to secretarial college. That was allowed or perhaps if you went to train as a nurse. That was another one that was more or less smiled upon. But to go on to university was quite a fight. Young ladies only went to train as nurses or teachers. They certainly didn't do anything else. Whilst I didn't break away from the teacher mould I certainly broke away and went to university. Even in so doing it was considered by my family that this was a waste of education because I would only get married and get children. *(Mrs. Conway, head teacher, Greenwood School)*

The perception that young women have more options and the freedom to choose what they want to do in relation to education, employment, and family intersected with how they were also located in relation to access to resources. Both school leavers and the young women in the YouthWorks program were seen as less likely to be able to take advantage of expanding options now available to young women because of their lack of resources.

As was the case with social class, it was common for confidence to be talked about in gendered terms across all the sites. In general, young women were seen as being empowered by the changes that have occurred to social conditions in the last thirty years and that this allowed them to confront their decisions with a substantial degree of assertiveness and determination:

I mean there's no doubt that a lot of girls about 25 years ago were—well it's not as though they were actually ever forced down you know in the sense you know, "You're a girl and you're not as good as the boys." It wasn't like that. On the other hand they didn't sort of have that confidence whereas now they realise that they can actually make a success of things.... In general I feel that there's a lot more confidence and togetherness around the girls as a group than the boys. I think as well professionally they know they can hack it now. The girls feel confident that they can become solicitors or they can become whatever they want to. *(Mr. Preston, head of sixth form, Ripley School)*

Compared to class and gender, discourses of race and ethnicity were drawn on less often as a way of understanding how young women were positioned in relation to options and choices. When racial and ethnic differences were spoken about, they translated into a difference of needs:

Shelley: Can the groups that you organise for young women be about whatever issues they have?

Geri: Yeah those issues and obviously with a large number of staff people are
            more interested in other things. Like myself and one of the other
            workers are interested in body image. Certainly for our black girls
            worker, that is a lot of what her work is based around because she feels
            that's what is important for the girls that she works with because of
            their culture and what it's like growing up as a young black girl in
            Chilton. *(Geri, youth worker, YouthWorks program)*

The effect of ethnic or racial difference was often constructed as deriving from the combined effect of its intersection with other relations of difference, mainly class and gender. At Ripley School, which has a mixture of
Asian, African Caribbean, and White students, the chances of continuing
with education were explained by the head teacher as being about an intersection of class, gender, and ethnicity. In the following example, ethnicity intersects with gender to affect whether young women advance to a
university, with class also intervening to increase the chances of this happening:

Mr. Preston: What tends to happen is when they reach the end of sixteen a lot of
            the working class children tend to leave. The ones that stay into the
            sixth form are predominantly middle class and predominantly
            white but not exclusively. You met some girls who are from an
            Asian background but they tend to be perhaps the slightly better off,
            if you like, of the Asian students.

Shelley: So class is a bigger difference than gender?

Mr. Preston: Well the one area is amongst the Asian girls who are restricted by
            their families. Their expectations are very much pulled back by that.
            They are told what they can do. The more liberal families will say
            "yes you can go to university" but amongst the Asian girls there is a
            problem because the families for whatever reasons want the girls to
            stay close to home, close to the family. Now the more liberal ones
            will say, "yes you can go to university no problem but you're going
            to go to one of these local ones" so in other words "you can live at
            home. We don't want you to live in a hall of residence." It's very
            difficult for me to say anything like, "I don't think you should do
            that." It's none of my business in the end but it's difficult for the
            girls because they are torn both ways.

Interviews with practitioners show how discourses construct difference
and are deployed within each of the places where young women's choices
about education, training, and career decisions are being made. Discourses about race, class, gender, and ethnicity operate to organize relations within those sites and the practices that constitute them. They also
serve as a way of positioning young women with regard to what kinds of
choices they have available and what they might expect to achieve. In
short, these discourses come to organize the relations they purport to de-

scribe. Furthermore, these accounts constructed by practitioners reveal how categorical identity is used as an explanatory device—as a way of describing individuals' similarity and as a way of locating particular individuals within general sets of relations defined by social categories such as gender, race, class, ethnicity, and age, which are assumed to exist as stable sets of patterns across time and space.

POSITIONING THE SELF—POSITIONING OTHERS

Because identity has been increasingly linked to notions of fluidity and choice, the young women in this study were asked about their own perceptions of available choices and about the limitations they perceived as being set on those choices. They were first asked to identify limitations faced by young women in general and then to identify the limitations they had experienced themselves. This exercise—the consideration of choices available to young women in general followed by reflection upon their own positions—revealed their understanding of how exclusion operates in both the categorical and ontological realms of identity. The discourses used by practitioners to situate these young women were also drawn upon by the young women themselves in their explanations for how and why choices might be limited. All of them were able to position themselves and other young women within the relations of race, class, gender, ethnicity, and age. The tendency, however, was to position the self in relation to the other, where the self was defined in a negative relationship to the other.[14] This differentiation was most evident in the movement made when speaking about the limits placed on young women in general, compared to speaking about the limits they felt impeded their own choices. In this movement, the self is differentiated from the other—it is *other* young women who are seen as occupying a distinctly different position from the one in which they position themselves. It is *other* young women who have limits placed on them. The following excerpts illustrate how the other enters into the narrative that defines the self with regard to gender, ethnicity, and class, and how these positionings are related to notions of choice.

Gender

In this first example, Jessica speaks about the social category "young women," but then identifies her own experience outside of that category. Young women are categorized as a group of people who are limited, but the self is defined as different from this group:

Shelley: What kinds of things do you think limit the opportunities for young
                women?

Jessica: They don't always get the same chances do they? They're still expected in a way to be staying at home having children. They don't want to promote women too high or give them too much responsibility because they think they'll be going soon to have kids and things. They just still are not in the lead. They're behind men.

Shelley: Do you think there is anything that has limited the kind of choices you've been able to make for yourself?

Jessica: In a way but not really especially in prison work where more women are coming in all the time. *(Jessica, nineteen years old, completing a GNVQ at Pearson College)*

In this exchange, the positioning of the self and the other within the discourse of gender is incongruous. It is *other* young women who potentially will come up against sexual discrimination in the workplace. Jessica makes this assertion, yet does not take up this position herself, even though her goal is to work within a prison setting—perhaps one of the most nontraditional careers to which a young woman could aspire. A similar response to the question is given by Lucy, who does not identify with gender relations as producing limits to her own choices, but does construct gender relations as affecting the organization of women's lives in general:

Shelley: What kind of things do you think limit the kinds of opportunities young women have?

Lucy: I don't know because I think that there is equality for women now more than there ever has been. So I don't know. There's not anything that gets in my way—being a woman—that stops me from doing anything.

Shelley: Do you think that there is anything else that gets in the way of young women having choices and being able to do whatever they want to do?

Lucy: Well like how women are perceived. Like men putting them down all the time. Like there's meant to be equality in the workplace but like if you have a baby or something and have to go on pregnancy leave it's a problem. I think as much as equality is a real definite the perception is different. *(Lucy, sixteen years old, completing lower sixth form at Greenwood School)*

In both of these discussions, gender is constructed as involving relations between women and men in which women are discriminated against, particularly in the workplace. However, gender is also constructed as being about increased equality, so while other women may be limited by their gender, both Jessica and Lucy do not identify themselves with this position but instead with one in which gender is about women being able to do what they want. This illustrates how discourses and the subject positions within them are simultaneously constituted in multiple and contradictory ways. Gender can be about *both* increased choice and discrimination. It is an identity category that is both fluid and structured.[15]

Ethnicity

Nonidentification with certain discursive positionings was also evident in association with ethnicity. Shayne, a seventeen-year-old from an Asian background, positions others but not herself in such a way that being Asian is about being limited in one's choices:

Shayne: I think that basically coming from an Asian view—I have a couple of Asian friends—and coming from them I think that what really hinders them is their background. Their culture which is really, really backwards I think. It is the way the people think within their communities. They think women are somehow inferior to men so in that case I think that in ethnic minority communities that hinders women.

Shelley: Do you think anything has limited the choices you've been able to make for yourself?

Shayne: So far no. So far I think I've done well with that. I've actually always wanted to go on and do A-levels and I've achieved that. I achieved it by passing by all my GCSEs which I was quite pleased with. So far I don't think I've limited myself or hindered myself in any way. *(Shayne, seventeen years old, completing lower sixth form at Ripley School)*

Even though Shayne herself is Asian and therefore would likely be discursively positioned in particular ways by others, she locates herself and her choices outside of the Asian community's influence. It is other young women, her Asian friends for instance, who she places in the same category—a position characterized by constraint deriving from the expectations associated with their ethnic background—but no reference is made here to her own ethnicity. Instead, she constructs her own ontological identity by locating herself outside of the relations within the Asian community that limit young women, and she also locates herself outside of the relations within the dominant White culture that may operate as a restriction on those who occupy the position of an ethnic minority.

Although most of the young women did not see themselves as having their opportunities limited by the factors that they believed limited other young women, there were several instances when a congruent relation was constructed between the self and the other. This recognition of unequal positionings within relations of power and privilege was often due to having experienced being positioned in such a manner by others, thus coming to inhabit those relations in a particular way. These young women were able to identify themselves as being positioned such that their choices were affected, whether through sexist attitudes in the workplace, by the traditions of their ethnic community, or by social class. The following examples illustrate the young women's recognition of how their lives were organized by social categories and the lived social relations these categories organize, within which they were embedded:

Claire: There are some men I don't like at work. You don't really want to hear what the men have been up to that night with their wives and girlfriends and a bit on the side and all this. You don't want to hear that.

Shelley: So they talked about it in that work environment.

Claire: They talked about it all the time. Constantly.

Shelley: That made you feel like it was a place you didn't want to be working in?

Claire: Yeah, I tried to ignore it but it just got to the point where I was chasing after one of them with a spanner telling him to shut up.

Shelley: So sexist attitudes about women?

Claire: Yeah I can't stand that and all these jokes like, "Why do women have small feet? To get closer to the sink" and all this. I don't find that very amusing. *(Claire, sixteen years old, career guidance center)*

Prea: I think it's society not seeing a woman as equal to a man. I think it's hard. You know like with me it's being Asian and everything. I get society's views and then I get the community's pressures as well. We have some people who think that a girl shouldn't go away from home, go to university. You know live that kind of life. They think like that. I'm lucky in that way because my parents are quite liberal in that way and they do understand. They look at what I want to do, my dreams and things but then they always think about what other people are going to say.

Shelley: So do you feel that sometimes there's conflict?

Prea: Yes definitely. I don't have that same sort of freedom as other people. Sometimes I wish they just didn't worry about what other people say. Just do what they want to do. I know my Mom has regretted a lot of things—things that she wanted to do but didn't because of what things people might say. I don't want to fall into that. *(Prea, nineteen years old, completing a GNVQ at Pearson College)*

In these two examples, the young women speak about limitations to their own choices as being about how they are positioned within a general set of relations that operate to place restrictions on young women's lives. This positioning has produced a particular experience that these young women seek to interpret and describe by employing discourses about gender inequality and, for Prea, the intersection of gender with her own ethnicity.

In all of the examples discussed here, sets of relations organized by difference are understood as one of the ways through which choices and opportunities are ordered. To understand the relationship between difference and the kinds of identities under production in this study, recognition of the dimensions that reside within the relationship between difference and identity is required. When the practitioners constructed their institutions in terms of specific relations of difference and social division, they did so at the macrolevel of analysis—at a level of abstraction where reference is made to patterns of social relations that persist over time and space (social class, gender, ethnicity, and age). The young women drew upon the same discourses also at the macrolevel, but only in relation to the general subject of "young women." At the microlevel of their own subjective experience, however, recognition of the self as this general subject began to fracture. There was a tension between these two planes—the subjective and the social, or the immediate and the abstract. This can be explained by appreciating that identity is about the disjuncture between those discourses that seek to inscribe the subject in certain ways and the ways in which the subject engages in the interpretative practices of identity formation. Identity is about both similarity and difference, correspondence and dissimilarity. It not only involves the ways in which subjects see themselves in the representations available, but also how they construct the meaning of those differences and position themselves and others through that understanding.

Taylor's (1998, 345) distinction between identity as a social category into which individuals are placed on the basis that they are perceived to share a position (categorical identity) and identity as one's own uniqueness (ontological identity) is a useful way of understanding how experiential diversity enters into the constitution of self and claims about individual selfhood. On the macrolevel, discourses are about the positioning of the abstract collective subject; for instance, the category of "woman" as opposed to actual, historical women whose experiences and, therefore, identities are disbursed across multiple axes of difference such that individual experience and identity are not reducible to the collective experience. According to Brah:

The relationship between personal biography and collective history is complex and contradictory. While personal identities always articulate with the collective experience of a group, the specificity of a person's life experience etched in the daily minutiae of lived social relations produces trajectories that do not simply mirror group experiences. (Brah 1996, 124)

A key difference between those young women who identified themselves with the position of the collective subject of discourses about gender, ethnicity, and class and those who did not was whether they were able to recount experiences through which they came to understand themselves and their relations within these discourses in particular ways. Experience is an important part of identification, not as a foundational category or as the medium through which an essential interiority is expressed, but as a process through which subjectivity is formed. To understand how difference is constituted relationally, we need to focus on historical contexts and discursively organized processes within which subjects become positioned, thereby producing their experiences. It is not individuals who *have* experience but subjects who are *constituted through* experience (Scott 1992, 25–26). We seek to interpret and explain experience using the meanings and categories made available within historically specific contexts. Through experiences embedded within practices, traditions, rituals, ceremonies, and institutional forms, individuals come to recognize themselves as participants in social relations (Taylor 1998, 342). In this way, subjectivity is constructed in a continuous process, an ongoing, constant renewal based on an interaction with the world. It is produced "not by external ideas, values, or material causes but by one's personal, subjective engagement in the practices, discourses, and institutions that lend significance (value, meaning, affect) to the world" (de Lauretis 1984, 159). Our identities are about our own interpretive histories.

Experience of difference is a site of contestation and a discursive space where "different and differential subject positions and subjectivities are inscribed, reiterated, or repudiated" (Brah 1996, 116). To posit that discourses produce experience and therefore identities is not a move toward linguistic determination, for there is never a perfect "fit" between the self and the various categories through which we come to understand and construct the self. The unity that identity suggests is not "an all-inclusiveness sameness, seamless without internal differentiation" (Hall 1996, 4). Instead, it is the "channelling of excess of meaning into a relatively structured form" (Jervis 1998, 325). This excess of meaning interrupts overdetermination and in this way difference allows for agency because although subjects are constituted discursively, there are conflicts among discursive systems, contradictions within any one system, and the possibility for the deployment of multiple meanings. Subjects do have agency, not as autonomous individuals exercising their free will, but instead as subjects whose agency arises through situations and statuses accorded them (Scott 1992, 33–34). Identifications are both partial and contingent, as Brah explains:

When we speak of the constitution of individual into subject through multiple fields of signification we are invoking *inscription* and *ascription* as simultaneous processes whereby the subject *acquires* meaning in socio-economic and cultural relations at the same moment as she ascribes meaning by making sense of these relations in everyday life. (Brah 1996, 117)

Although Giddens is criticized for privileging unity over difference within his theory of reflexive identities, it is important to recognize that deconstruction of the unified subject into multiple selves does not mean that the subjectivity escapes coherence. Pieces, fractures, and divisions may well constitute the subject, but these fragments do not defy classification or unification into relations based on sameness. As Taylor argues, there is a need to understand identity not simply as unitary but nevertheless as possessing unity:

We need to understand the way in which, on the one hand, individuals build a sense of coherence through their multiple social identifications, and, on the other, the way in which categories of identity act back upon their incumbents, often ascribing ontological characteristics to their members. (Taylor 1998, 341)

This makes it possible to talk about concrete identities and subjectivities that are neither completely fragmented nor simply unified wholes but are coherent unities embodied in concrete, historically located individuals (Taylor 1998, 340). Brah indicates that difference operates within identity when she points out that identities are marked by the multiplicity of subject positions that constitute the subject. Therefore, identity can neither be fixed nor singular, but instead is a "constantly changing relational multiplicity," which, although in a state of flux, does assume "specific patterns, as in a kaleidoscope, against particular sets of personal, social and historical circumstances" (Brah 1996, 123).

CONCLUSION

This chapter has shown that identity is intrinsically about difference, where difference has multiple and complex dimensions. Difference is about the broadening outward of traditional parameters of social relations, such as gender, in which choice becomes an aspect of identity formation. It is also about relational economies through which self and other become positioned, and about individual diversity across time and space. In the first instance, difference is used by both the young women and the practitioners as a way of organizing an understanding of how social relations are structured across time and space such that there is consistency in what it means, for instance, to be a woman or middle-class. Difference translated into a particular relation to choice; thus, social relations are partly defined by a relational economy within which choices are differentially distributed. The idea of difference is utilized by individuals to account for how choices are structured; in other words, how one is located within relations of difference shapes and influences life chances. In short, difference as social inequality is a concept that people employ in their everyday interpretations of the social world. These constructions of social relations refer to categorical identifications—abstract collective subjects. Reflexive modernization undertheorizes these dynamics in asserting that a do-it-yourself biography is rapidly replacing ascribed biographies.

Despite the assignation of particular meanings to social relations and a structuring of relations through difference, many of the young women in this study exhibited, at the level of ontological identity, a more individualized account of the self. While recognizing that the other was constrained or limited, the autonomy of the self relied upon being different from other young women who face social inequality. Here, ontological identity signals the movement of identity away from broad social categories toward the expression of a self that is defined by one's own unique experience.

The operation of categorical and ontological identity, which is expressed in these accounts as relations of sameness and difference, reveals that the process of identity construction is simultaneously about stability and flux. For example, gender relations were often constructed as relations of difference, in which the autonomy of woman as man's other was restricted but gender was simultaneously about relations that had transformed significantly. The young women employed both definitions in the interpretations and constructions of their own experiences. The understanding of inequality being embedded in social relations and the ways in which these relations transform indicate that there is a high degree of reflexivity at work in these accounts. This could imply that this ability to reflect upon social conditions of existence might support conditions of further transformation, as when the young women refuse to identify their own experience with the collectively oppressed subject "woman" in favor of asserting their own difference, based upon individualized experience. This theme reemerges in chapter 7, in a consideration of feminism and identity politics. Furthermore, the awareness of changing patterns of gender relations indicated by both the practitioners and the young women supports the assertion that social relations of industrial society are being remodeled and becoming more fluid. This is an important consideration because identity is relative to constantly shifting external contexts, which means that identifications can transform as the significance of patterns of relations shift.

Giddens, by emphasizing the centrality of choice in this theory of identity, presumes that experiences that come to define the self are chosen, but as Scott argues, it is not individuals who *have* experience but subjects who are *constituted through* experience (Scott 1992, 25–26). The statement "we are what we make ourselves" is a process that is embedded within practices, representation, social relations, and so forth within specific historical and local contexts. Individualization is still shaped by patterns of social inequality, as is apparent within the institutional contexts constructed by practitioners in this study (schools, youth training, workplaces, the family, etc.), where ways in which discursively organized experience produces different identities.

Recognizing the operation of social categories like "woman" and one's identification with that category is a process inherently linked to one's experiential diversity or uniqueness. Indeed, understanding one's positioning within social relations often provides a basis for understanding one's ontological and categorical identities. Identities are never complete or whole but are in constant movement, such that things like gender discrimination or racism might in certain contexts or moments come to have a greater impact on the identities they produce than in other contexts. Coherence is a temporary moment, recognitions are fluid, and nonrecognition is not necessarily misrecognition.[16] It is possible to understand how certain relations work without that specific dynamic being descriptive of the most salient aspect of one's own relation to self within a particular context. Indeed, it is important to see difference as an extensive multiplicity—an affirmative conceptualization of difference that does not rely upon negation of the other, but as a positive articulation of the self's interconnectedness with others.[17] This way of thinking about difference affects the possibility of thinking about identity also as a creative possibility.

In chapter 6, the effects of processes of differentiation are considered in relation to the expanding possibilities for constructing oneself with regard to others within the context of intimacy. The idea of having an expanded range of choice of how to organize one's life is explored through a discussion with the young women about their feelings and attitudes toward marriage, child rearing, and domesticity. Specific attention is given to the ways in which a construction of the self as autonomous produces a series of conflicts and problems for the pursuit of interconnectedness and commitment to an intimate partner. Giddens's concept of the "pure relationship" is used to evaluate this discussion. The strategies that were developed are interpreted as an expression of the "right to difference" set within the context of expanding possibilities for lifestyles indicated by shifting and fluid patterns of family and intimate lives. This "right to difference" is about the right to make individual decisions and choices, whereby a "recognition of diversity and a respect for individual differences opens the way for new definitions of autonomy and authenticity" (Weeks 1995, 142). This is a right that is fundamentally about respecting different ways of being human and recognizing the various ways that potentially exist for achieving self-defined ends.

NOTES

1. This is not to suggest that multiple ways of making identifications were not possible in modernity. Indeed, modernity, as a historical epoch is characterized by a proliferation of identity schemes (Calhoun 1994, 12). However, the multiplication of possible identity schemes has become a more central focus for theorizing identity within postmodernity addressed particularly by poststructuralist theory, which allows for an interrogation of the multiple and shifting processes implicit in identity construction.

2. The conceptualization of difference is developed by Barrett (1987) in a useful discussion of how difference has been deployed in feminist writing and debate. Barrett also discusses the use of difference in modern psychoanalytical accounts of

sexual difference. Refer also to Brah (1996, 95–127) for a useful analysis of difference, diversity, and differentiation.

3. The meaning of "fragmentation" and the ways it is used in social theory are problematized in a discussion by McRobbie (1994, 27–29). Responses to fragmentation have different implications for one's analysis. For some theorists, fragmentation induces a nostalgic longing for a return to totality, while for others it is celebrated and aligned with the subaltern experience.

4. For discussions of identity that rely upon the notion of difference as a relation, see Anthias (1999), Brah (1996), Hall (1996), and Rutherford (1990).

5. Spelman offers the useful point that the oppressions one experiences are not a question of *quantity* but *quality* so, for example, racism experienced by Black women does not add an extra burden to sexism but a qualitatively different burden (Spelman 1990, 123).

6. On the other hand, theorists such as Spivak (1987, 1990) argue that "strategic essentialism" can be a useful strategy in developing a politics based on identity.

7. Taylor (1998) discusses this in relation to welfare discourses and the problems that social identity as a product of difference and similarity pose for social policy.

8. Hall argues that identity bridges the gap between the inside and the outside, or the personal and public worlds. Objective places here refer, in sociological terms, to structures or patterns of social relations that persist over time. Social categories provide a means for embedding the subject within the social, but are never determinate.

9. Bradley's (1996, 19) definition is useful here. Class is a social category that refers to lived relationships surrounding social arrangements of production, exchange, distribution, and consumption. Class is not just confined to economic relationships in this definition, but extends into a broader web of social relationships defined by, among other things, lifestyle, educational experiences, and patterns of residence.

10. The GNVQ in health and social work at Pearson College was also constructed by the tutors as a place within which one's social class had repercussions. For example, working-class families were said to be less supportive of their daughters pursuing a qualification than middle-class families.

11. These dimensions are reflected in Hall's (1992, 276) definition of identity, where the objective refers to patterns of social relations that exist over time and the subjective refers to the individual's perception of the self and how he or she fits into those sets of external social relations.

12. He mentions the GNVQ in health and social care as being particularly gendered, that is, pursued predominantly by young women, with participation by young men as rare.

13. The young women who came to the further-education college to complete this GNVQ were described as predominantly wanting to pursue careers in nursing or social work. However, many of the young women interviewed claimed that they wanted to use the qualification for entry into police work, prison work, and probation services.

14. The structure of the relationship follows the form: I am what I am because I am not that (the other). The self is defined against the other.

15. This tendency is argued in Bradley (1996, 7). Her point is that the meanings of social categories that organize social relations can change over time.

16. The term "misrecognition" implies that the subject fails to realize or understand his or her objective position, supporting the notion that there is a reality that exists outside of an actor's understandings, for example, in explanations utilizing the idea of false consciousness. Misrecognition is not used here because it contributes to a denial of agency. "Nonrecognition," on the other hand, suggests that the subject does not identify with a particular position within a specific set of circumstances. This term does not suggest that a position of inequality is irrelevant, but that a specific positioning is not relevant to the particular situation at hand, thereby allowing recognition to be made in other moments, places, and situations.

17. This way of thinking about difference is influenced by the work of Doreen Massey, as presented at the University of Leeds, Centre for Interdisciplinary Gender Studies, Annual Lecture (October 11, 2001).

Chapter 6

Intimacy and Individualized Biographies

> I think time has changed everybody's ideas ... because when my
> Mum was young I think everybody thought you go to school, you get
> married, you have kids, you look after the home and you can have a
> career but there wasn't as wide a choice in what kind of careers or the
> ways you could carry on your life. I think they were slightly restricted
> whereas today there doesn't seem to be that straightforward pattern.
> Everybody seems to be doing it in a different way. There's not as much
> pressure to have children when you're say twenty. A lot of people now
> seem to be thinking that they'll have their career first and then later on
> maybe in their thirties they'll look at having kids because there are
> choices now. They are slowly becoming more open.
>
> Mel, sixteen years old, completing lower sixth form
> at Greenwood School

In her description of the increasingly diverse ways of navigating the complex interrelationships between education, careers, marriage, domestic responsibilities, and having children, Mel has offered a rather compelling evaluation of the state in which relationships are purported to exist within conditions of reflexive modernity (Beck 1992; Beck and Beck-Gernsheim 1995, 1996; Giddens 1991, 1992). It is generally recognized that the organization of the private realm and the relations that constitute it have undergone tremendous transformation in the past thirty years. Key issues taken as indicators of change include the growth of domestic partnerships; decline in the popularity of marriage; and increases in the rates of divorces, remarriages, stepfamilies, single parenthood, joint custody, abortions, and dual-career households (Jagger and Wright 1999, 1). Factors such as these have influenced the study of intimacy and family relations from a perspective that suggests that family practices are becoming more diverse and fluid (Morgan 1996; Silva and Smart 1999).[1] One of the outcomes of transformations to the practice and organization of intimate relationships concerns the increased "diversity of family practices which need not emphasise the centrality of the conjugal bond, which may not insist on co-residence, and which may not be organised around heterosexuality" (Silva and Smart 1999, 1).

For young women, these transformations to practices of intimacy create the context within which they must attempt to incorporate intimate relations[2] into their individualized narratives and manage the tension implicit in the construction and enactment of a narrative that is simultaneously about autonomy and affiliation. In order to do this, they may evaluate the models on hand—the biographies their mothers have led, for instance—and choose to either follow these established paths, reject them, or reconfigure them according to the set of values, goals, and costs deemed most relevant to their own lives. This chapter explores the ways the young women who were interviewed conceptualized intimate relationships; the models of intimacy they were constructing for themselves; the dissonance that intimate relationships produced; and the strategies they employed for reconciling the conflicting demands of education, career, marriage, domesticity, and child rearing. The choices that these young women are making with regard to how they want to live their intimate relationships are analyzed with the objective of understanding what implications a self defined by autonomy may have for the positioning of oneself within intimate relationships.

MAPPING INTIMACY

Although the organization of intimacy is diversifying in late modernity, its significance is said to be intensifying rather than diluting. Both the diversifying tendencies and the increased emphasis that people are placing on intimate relationships are connected to processes of detraditionalization. As external references and authorities lose their influence, the individual becomes responsible for defining and choosing how to organize their own intimate relationships, but because these same sets of conditions produce uncertainty, the intimate relationship is sought out as a refuge—a space within which to explore oneself through mutual self-disclosure. In this regard, theorists of reflexive modernization argue that intimacy is becoming a central aspect of identity (Beck and Beck-Gernsheim 1995, 51; Roger 1996, 86–87).

Marriage is one form of relationship that has been affected by a transformation in the ways people seek out intimacy. Whereas marriage was historically "first and foremost an institution *sui generis* raised above the individual," there has been a shift toward it becoming a product constructed by those involved (Beck and Beck-Gernsheim 1996, 33). Central to this reconstruction is the questioning of forms that were once taken for granted because

It is no longer possible to pronounce in some binding way what family, marriage, parenthood, sexuality or love mean, what they should or could be; rather these vary in substance, exceptions, norms and morality from individual to individual and from relationship to relationship. (Beck and Beck-Gernsheim 1995, 5)

As Mel, quoted previously in this chapter, points out, there are now more choices available to young women and a general openness to charting one's own course. Her description reflects the theoretical contention that new family practices are emerging as the influence of dominant models diminish along with rigid, pre-given paths of living (Silva and Smart 1999, 4). As Morgan (1996) suggests, individuals no longer passively accept pre-given models and family structures, but are actively creating new ways of handling family relations and routines. Indeed, all of the young women interviewed here identified the extent to which the conditions under which they were having to confront decisions about their lives had changed in comparison to the situation their mothers had faced when they were a similar age. When asked if they thought their life would be different from their mother's, the overwhelming majority agreed it would be. This was primarily attributed to the different ways education, careers, marriage, child rearing, and parenting would have a bearing on their lives. Within these areas—the traditional split between public and private spheres—they felt the most dissonance with the lives their mothers had lived. Stress was often placed upon the life she had *been able* to live rather than the *choices* she had made. Indeed, the young women often commented upon the lack of choice available to their mothers—a lack of choice and options that had significantly constrained their mothers, but that they felt contrasted sharply to their own level of access to opportunities. In this regard, the models lived by their own mothers were described by young women as constituting the most traditional means of negotiating intimacy and autonomy. The characteristics of such a model included limited choices, self-sacrifice, regret, and dependence on a male partner. It is not surprising, therefore, that almost all of the young women rejected the notion that they might follow the same path:

Lauren: My Mum was twenty-two when she had me. She was married to my Dad and they'd been together since she was fifteen and all that kind of school romance stuff and she's always been a housewife and tied down and she wishes she hadn't done that. She's never been bothered about travelling and I am.... My Mum is very family oriented whereas for me it's like "I live here and here and here and this is where I venture." So I think our lives are completely different. *(Lauren, nineteen years old, career guidance center)*

Prea: My Mum does everything in the house. She manages everything and I
           don't know how she does it. She does the cleaning, she works, she
           manages the finances and everything. I mean she never, ever questions
           my Dad. She will not say a thing. I tell her to say something.... She has
           not once stood up for herself ever and I wish that she would. *(Prea,
           nineteen years old, completing a GNVQ in health and social care at Pearson
           College)*

Caroline: My Mum and Dad they've got a relationship where they're partners in
           business but my Mum does everything at home like cooks and things
           like that and they don't do things together like I would in a
           relationship. They're very happy with how they are because it has been
           like that from the beginning but I wouldn't want to be like that. I want
           to be in an equal relationship and do a lot of things together. *(Caroline,
           nineteen years old, completing a GNVQ in health and social care at Pearson
           College)*

These young women expect to be able to insist on having equality within
their relationships and, unlike their mothers, they assert that they will
have a greater degree of freedom to live their lives as they want, not only
within the context of their relationships, but also with regard to the effect
their intimate relationships will have on the choices they make in other
areas of their lives. The emphasis they place on equality reflects the way
women's biographies have become more individualized, as ascribed gender roles have transformed in late modernity. Beck (1992, 110–11) argues
that women have been freed from the traditional traits ascribed by femininity and identifies five conditions that have led to shifts in the structure
of women's biographies. These include (1) increasing life expectancy,
which constitutes a demographic liberation from the role of childbearing
and rearing; (2) the deskilling of housework, which has directed women
outside the home in search of fulfilling work; (3) availability of contracep-
tion, supporting intentional motherhood; (4) growing divorce rates, which
translate into a condition where women cannot necessarily rely upon a
husband for financial support; and (5) the equalization of education opportunity, "which is among other things also the expression of a strong *career* motivation" (Beck 1992, 111).

   Transformations to women's roles, however, produce a series of conflicts and contradictions that may have a destabilizing effect on intimate
relationships. What Beck terms the "individualisation spiral"—labor
market, education, mobility, career planning—has a pronounced effect on
the family as the family becomes a "continuous juggling act with divergent multiple ambitions involving careers and their requirements for mobility, educational constraints, conflicting obligations to children and the
monotony of housework" (Beck 1992, 111). According to Beck and Beck-
Gernsheim:

The new factor altering love and marriage is not that somebody—meaning the
man—has become more himself, more individual in the course of modern

times.... What is new is the individual *female* biography, freeing the woman of family duties, and sending her out into the world with an impetus which has been increasing since the 1960s ... as long as it was only the man who developed his potential and the woman was complementarily obliged to look after him and the others, family cohesion remained more or less intact—at the cost of her own interests or personality. (Beck and Beck-Gernsheim 1995, 61)

The young women interviewed were aware that they will not have to be confined to the role of housewife, they can demand equality within their relationships, and they enjoy a significantly greater scope of freedom to decide how these relationships will fit into to their life trajectories than women have had previously. However, given that they have the option of rejecting the traditional routes that their mothers were more compelled to follow, what alternatives are they formulating as potential replacements? The constructions emerged according to four different patterns: traditional, deferred traditional, negotiated, and nontraditional.[3]

Traditional Intimacy

The traditional pattern is most closely aligned with the expectations of traditional femininity.[4] This model was adopted by only a small minority of the young women for whom aspects of it seemed appealing. Jessica, for instance, expressed frustration at how long it would likely take to arrive at her goal of having a home, a marriage, and children:

It quite worries me actually because I always sort of think, "When am I ever going to [get married]?" If you have to go through all these 6 or 7 year relationships before you do get married then what age am I going to get married at? (laughs) But I do want to get married. I have my image of the perfect marriage with the perfect little house, and little kids and I've always wanted to do that. I mean if it were up to me now, I could happily drop everything [education, career goals]. *(Jessica, nineteen years old, completing a GNVQ in health and social care at Pearson College)*

Sarah was also willing to accept the constraints of marriage and domesticity because she saw this as not only a viable alternative to having a career, but also as a choice that *should* exclude working outside of the home. She admitted that having a career, a marriage, and children would be difficult, but only for women who want to be "really successful" outside the domestic sphere. These women, she argued, shouldn't have children because they are too busy to spend enough time with them. Specifically, she identified the "high-flyer" type of woman as such a person, which she herself was not "bothered to be":

I'm not bothered when I get married and have kids to be the one who goes out to work. I'd rather just take a back seat and just look after them—put them first because I'll be sharing my life with someone. It won't just be me all the time. There'll be a husband and children first so in that way my life will change—not putting myself first. *(Sarah, sixteen years old, completing lower sixth form at Greenwood School)*

Sarah's comments may well produce unease for their construction of women's paid labor as being more a case of personal indulgence rather than essential to the maintenance of the household. One effect of this attitude is the reinforcement of traditional stereotypes that tie men, as earners, to the public realm and women, as unpaid housewives, to the domestic realm. Furthermore, this attitude suggests that for women, working outside the home is a choice that can be rejected. Yet, while interpreting her narrative in this way produces these effects, her position may also be read through the lens of choice and autonomy. Choosing not to be the "high-flyer" type of woman is the other side of the coin, where seeking out a career for matters of individual satisfaction is counterbalanced by the assertion of the equally valid option of choosing not to. In this regard, these comments may be indicative of strategies to evade or resist the normative constraints of enacting a relation to the self that is defined by a privileging of independence over intimacy.

Deferred Traditional

In this model, most of the traditional aspects of women's domestic roles are retained—getting married, having children, staying at home to care for children, and sacrificing one's career—but rather than adopting this arrangement in their early twenties, as many of their mothers had done, the young women who deployed this model expressed a determination to defer it to some point in the future when they would be prepared to *choose* to enter into it:

Lynn: I mean ideally I would like to get that ideal family concept. You know, husband, kids, husband coming home for tea but not until I've done what I want to do because if I get married and have kids I'm going to think back, "Oh I wish I would have done that." So I want to do things and then if I want, to settle down. *(Lynn, eighteen years old, completing a GNVQ in health and social care at Pearson College)*

Shayne: Oh yeah. I think I will get married. I mean I can't see myself having dozens of children but 2 would be nice. A part of me thinks marriage, nice husband, nice home, respectable life but part of me thinks career woman and I'll be successful. I think I could have a bit of both. I think if I knew I was going to get married later on as long as I'd done what I want before getting married. Like if I'd done a law degree and practised for a year or so and am happy with that. Even if I married into a family where I liked the guy but he was slightly strict I think because I'd done what I wanted to do with my life, I could sacrifice further for them. If I hadn't the opportunity to do that already I wouldn't stand for it. *(Shayne, seventeen years old, completing lower sixth form at Ripley School)*

The main feature of this model is having one's own life first before making the sacrifices perceived as inherent in committing to a partner and having a family. There was a perception of an almost inevitable loss of one's autonomy in the way this model was constructed. Being able to pursue education and career goals, to enjoy independence, and to establish an identity were held up as important objectives, but ones that had to be achieved prior to accepting the constraints of domesticity and intimate commitment. As such, life trajectories for these young women were defined by two separate phases—one defined by autonomy and the other by sacrifice—thus combining the logics of their own life narratives with the logic perceived as underpinning their mothers' narratives. For example, Mel, a sixteen-year-old sixth-form student at Greenwood School, explained that she did want to eventually have children, but not straight after marriage, as she would want to "establish me as a person and not as a mother or somebody who is related to another person." The value of autonomy and the need to preserve it as long as possible were the primary reasons for devising deferral of commitment to a relationship as a strategy for incorporating intimate relationships into their life trajectories.

Negotiated Traditional

The negotiated model of intimacy follows the same logic as the strategy of deferred traditional—the need to establish one's own identity prior to commitment—however, in this model, making the commitment to marriage and having children was not seen as irreconcilable with maintaining autonomy and independence. Instead, it emerged that these young women perceived an inherent conflict between the workplace and the domestic realm, and between asserting their own desires and managing the expectations of others. They believed that working through these conflicts would necessitate a number of negotiation strategies. Generally, the young women who adopted this model were attempting to reconfigure the traditional model in order to arrive at a compromise that would maximize the satisfaction that could be derived from being *both* in a committed relationship and having one's own separate existence. In these cases, the young women expressed a determination to avoid the potentially negative or constraining consequences of domesticity:

Shelley: Do you see yourself getting married?

Nikky: Yeah but I don't want to just stop things because I get married. I want to carry on doing what I want to do but getting married isn't going to stop me. It's just another thing that I want to do. *(Nikky, sixteen years old, completing lower sixth form at Greenwood School)*

Here, marriage is constructed as potentially limiting to one's range of opportunities, but unlike in the deferred traditional model where constraint is perceived as almost inevitable, there is the expectation of being able to resist and negotiate these constraints. One of the most frequently cited problems that would have to be resolved was the performance of domestic roles. As Joanne explained, she doesn't mind who does what around the house as "long as he does his share and doesn't leave it all to me like if I'm cooking and cleaning then he can look after the children or when he was cooking then I'd take care of them." Very few of the young women assumed that equality within the domestic realm could be taken for granted, and they expected to have to work to ensure it. For example, when it was suggested to Sasha that her husband might expect to her stay at home, she worked out a strategy in her narrative to combat this possibility:

I'd go, "I'll pretend I didn't hear that!" I'd educate him before we had children about stuff like that. I mean you forget don't you? Like if I said to him on the wedding night, "Listen when we have children this or that," he'd probably forget by the time we had them. I said to my sister, "You have got to get it written down. Get him to sign it!" She said, "It doesn't seem like marriage then. It seems like a contract." That's how it's got to be but I think it depends ... hopefully my husband isn't that narrow minded and I wouldn't stand for it. *(Sasha, seventeen years old, completing lower sixth form at Ripley School)*

Compared to the other models of intimacy, negotiated traditional must accommodate a considerable level of ambivalence, which is produced by the knowledge that wanting to maintain one's own identity and entering into a shared commitment with an intimate partner will require a degree of reconciliation. Overall, however, it was the model most often adopted. What these young women are identifying are the inherent contradictions of traditional forms of intimacy and the problems that individualization processes produce for the goals of connecting with another person while preserving self-autonomy.

From the perspective of reflexive modernization, the conflicts that must be continually managed by the individuals involved in an intimate relationship can be linked to contradictions inherent in processes of modernization. In this analysis, modern industrial society is premised upon the opposition between wage labor and household labor and the corresponding ascription of male and female roles. Insofar as industrial society depends upon the separation of these roles, it is also dependent upon gender inequality; however, these inequalities violate principles of modernity[5] and as modernization proceeds, become increasingly problematic (Beck 1992, 104). As ascribed gender roles dissolve, along with their constraining influence, biographies become ever more individualized with the implication for intimate relationships that two labor-market biographies must be accommodated. Problems arise specifically within the domestic realm because the traditional organization of the family presumes gendered inequality inscribed in different gender roles. One of the many questions that emerges from this set of conditions is how to find a balance between autonomy, the pursuit of one's own goals, and the desire to make a commitment to another person who is also equally engaged in constructing an individualized biography. Beck and Beck-Gernsheim explain:

What appears to be an individual failure, mostly the fault of the female partner, is actually the failure of a family model which can mesh *one* labour market biography with a lifelong housework biography, but not *two* labour market biographies, since their inner logic demands that both partners have to put themselves first. Interlinking two such centrifugal biographies is a feat, a perilous balancing act, which was never expected so widely of previous generations but will be demanded of all coming ones as more and more women strive to emancipate themselves. (Beck and Beck-Gernsheim 1995, 6)

In the post–World War II period, not only have traditional gender roles destabilized, but also the distinction between public and private spheres.[6] Examining the relation between these spheres reveals that changes that have occurred in the organization of the nature of work are associated with changes in the organization of the family. Crompton, Gallie, and Purcell (1996, 37) identify three main changes to the realm of employment that have had a significant impact upon the organization of work and family: (1) the shift to a service economy, (2) the impact of technological changes and information technologies, and (3) the decline of the male breadwinner or single-earner model of employment and household.

A further tension to be managed is the discrepancy between a growing consciousness of gender equality and the resilience of structured gender inequality, as well as the gap between female expectations and the reality of unequal distribution of rewards and opportunities. In considering the increased range of choices regarding how to live one's life, it becomes apparent that there are distinct choices available and that the navigation of these choices leads to different consequences for men and for women—one of which is the reproduction of gendered inequality. Thus, the negotiation of choice is also about the reconfiguration of identity, for as Jagger and Wright (1999, 5) remind us, "addressing gender-based inequalities in heterosexual family relationships, and the sexual division of labour from which they spring, involves changing prevalent understandings of femininity and masculinity and the construction of gender identities."

These factors mean that daily life becomes infused with questions about roles and responsibilities, including domestic tasks. These might range from who does the washing up, to more complex conflicts rooted in issues surrounding mobility and personal career sacrifices, such as might be the case where one partner wants to move to another geographical location to accept an employment opportunity. What happens to the other partner when such a choice arises? Whose interests, priorities, and commitments matter most, and if both hold equal weight, how are these choices to be managed? The model of negotiated traditions constructed by most of the

young women in this study highlights the dynamics of individualized biographies and their recognition of the contradictions that remain in the organization of female and male biographies and their traditional location in
two different spheres.

Some evidence indicates that these young women are quite right to
expect that equality will have to be negotiated in their personal relationships rather than be taken for granted. In a review of research that has
addressed the extent to which married or cohabiting couples have
moved away from the traditional arrangement of man as "bread-
winner/head of household" and woman as "housewife/domestic ser-
vant" toward more egalitarian and symmetrical partnerships, Jamieson
(1998) found that much progress is still required if equality is to be established. As an indicator of equality, a much-studied factor has been the division of domestic work by couples and their distribution of total income
within the household. Findings suggest that, "heterosexual coupledom
remains surprisingly organised around man-as-the-main-earner and
woman-as-domestic-worker/carer despite the prevalence of dual-earner
households" (Jamieson 1998, 137). While equality may be a conscious goal
of both partners, evidence exists that many couples continue to reproduce
gendered inequality through a division of labor that finds women performing the majority of the household chores. Jamieson argues that the resilience of these patterns is evident in the ways that justifications and
explanations were produced by many couples in the studies reviewed to
account for the fact that their relationship was not as egalitarian as they
might have claimed. Although a model of intimacy grounded in traditional gender roles may be destabilizing in late modernity, an unequally
gendered division of labor seems to provide much potential for conflict
and discord, as these young women suggest in invoking a model that is
premised upon negotiation.

Nontraditional Alternatives

The final model that emerged as a framework for structuring intimacy
was one in which the conventions of marriage and domesticity were most
outwardly challenged and replaced with distinctly different models.
These reconfigurations suggest that traditional forms of intimacy were not
taken for granted as the way one should live, but instead challenged and
therefore made to seem less like facts and more like a matter of individual
preference. Beck and Beck-Gernsheim (1995, 35) argue that as private lives
become increasingly open to questioning, the concomitant need for the invention of solutions to newly emerging challenges arises. These alternative models for intimacy reveal what these young women perceived to be
viable options for living out their intimate relations.

The least extreme form of challenging convention was based upon a
perceived desirability of living together as an alternative to getting mar-

ried. As in the other models, the goal was to find a partner to share one's life with, but on a different set of terms that originated from within the relationship and not from the imposition of external conventions. These types of relationships are most closely aligned with what Giddens argues is an emergent form of intimacy in late modernity—the "pure relationship." The legitimacy of these relationships relies less upon external validation and more upon what the individuals involved perceive as desirable. For example, Georgia and Shannon question the immediate legitimacy that the institution of marriage grants to relationships:

Georgia: I see myself with somebody. I'm not sure about the ring on the finger but I see myself living with someone and acting like a married couple. I'm not sure that I really see the point in marriage because you're going to be together, living together and I don't know if you need a ring and 10,000 pound debt or whatever it costs now to get married just to say that you love him or that you're going to be with him so I don't know if I am going to get married but I see myself in a relationship. *(Georgia, eighteen years old, completing a GNVQ in health and social care at Pearson College)*

Shannon: You can show just as much commitment to a person living with them as you do getting married but it's just people's views that you should get married. Like my Mum says, "Oh you have to get married!," and I say, "Why Mum?" It's just to make them feel better really, your getting married but at the end of the day you don't have to anymore. *(Shannon, nineteen years old, completing a GNVQ in health and social care at Pearson College)*

Both of these young women challenge the notion of a legitimate relationship as one that necessarily culminates in a formal marriage. However, it could be argued that this strategy only minimally undermines the traditional organization of intimacy, as it still to some extent approximates the characteristics of conventional marriage. Anna, on the other hand, proposes quite a radically different option derived from a critical assessment of societal expectations. Her ideal, however, was far from typical:

I don't think that I will get married but I might live with someone. I don't think that I will have children of my own. I'll probably adopt. I just want to live a kind of family that isn't—well, I'd want one that's more like a commune I suppose where people are individual but just living together and just sharing their lives where there's no set roles.... I really hate any kind of restrictions ... and when it comes down to it you've been gunning for Oxford or whatever and the school is trying to channel you into doing this and you wake up one day and think, "I'm not happy and I don't want to do this and this is my life and why the hell am I doing this just because society is telling me I have to do it?" *(Anna, eighteen years old, completing lower sixth form at Ripley School)*

Brenda, a nineteen-year-old who has a sixteen-month-old daughter, offered one further example of a nontraditional construction of intimacy. In many ways, Brenda's narrative fits the traditional mold: She has had a baby at a young age. She is living with her boyfriend (the baby's father). Their goal is to buy their own home and get married. What makes her narrative unique, however, is the way marriage is self-consciously structured into it in a reversal of the traditional order of life events. Marriage, while part of the picture she constructs in her narrative, is incorporated as an endpoint rather than as a beginning. It is positioned as the event that will eventually be appropriate for her once she has secured a career, a home, and "everything that she wants to do with her life." In contrast, the model of deferred tradition involves getting married as a deferred event that then sets into motion a sequence of events—mainly having children, leaving full-time employment, and making self-sacrifices for the sake of one's family. For Brenda, who wants many of these same things—a committed relationship, a child, a home—the necessity of entering into a marriage first is not perceived as a requirement. Brenda critically and consciously reconfigures the relationship between commitment and marriage. In her model, two people don't first get married—formally committed—then build a life together. Instead, they build a life together and then eventually consider marriage; thus, the conventional temporality of intimacy organized within the conventions of the life course is reconfigured. In Brenda's following comments, there is also the suggestion that marriage in itself is a problematic goal because it often doesn't last. If marriage is something that she considers to be necessary not so much for her and her partner, but more so to impart certain advantages to their daughter, then there is also a hesitancy to enter into marriage derived from the knowledge that relationships break down. If one cannot assume that marriage lasts, then why use it as a point of departure for making a life together?

Shelley: Do you see yourself getting married?

Brenda: I'd like to but not for me but for my little girl. So she's got a married Mum and Dad maybe.

Shelley: When is a good age for you to get married?

Brenda: When I've got my career and I've got my house and I've got everything that I want then I'll do it.

Shelley: Why would you wait?

Brenda: Because I want those things before I get married. I suppose with the situation I'm in now with my boyfriend is near enough to marriage because we've got a little girl and we're doing the things we want to do but I think it's taking that step into marriage. That document where you've got to if you want to separate go through a divorce and everything and it's a real proper commitment. I'd rather do it when I've got everything that I want to do in life. *(Brenda, nineteen years old, career guidance center)*

In summary, the four models of intimacy mapped out here indicate that to a certain extent destandardization of the organization of intimate relationships is taking place whereby the freedoms open to individuals to define the parameters of intimacy result in an expansion of a sense of individuality and personal autonomy (Cheal 1991, 133). The extent to which these young women were able to construct for themselves ways of negotiating relationships while still preserving their individual identities serves as an indication of how a greater degree of choice is available to them compared to their own mothers. However, the models that were constructed do not support the suggestion that traditions have disappeared altogether. Instead, it is the case that continuity resides alongside diversity in intimate relations and family life (Silva and Smart 1999, 4). Certainly, many aspects of traditional arrangements of parenting, partnering, and sexuality are reproduced in these narratives, while coexisting with a reflexive engagement with conditions that allow for individual choice.

"POST-COUPLEDOM"

Intimate relationships were an important aspect of the narratives these young women were constructing. Whether through an acceptance of traditional relationship arrangements or via a critical reconfiguration of those traditions, these young women did see themselves as entering into some form of commitment with a partner at some point in their future. In one respect, this acceptance of forming a committed, monogamous relationship as an ultimate goal in life undermines suggestions that increasing numbers of young people are choosing to be single—a form of lifestyle that is supposedly becoming increasingly attractive to young people (Heath 1999, 554). Opting out of "coupledom" could also constitute one way of negotiating intimacy in late modernity, and although these young women did not take up this alternative as a long-term strategy, the idea of being single in the short term was often seen as both an acceptable and appealing choice to make. Indeed, to construct being single as a *choice* is significant because one of the strongest connotations of being single, historically for women in particular, is that it is not a choice but instead an unfortunate position in which one finds oneself as a result of a relationship breakdown or simply the product of one's inability to find a suitable partner—in short, an undesirable status that one would not choose to inhabit.

Attitudes toward being single emerged in discussions regarding a fictional scenario that described a young woman's dilemma about a troubled relationship with her boyfriend.[7] The responses to this situation were nearly equally split between advising to end the relationship on one hand,

and on the other, to first attempt a negotiation with him before breaking it off.[8] The choice to be single was seen as a viable solution to the dilemma because it would allow the young woman in the scenario to embrace independence. The value of this independence was measured against the degree of hassle and constraint that was perceived to characterize relationships with men. In the following example, Lynn doesn't reject the idea of being in a relationship, but points out that staying in a relationship can often be due to social pressure and that underlying this pressure is the inability for many people to understand being single as a choice. Similarly, Claire explains why being single is a desirable choice to make:

Lynn: I think that if she isn't entirely happy she should look at why she isn't happy and if she can't get rid of what's making her unhappy, like his attitudes won't change, then she should get rid of him and she should have someone positive in her life. If they can't even decide where they're going out then god! You know what I mean? You're supposed to give and take in a relationship and I think she may be insecure but she'll be able to cope on her own definitely because once you get out of the routine of being in a relationship then you realise that it may be socially acceptable to have a boyfriend but without one you can get rid of the pressure. Like with me I always get asked, "Don't you have a boyfriend?" and I say, "No." "Well, why not?" "Because I don't want one." When you're at a point in your life when you don't want one some people find that very hard to grasp. *(Lynn, eighteen years old, completing a GNVQ in health and social care at Pearson College)*

Claire: I like being single because I do what I want to do. I don't have to ask permission to do it which is what I had to do with my ex-boyfriend. I'd phone him up and say, "Do you mind not coming down tonight? I fancy going out with my mates" and he'd argue with me, then I'd say, "Okay come down if you want but I won't be in." *(Claire, sixteen years old, career guidance center)*

In discussing this relationship scenario, the value of achieving and preserving one's independence was asserted and reconfirmed. This issue was at the heart of the dilemma—how to be in a relationship without losing one's identity and autonomy. Preservation of an independent identity was pursued through a variety of strategies that had their efficacy in that they served to decentralize the importance of the relationship. While it was perceived that maintaining the relationship was an acceptable goal, it was often suggested that it would be best for the young woman in question to focus on other aspects of her life so as to limit the impact the relationship with her boyfriend would have on her. This involved shifting her focus to other kinds of intimate relationships like friendships, "because boyfriends come and go but friends are always there." Spending less time with him, therefore, and instead concentrating on friendships was seen as a way to explore and assert one's self reliance:

Lucy: The thing I don't like about relationships is having to answer to some-
           one else and always seeing what they're going to do. Boyfriends always
           have this problem with me because my friends have always been more
           important to me than they are. They say choose your friends or me and
           it's always been my friends. *(Lucy, seventeen years old, completing lower
           sixth form at Greenwood School)*

Emilia: I think sometimes [being in a relationship] you can neglect your friends
           which is stupid especially at my age because it shouldn't be what all
           your attention is focused on. It should be friends, developing your own
           personality, doing well in school. *(Emilia, seventeen years old, completing
           lower sixth form at Ripley School)*

Lianne: I just finished with my boyfriend about 3 days ago. It was my decision. I
           just didn't want to go out with him anymore. I just want to concentrate
           on getting a job and things, have some fun and freedom and spend time
           with my friends and family. *(Lianne, sixteen years old, career guidance
           center)*

One of the ways it can be considered that intimacy is transforming,
then, is in questioning the desirability of entering into a committed relationship at all. This idea, expressed here by these young women, is beginning to emerge in popular culture in the representations of and,
arguably, the idealization of single lifestyles. The "New Singletons"—
people in their twenties and thirties who live alone and choose not to get
involved in a relationship—have been interpreted as indicative of the
beginning of a vast social change in which marriage and commitment
are no longer held as the ideal. In relation to debates regarding the declining significance of the family, Morgan makes the point that the single-person household is one of the most rapidly growing household
types, which he defines as being a key feature associated with late
modernity (1996, 197). In a newspaper article about "post-couple"
Britain, single women are held as the future, in which there will be more
single-person households than any other kind (Rayner 2000, 1). This actively chosen lifestyle is attributed to increased affluence, lower rates of
marriage, and the rise in relationship breakups. In this article, single
lifestyles are constructed as an ideal in which people consciously choose to
steer clear of emotional commitments, avoid parenthood, and instead commit to being alone. It is speculated that this new attitude will have vast
transformative implications, particularly for consumption and lifestyle
patterns. While these young women chose to be single as a strategy for negotiating and resolving problematic romantic relationships, these findings
do not necessarily support the contention that more young women will ultimately choose "singledom" as a long-term lifestyle. The value of choosing to be single in this study was primarily a short-term strategy—the
value of which was to be found in the independence it allowed—however,
as discussed earlier, all of the young women perceived themselves as be-

coming involved in some form of committed, intimate arrangement in the long term.

NEGOTIATIONS

The relationship scenario was interpreted as being not only about the importance of autonomy, but also equality. While simply leaving the relationship was one way of resolving the conflict, just over half of the young women advocated embarking on a process of negotiation with the boyfriend in order to establish equality within the relationship. As in the negotiated traditional model discussed earlier, tactics of compromise, bargaining, and mutual concessions were suggested as the best way to secure both individualism *and* partnership. Intimate relationships were often perceived as the site of conflict and a space within which male dominance had to be resisted. This is interesting because while the young women tended to assert that they as a gender were gaining more power and equality in general, intimate relationships were often seen as one area in which men still resisted treating women as their equals—thus the need for ongoing assertion of one's self-identity. Lauren's following comments highlight the tension perceived to be at the heart of intimate relationships, a tension rooted in male dominance:

They run you down so much you feel like you can't get anyone else so you have to cling onto this person. They make you feel that they are the only person in the world that will ever care about you, will ever think that you are pretty. So if someone tells you something often enough you will believe it. So he's probably telling her, "You won't get anyone else" blah, blah blah so she thinks she won't and she has to stay with him but it's just his way of making sure she doesn't leave him. *(Lauren, nineteen years old, career guidance center)*

It was more unusual for the young women to declare that equality within intimacy was just as important to young men. Anna's comments, for example, were in the minority because she insisted that young men's attitudes toward female autonomy have transformed such that it is a quality now regarded as a positive asset to a relationship:

I think a lot of boys find it [feminism] attractive actually because it's something to which they can relate. I think that most boys don't like having a relationship with someone they can't talk to. That may be just the boys I associate with but I think in the long run if someone is actually going to be your partner, given the way society is now, there is much more the idea that you have a relationship that is emotional and that you're talking.... Now it seems you have to spend more time as a couple and going out together and doing things as a couple as opposed to being man and wife. You tend to be more equal. *(Anna, eighteen years old, completing lower sixth form at Ripley School)*

Although Anna's comments are unusual because she asserts that young men are attracted to feminists, her comments do reflect a perception shared by many of the young women that a central part of being in a relationship is engaging in mutual disclosure of emotions and being able to express oneself. Negotiation and compromise were viewed as inherent aspects of a successful relationship and as such, being able to talk to your partner and develop open lines of communication were identified as essential to a successful relationship. This particular construction of intimacy is indicative of what Giddens terms "confluent love"—the central feature being the presumption of equality in emotional give-and-take. Intimacy is dependent upon the extent to which the partners are willing to reveal themselves, their feelings, their needs and concerns, and make themselves vulnerable to each other. These principles were apparent in the responses to the relationship scenario:

Mel: I think Sarah should speak to her boyfriend and come out plainly with what she thinks and if there is a basis for the relationship then the boyfriend will listen and see if they can come to some compromise. *(Mel, sixteen years old, completing lower sixth form at Greenwood School)*

Lianne: Trust and communication are important. If you can't trust someone then I don't see the point at all. You've got to be able to talk. If you don't want to see him one night then say, "I'm going out with my friends." You can trust him and he can trust you and that just makes you appreciate each other and not seeing each other all the time, every day. *(Lianne, sixteen years old, career guidance center)*

In these examples, the young women are advocating open communication as a strategy that would allow one to be in a relationship, while also retaining individuality and autonomy. The form of intimacy suggested here has certain parallels with Giddens's pure relationship, which depends upon a form of intimacy constituted by ongoing negotiation and communication. The lack of external reference points such as familial obligations, kinship ties, and social roles and duties means that the relationship is freely chosen; in order for it to survive the conflicts and contradictions accentuated by processes of individualization, a constant appraisal of its internal dynamic is necessary. This entails a commitment on the part of both individuals to developing and maintaining the quality of the relationship. Since the relationship may be as freely exited as it was entered, it cannot be taken for granted and must be worked at by both partners through mutual trust and disclosure. Commitment means a willingness to do this work, but only until the rewards and satisfactions delivered by the relationship cease or are deemed inadequate. Thus, "the possibility of dissolution … forms part of the very horizon of commitment" and the relationship is acknowledged as only "good until further notice" (Giddens 1991, 187).

While Giddens stresses that intimate relationships are becoming less tied to external reference points and more attuned to an internally referential dynamic, it would be an error to overstate this point, particularly with regard to the values that are being deployed in these young women's narratives. In seeking to create models of intimacy that can accommodate the identity under construction, the values that underpin these models do not spontaneously emerge from within the relationship itself but are very much universal principles. These values are invoked as standards for norms of conduct to which the relationship is expected to conform. In other words, when they invoke the abstract ideals of trust, honesty, respect, and equality in their narratives, they are constructing a framework for intimacy that relies upon values that exist prior to any particular relationship; therefore, these models for intimacy do rely very much upon an engagement with external reference points.[9]

One of the central challenges characteristic of the pure relationship, Giddens argues, is the contradiction posed by the need for commitment to sustain the relationship, on the one hand, and, on the other, the knowledge that relationships are far from durable. Some kind of guarantee that the relationship will last for an indefinite period must be provided to one's partner; however, where marriage was once taken for granted to be a lifelong commitment or a "natural condition," inherent in pure relationships is the fact that the relationship can be terminated, more or less at will, by either partner at any particular point. The paradox is that commitment is necessary for the relationship to last, but "anyone who commits herself without reservations risks great hurt in the future, should the relationship become dissolved" (Giddens 1992, 137).[10]

While the value and, indeed, the desirability of negotiating an intimate relationship were upheld by these young women, this attitude was often expressed in the face of knowing that relationships are not necessarily forever. This was apparent in the narrative of nineteen-year-old single mother Joanne, who is ambivalent about the prospects of marriage being able to offer her the security she feels she needs, not only because of the breakdown of her previous two relationships,[11] but also because of the impact the divorce of her own parents had on her. She wants to believe that marriage would be a positive thing for both her and her son, Jason, but sees it also as a potential risk because of the damage that occurs when relationships don't last. However, her comments also highlight something that Giddens overlooks in his analysis of the pure relationship—that investment in a relationship is not only about how it serves the interests of each individual. There is also another category of persons whose interests are very much at stake, but who do not command the resources or autonomy to protect themselves from the effects of the end of a pure relationship.[12] In the following narrative, Joanne contemplates what marriage would mean for *both* herself and her son:

Jason would have a brother or sister and someone would be there for me and Jason. It does scare me a bit though. When I met Wayne it was like, "I want to marry you," but now I don't know. I think I'm scared to. I don't know. Like my Mum and Dad getting divorced. I was ten when they got divorced so my brother was younger and he got all the attention and I was left to deal with it on my own.... I'd live with someone and probably get engaged and maybe in years and years and years I could maybe get married but I want to make sure it's right because I don't want to put Jason through what I had to go through. *(Joanne, nineteen years old, YouthWorks program)*

Of the thirty-three young women interviewed, four had children, and this was a significant influence on the way they constructed intimacy. Their own relationship to intimacy was mediated by their relationship to their children; therefore, intimate relationships were evaluated by these young mothers not just in terms of the potential impact on themselves as individuals, but also in terms of the potential impact on their children. The reflexivity in operation here is about evaluating what is in one's own best interest; however, the issue of how interests are constituted demands recognition that the interests in question are not about an isolated individual. It is likely that "interests" do not exist independently of the interconnectedness of relations that constitute one's identity. Individual interest can rarely be isolated because the constitution of the self through relations with others is not clearly demarcated from the social field of interconnections within which the self is embedded, nor can it be contained within a discrete boundary where one can clearly mark off a territory where one's own interests solely exist independent of one's multiple relations. This begs the question, Where do my interests end and the other's begin? Giddens's model of the pure relationship does not acknowledge the relational aspects of any decision or choice that one makes or the complexity of the intertwining of interests that are involved in life-choice deliberations.

The proposal that intimate life is undergoing a restructuring in late modernity was also evident in the ways the practitioners spoke about the tensions inherent in the conditions under which young women were negotiating their choices. The main source of the confusion and conflict that young women were seen to be experiencing was attributed to the clash between domesticity and careers. According to Mr. Preston, head of sixth form at Ripley School, young women were ambivalent about how to fit partners and children into their other goals, such as pursuing careers and individual achievement: "They don't want to get married like Mum and Dad but on the other hand if they meet someone nice they would like to stay with them." These comments suggest a lack of alternative models, an unavailability that leaves them to navigate a course on their own. Mrs. Conway, head of Greenwood School, suggested that one alternative is the rejection of husbands and marriage altogether. According to her, although there was a time when young women asserted that they would have it all—career, family, house, and husband—young women are now rejecting that for something altogether different:

They don't want to be superwoman.... What's now emerging is that you can have your career and indeed you should have your career and you can have a designer child. Forget the husband and family bit, which I find absolutely amazing. When you talk to the sixth formers about what they want, they want a child but they don't want a husband. They want a career and one child actually. It will be theirs and theirs alone. They seem to think that won't bring the responsibility of family with it. That that's easier to manage.

Mrs. Conway's assessment is echoed by the analysis made by Beck and Beck-Gernsheim, where they argue that as intimate relationships become less durable, people seek to find ways of being close to someone else— often a child. Whereas once men and women turned to each other to find themselves and make love the center of their existence,

We have now reached the next stage; traditional bonds play only a minor role and the love between men and women has likewise proved vulnerable and prone to failure. What remains is the child. It promises a tie which is more elemental, profound and durable than any other in this society. The more other relationships become interchangeable and revocable, the more a child can become the focus of new hopes—it is the ultimate guarantee of permanence, providing an anchor for one's life. (Beck and Beck-Gernsheim 1995, 72–73)

The tutors at Pearson College made similar assessments of the ambivalence young women have toward marriage and family. It was their perception that no longer do young women think of their education and training as a means of pursuing a career to "tide them over until they get married and have children," but they are beginning to question the assumption that they will get married at all. As Rose, a tutor on the GNVQ in health and social care, explained, many of the young women expressed the desire to have children, but to wait until they were in their mid-thirties and not necessarily within the context of a marriage. She qualified her comments, however, by saying that the young women were adamant about marriage and children not being a priority.

CONCLUSION

The young women in this study were not taking for granted that their life trajectories would follow an orderly pattern of education, jobs, marriage, children, and domesticity. In this regard, the routes they constructed for themselves tended to contrast significantly with the patterns they perceived their mothers to have followed. This shift in the form of their narratives is due largely to their perception of having more choices and opportunities available—a condition that allows them to construct their individualized biographies according to values, goals, and convictions consistent with their own narratives, instead of being derived from an expectation that life follows a uniform pattern practiced by everyone. One of the dominant values that informed the process of incorporating intimacy into their trajectories was autonomy. While intimate relationships were lent significance and certainly constituted part of the future, the value of autonomy, also central to the young women's narratives, provided a source of ambivalence, as autonomy and intimacy were perceived as incompatible. The way they presented their goals represents a logic of "both/and." The main obstacle to overcome within this problematic was the maintenance of a self outside of an involvement in a relationship.

Certainly, there are aspects of the young women's idealized constructions of intimacy that are consistent with Giddens's analysis of relationships in late modernity. However, there is also a considerable degree of tension within these narratives that is derived from the context within which these young women know intimacy is embedded—a set of social structures and practices that are organized through gendered relations of power and expressed within heterosexual intimate relations. For instance, the dynamic inherent in the most common model—negotiated traditional—is very much about autonomy and individuality, but it is also very much about the way gendered relations of power and inequality more generally come to bear upon the space that is about two people working out their relationship. Not only does Giddens's analysis fall short of theorizing this important point, but he also fails to acknowledge the substantial feminist literature that allows for a more thorough analysis of this dynamic.

The models of intimacy and negotiation strategies discussed by the young women are constructions rather than concrete practices. It is difficult to know how the values underpinning these constructions will affect the way these young women live out their future relationships, but this makes the values and ideals expressed here no less relevant. First, there is no discrete or uniform demarcation between what people say and what they do. Furthermore, consistency between these two aspects of agency varies with the mediating influence of many factors, such as both time and space, making it very difficult to predict in advance when what they say and do will seem contradictory. Second, the significance of the values constituting intimate spaces is also related to the private/public relationship. Although there has long been a line drawn between the private and the public spheres, the location and nature of this boundary shifts, and indeed the very division has been increasingly challenged (Morgan 1996). The ideals and values that govern the subjective meaning of intimacy within what is seen as private life are inextricably linked to the public sphere.[13]

Weeks (1995) makes the important argument that it is vital that problems generated in the realm of intimate life should reach the political agenda:

"Private life" has generated the social movements, around sex, gender, race, the quality of life, which have significantly changed the political agenda—and in so doing have shifted the boundaries between public and private. They have also, as we have seen, affected the ways in which we try to define our personhood, and our identities—identities which themselves dwell on the borderlines of the public and the private—and have thus begun to change the meaning of what it is to be an individual in society. (Weeks 1995, 136)

Expressions of the value of autonomy, respect, and freedom within the narratives created here constitute "rights of everyday life," specifically a right to difference (Weeks 1995, 140–47). Within the context of an increasingly pluralistic culture, the right to equality is being replaced by the right to difference—which can be interpreted as an endorsement of the right to make individual decisions and choices—whereby a "recognition of diversity and a respect for individual differences opens the way for new definitions of autonomy and authenticity" (Weeks 1995, 142). This is a right that is fundamentally about respecting different ways of being human and recognizing the various ways that potentially exist for achieving self-defined ends. Giddens (1992, 184–204), in a much more ambitious argument, similarly links the private with the public domain when he argues that the transformation of intimacy and democratization of the private realm has consequences for the wider social order:

The advancement of self-autonomy in the context of pure relationships is rich with implications for democratic practice in the larger community.... In positional bargaining—which can be equated with a personal relationship in which intimacy is lacking—each side approaches negotiation by taking up an extreme stance.... Global relations ordered in a more democratic manner would move towards principled negotiation. Here the interaction of the parties begins from an attempt to discover each other's underlying concerns and interests, identifying a range of possible solutions. (Giddens 1992, 195–96)

Within the context of theorizing transforming patterns of intimate relations and changing family forms, rights to difference are important because they allow the development of an understanding of the ways family practices are being carried out, which avoids interpreting change as the breakdown of the family or as an indication of moral decline (Jagger and Wright 1999, 10; Silva and Smart 1999).[14] From the point of view of policymaking, Silva and Smart (1999) argue that theorizing fluidity and shifts in family configurations can inform ways for institutional supports and policy frameworks to enhance autonomous choices in living arrangements. Understanding changing family forms is also linked to understanding transformations to gendered identities because, as Marshall (1994, 132) points out, transformations to family arrangements implicitly involve transformations to gendered identities and the gendered inequalities that the "family, both as an institution and in practice, may sustain" (Jagger and Wright 1999, 5).

There is considerable debate over whether relations such as gender, ethnicity, and class, which are articulated through intimate relationships, will be affected by transformations in how individuals organize and practice their intimate relationships. The narratives constructed here do tend to reproduce heterosexuality and fail to question the normativity of these practices or fully destabilize the ways in which they organize sexuality. As for the destabilization of gender, for instance, Jamieson (1999, 481) argues against the likelihood that male privilege will be substantially undermined through transformations of heterosexual intimacy. Indeed, she is very skeptical about the potential a democratization of the personal has to effect wider transformations to social relations. However, this argument fails to adequately acknowledge the wider sociohistoric context within which these issues are located. We already know that these young women are aware of the vast social transformations that have affected the context of their daily lives in comparison to the relatively more constrained conditions within which their own mothers confronted questions of identity. Vast transformations to the ways in which gender is perceived have occurred. McRobbie's (1999, 46–61) work, for instance, shows how discourses around intimacy in young women's magazines have altered significantly. Where the emphasis was once upon romance and passivity, femininity is now more likely to be defined by an active female sexuality. These shifts are about what McRobbie terms "the social relations of sexuality," which underpin representations and also make possible the invention of new practices and identities for those who come to inhabit these emergent relations. The personal realm of individual choice is intrinsically linked to relations, practices, and knowledges that constitute the public in a reciprocally constitutive relationship. In addition, to deny that intimacy is being performed in many new and creative forms relies upon a rather simplistic assessment of the relationship between those intimate spaces of everyday life and wider public spaces. Indeed, Jamieson's argument, by denying the link between heterosexuality and wider social processes, tends to reproduce the private/public binary that feminism has long since undermined. Ultimately, these debates do raise questions about the relationships between individual narratives and social change—an issue that is examined in the next chapter.

The pursuit of intimate relationships by the young women in this study, no longer bound by the same set of expectations faced by their mothers, was designed according to a set of patterns that exhibited characteristics of both old traditions or forms of intimacy and newer rules that seek to reinvent ways of being in a relationship. The old social forms, lived by their mothers, are destabilizing, but a desire for intimacy remains. Although these young women are left to navigate a series of contradictions, they are doing so within a set of conditions that allows for different routes to be constructed. The tensions they experience in navigating the contradictions have produced a set of strategies, the most common being a perceived need to develop ways of negotiating equality and reciprocity within the relationship. Unlike their mothers, who were seen as having settled for less than they should have, these young women asserted the right of opting out if their conditions were not met. The ideal relationship is one in which intimacy is based on equality, commitment is negotiated, and being in a relationship is ultimately not taken for granted but seen as an active choice.

The implications of the autonomous self and its connection to a right to make one's own choices are further examined in the next chapter in relation to politics. Dimensions of difference continue to be explored, where the notion that identities can be constituted within uniform categories is examined in relation to the project of feminism. Generational difference, as illustrated in chapter 7, means that young women have different options. The implications of age as a source of difference between women are explored, and it is suggested that a politics of identification must be embedded in the practices of everyday life, whereby it is possible to find localized resistant identities at work. Like the construction of the intimate self, this is a self that is based upon a right to self-determination. The link between this right to choice and individualism is discussed as a hybrid of Giddens's emancipatory politics and life politics—a hybridity that can be thought of as constituting a postfeminist politics.

NOTES

1. Silva and Smart (1999, 1) make the important point that increased diversity in the ways people choose to live their intimate lives can be interpreted in two distinct ways: either as a symptom of moral decline contributing to the end of the conjugal, nuclear family; or, more positively, as changes occurring in "relation to evolving employment patterns, shifting gender relations, and increasing options in sexual orientations." This latter model views the family as a fluid set of practices and relations that does not remain stable but changes in relation to wider social trends. Shifts in patterns of intimate relations, therefore, are not to be interpreted as signs of moral decline—a position often reflected in conservative ideology. This point highlights the discrepancy between the family as an ideal type (what it ought to be) and the actualities of how families are organized. Barrett and MacIntosh (1991) also make a distinction between the family as a social and economic institution and the family as an ideology. Jagger and Wright (1999, 3) argue that both of these aspects can be distinguished from the empirical realities of individuals and their families.

2. Intimate relationships include friends, family, and partners. The focus in this chapter, however, is on heterosexual, monogamous relationships and their construction. This is not to assume that all of the young women in this study were heterosexual. Nor is it the intention to perpetuate the heterosexual nuclear family as a normative ideal and extension of what Butler (1993) terms "heterosexual hegemony." See Jagger and Wright (1999, 10) for an examination of this issue. The discussion of relationships with the young women in this study was restricted to heterosexual relations because no other model of sexuality emerged in their accounts. None of them mentioned homosexuality as an alternative to heterosexual relationships, and although it would seem that the norm of heterosexuality operates to define sexuality at the exclusion of other alternatives, it is not the intention of this analysis to suggest that identification with other forms outside the constraints of heteronormativity is not possible.

3. These models, like the construction of the nuclear, heterosexual family, constitute ideal types that in practice may overlap with other models and do not necessarily translate directly into ways people live their lives. For purposes of analysis, this scheme indicates how the young women were constructing ways of practicing intimacy rather than accepting pre-given models. The expression of diverse models for practicing intimacy, however, supports Cheal's claim that since the 1970s, in most Western countries, processes that contributed to the standardization of the family life cycle have either stopped or reversed, resulting in an increasing proportion of household configurations that depart from the normative pattern of family life (Cheal 1991, 124).

4. More specifically, the expectation that the woman performs the duties of housewife, while the man acts as the main wage-earning head of household (see discussion in Jamieson 1998, 138–57).

5. Beck (1992, 14) argues that industrial society rests upon a contradiction between the universal principles of modernity—civil rights, equality, functional differentiation, methods of skepticism—and the structure of its institutions in which these principles can only be realized on a partial and selective basis. The consequence of this contradiction is that industrial society destabilizes itself through its very establishment—"continuity becomes the 'cause' of discontinuity" (Beck 1992, 14).

6. The tendency in sociological analysis has been to perpetuate the distinction between work and home within industrial society (Morgan 1996, 15). However, the distinction between the gendered spheres of public and private, work and family, or employment and household is somewhat false. As argued by Silva and Smart (1999, 7), "only recently has mainstream sociological analysis of family life and intimacy begun to reject the traditional presumption that the family is an institution which is separate from other social institutions." For a discussion of the private/public division within modernity, see Cheal (1991, 81–118).

7. The scenario presented was as follows: Sarah currently has a boyfriend that she has been with for the past eight months. She spends most of her spare time with him. They have been fighting a lot lately because he always decides what they're going to do when they go out. Her friends tell her to just break it off. They

say she is just insecure. Sarah admits that she isn't totally happy but she has always had a boyfriend and doubts if she really would be happier on her own. What should she do?

8. Seventeen of the young women advised negotiating with him as the first strategy, while sixteen advocated breaking it off.

9. See Jamieson (1999, 486) for a discussion of this issue.

10. The very nature of what women have to risk by entering into a relationship is itself changing. The transformation of a woman's position within the labor market is of particular relevance in this regard. For instance, a woman's social and economic status has become less dependent on the status of her husband. Therefore, as Silva and Smart (1999, 6) argue, the more women come to appreciate this and achieve more secure routes to a decent standard of living than what marriage can provide, the more marriage and intimacy will destabilize. If a marriage did not provide the expected satisfactions in terms of identity, affection, sexuality, and so on, then a woman could leave the marriage without risking a decline in her standard of living.

11. The first of these relationships was with the father of her two-year-old son. At the time of the interview, she had recently split up from another relationship and had experienced a miscarriage.

12. For critiques of Giddens on this point, see Bauman (1993, 336) and Smart and Neale (1999).

13. For example, there has long been an association between the family and moral order (Jagger and Wright 1999, 10). Controversy often surrounds the formation of family life and how people choose to live their intimate relations. These moral debates often center on what the family *ought* to be in comparison to what *it is* (Silva and Smart 1999).

14. For a discussion of how postmodernism has affected the sociological project of theorizing the family, see Cheal (1991).

Chapter 7

Emergent Feminist Identity(ies):
The Micropolitics of Postfeminism

The propensity of young women to espouse opinions compatible with a feminist viewpoint yet at the same time express an almost complete non-identification with feminism is certainly not new. The intergenerational currency that feminism has come to lack has been a recurring problem that continues to bring to bear questions regarding the relative success or failure of second-wave feminism.[1] A recent manifestation of such an evaluation of the significance of second-wave feminism for young women surrounded the release of Germaine Greer's book, *The Whole Woman.* Reviews of the book and articles about Greer in the popular press at the time of the book's release contained questions such as, "She's back. But does she still matter?" and "Is she relevant to young women?" In one specific instance, these kinds of questions were embedded in the structure of a page layout in a national newspaper that contained an advertisement for a talk by Greer, promising, in relation to her book, a discussion of the "future of feminism." Set provocatively alongside this advertisement was another one for Natasha Walter's book entitled *The New Feminism,*[2] described as "feminism for a new generation." The underlying message here is not only that generational differences exist with regard to feminism, but that those differences are often in opposition to each other.

In seeking to analyze how young women engage with the possibilities they confront in fashioning an identity in late modern society, it has been obvious that an important aspect of this analysis is the influence of second-wave feminism. This influence is complex and is at least dual in its significance. The first aspect of feminism that is relevant to consider in relation to the lives of young women involves the role feminism has played in bringing about changes to the social order, which in turn have resulted in young women having more choices available to them compared to previous generations. The second mode of influence is the extent to which feminism as a discourse has entered the mainstream, becoming what Erica Jong has said in relation to young women, "is the whole climate of their lives, the air they breathe. It hardly even needs a name anymore" (Jong 1999, xix). Feminism is available for use as a potential resource in navigating the very choices it has helped to create, but as made evident by the debates around Greer's current relevance, the nature of the relationship between feminism, young women, and life choices demands further consideration.

DIFFERENCE, FRAGMENTED FEMINISMS AND THE "POSTFEMINIST SELF"

The aim of this chapter is to arrive at an understanding of the identities that the young women interviewed were producing and the implications of this relation to self for the current state of feminism. This requires the following: first, an examination of the problem of difference, specifically in relation to age as an undertheorized source of fragmentation within feminism; second, to frame this problem in the context of debates surrounding the meaning of "postfeminism"; third, to assess the extent to which the self-constructions of young women at the turn of the twenty-first century can be deemed feminist or postfeminist; and finally, to relate these issues to the context of late modernity and the tension between emancipatory politics and life politics.

In relation to diversity contained within the category "woman," it is becoming apparent that age is an increasingly significant source of difference. For example, Sylvia Walby in *Gender Transformations* examines the high degree of success young women in the 1990s enjoyed in both education and employment, and concludes that age is a major differentiator of women's employment patterns because younger women have gained access to education and employment with considerably more success than older women (Walby 1997, 55). Therefore, it is age that most clearly shows the increasing polarization in the experiences of women, which implies that there is an immense differentiation between the lives of younger and older women as the result of social conditions that have transformed dramatically in the past thirty years (1997, 59).

In Britain, young women are now outperforming young men at primary school, secondary school, and into higher education as well. They are getting better results in both GCSEs and A-levels, and they are making great gains in entry to traditionally male-dominated fields (Roberts 1995, 47).[3] As recently as ten years ago it was young men who held the advantage in educational attainment, but now young women are more likely than men to participate in further education (Walby 1997, 44). It is interesting to note that the areas of choice identified by the young women in this study as being most central to their lives, as discussed in chapter 3, tended to be these same areas where large gains have been won by and for women. Education and career options were very important to these young women, whether they were aiming for university degrees to be followed by professional careers or seeking to enter the workforce as soon as possible via training schemes or apprenticeship programs. In view of these kinds of shifts in gender relations and social structures, age will continue to provide a source of difference between women, which implies that these conflicts will continue to provide sources of fragmentation for feminism.

One of the central topics addressed throughout this study has been how these young women defined and engaged with the choices they had available to them as part of their reflexive "project of the self." For young women in contemporary society, processes of individualization and detraditionalization mean that not only are a wide range of options available to them in terms of their self-definition, but that an active negotiation of positions that are potentially intersecting and contradictory is necessary. How is the navigation of choices available to young women related to generational difference and the debates about the currency of feminism in the late modernity? In the biographies produced by these young women, is it possible to claim evidence of the viability of feminism for this generation? In the analysis of the interviews, generational difference appeared to be of consequence because, for example, very few references were made to feminism at all and yet the values invoked were entirely consistent with a feminist perspective. A consideration of this absence requires an inquiry into the meaning and significance of "postfeminism."

The consequences of generational difference for a unified feminist movement are often framed within the context of an antagonistic relationship between younger and older women in which references are made to "bad daughters," and "lifestyle feminists" versus "victim feminism." Generally postfeminism is approached with guarded skepticism by second-wavers, while a younger generation of women display resistance to adopting an identification with a form of feminism they feel has no relevance to their daily lives. This friction is largely a variation of an issue that feminism has had to confront before, that is, the problem of difference.

AGE AS A SOURCE OF DIFFERENCE

The recognition of exclusionary tendencies and the presumption to speak for all women within feminism marked a significant turning point in the development of feminism, both as a body of theory and a political movement (Hooks 1981; Riley 1988; Spelman 1990). By challenging the unity of the category "woman," the biases inherent in early second-wave feminism were exposed, thus forcing a critical reappraisal of assumptions underlying feminism as a form of identity politics. Judith Butler has effectively framed the problem of difference for feminism as one of (mis)representation. The goal of feminism has been to represent the interests of women and in so doing has laid claim to the existence of a female subject who can be represented, but pitfalls are inherent in such a strategy. According to Butler:

The domains of political and linguistic "representation" set out in advance the criterion by which subjects themselves are formed, with the result that representation is extended only to what can be acknowledged as a subject. In other words, the qualifications for being a subject must first be met before representation can be extended. (Butler 1990, 1–2)

Feminism claims to represent a subject that itself constructs. The paradoxical consequence is that feminist goals risk failure by a refusal to take into account the constitutive powers of feminism's own representational claims (Butler 1990, 4). In short, the subject of feminism is produced by a discourse that claims to represent it, and this representation is possible only at the expense of the exclusion of other identities. Ultimately, the fragmentation within feminism and the opposition to feminism by women who it claims to represent are indicative of the limits of identity politics. In response to those who would suggest expanding the scope of feminism to make it more inclusive, Butler (1990, 5–6) argues, "what sense does it make to extend representation to subjects who are constructed through the exclusion of those who fail to conform to unspoken normative requirements of the subject?"

The problem of making feminism more inclusive has been one that feminists have taken very seriously and continue to struggle with. Increasingly, the literature makes reference to "feminisms," recognizing the extent to which the category "woman" is characterized by difference rather than equality in terms of race, class, sexuality, nationality, and religion, to name but a few of the intersecting discourses that constitute women's simultaneous positionings. While difference has become acknowledged as one of the most serious challenges facing an increasingly fragmented feminism, the issue of generational or age-based difference remains undertheorized.[4] Indeed, a consideration of the voices and concerns of young women has, until recently, been virtually absent from academic debates. This absence was addressed in a recent issue of the journal *Signs*, devoted to the topic of "Feminisms and Youth Cultures." The motivation for the issue was

To interrogate how the lived experiences and cultural products of youth articulate, reflect, and transform feminisms, as well as how feminisms and associated analyses have themselves transformed those same lived experiences and cultural products. That is … how can an analysis of youth cultures innovate and renovate interdisciplinary feminist studies? (Bhavani, Kent, and Widdance Twine 1998, 575).

Thus, we return to the question: What can we learn about the relationship between young women and feminism?

IS POSTFEMINISM ANTIFEMINISM?

Intergenerational disagreement about what constitutes a feminist issue or a feminist identity has been a central feature of debates in which the meaning and significance of postfeminism is assessed. From one position, postfeminism is constructed as a thinly veiled form of antifeminism. Writers such as Susan Faludi or Marilyn French implicate the work of Naomi Wolf and Katie Roiphe, for example, in a backlash against feminism. While this younger generation of writers attempts to deliver new perspectives on some of the old problems confronted by feminism, their theories are often seen not only as flawed versions of real feminism, but as contributing to a hostile climate for feminism full stop.

Postfeminism is often construed as antifeminist on the basis that it is seen to create the false impression that equality has been achieved, thereby encouraging young women to pursue their individual freedoms at the expense of a collective female identity. From this perspective, the problems that young women encounter in achieving their goals are constructed as individual challenges, rather than political problems that are best faced collectively. Writers such as Wolf are criticized for placing responsibility for resistance in the hands of individual women in what amounts to a liberal individualist politics (Whelehan 1995, 220). Furthermore, it is argued that postfeminism promotes an image of feminism as being responsible for the unhappiness women experience as a result of trying to have it all, rather than as a movement that provides solutions to the problems women face. Faludi argues that, regrettably, in a postfeminist climate, feminism as an oppositional discourse has lost its currency because it is seen as "so seventies." Postfeminism from this perspective, therefore, means not only that women have arrived at equal justice and have moved beyond it, but also that they simply are beyond even pretending to care. This indifference, Faludi contends, may deal one of the most devastating blows to women's rights yet (Faludi 1992, 95).

While an older generation of feminists expresses disappointment about the ways in which a younger generation of new feminists like Wolf or Walters engages in feminist issues, this younger generation argues that the terms and conditions of so-called old feminism are no longer pertinent and carry harmfully proscriptive overtones. It is useful to return to Butler's (1990, 5–6) argument about the futility of extending representation to subjects who are constructed through the exclusion of those who fail to conform to unspoken normative requirements of the subject, because this point about difference and the normative nature of discourse can be extended to the issue of young women's nonidentification with feminism. For example, Naomi Wolf recounts her experience of exclusion:

My friends and I are all self-defined feminists. But we know that if we were to stand up and honestly describe our lives to a room full of other feminist "insiders"—an act that should illuminate the route to female liberation—we could count on having transgressed at least one dearly held tenet on someone's list of feminism's "do's" and "don'ts." (Wolf 1993, 68)

The entrenchment of these two positions seemingly results in a frustrating and most unproductive stalemate. However, there is a body of literature that now attempts to move beyond the negative evaluation of postfeminism to a framing of the concept in more productive terms. Brooks (1997), for instance, argues that postfeminism is not antifeminism, but an *expression of a stage* in the constant evolutionary movement of feminism. As a conceptual frame of reference, it encompasses the intersection of feminism with a number of other antifoundationalist movements including postmodernism, poststructuralism, and postcolonialism. As such, it is the expression of a critical interrogation of the foundations of feminism, the goal of which is to address the conceptual shift that has occurred within feminism from debates around equality to a focus on debates around difference and how feminism might come to terms with difference.

The prefix "post" is used here not as a signifier of a complete break in previous social relations or as the overcoming of oppressive relations, but instead as implying a *process of ongoing transformation*. This represents not a depoliticization of feminism, but instead a political shift in feminism's conceptual and theoretical framework. Postfeminism does not assume that patriarchal discourses and frames of reference have been displaced, but signals a reflexive consideration of this context that takes as its point of orientation a critical engagement with feminism's own frameworks. Thus, a challenge to various hegemonic assumptions of earlier feminist epistemologies and underlying assumptions is made and new spaces are opened up.

The focus of the following analysis is based on the assertion that the young women in this study were creating politicized identities, and that this is relevant to processes of ongoing transformation to gender relations. These identities are examined in relation to both versions of postfeminism. On the one side, postfeminism as antifeminism frames young women as depoliticized actors espousing liberal individualist politics in the pursuit of individual goals. Such a position relies on a politics founded upon a feminist identity that young women are seen to lack. On the other side of the debate, postfeminism is interpreted as constituting a reflexive engagement with the limitations of hegemonic forms of feminism in order to understand how feminism is shifting and evolving. This commitment reflects the position expressed in the *Signs* special issue on female youth cultures, namely, a sustained engagement with the question of how the study of young women might renovate feminist studies. How might we interpret young women's constructions of self as a form of political agency? How might we understand their engagements with choices and the creation of their own identities as expressing a politicized agency within conditions of postmodernity? These questions are tied to the point McRobbie makes when she argues that

Politics occurs in the act of breaking away from the claim to be represented. New, emergent or otherwise excluded identities emerge from this discourse of rejection and repudiation. "This is not us," they are saying. And in saying so there is also a question of who indeed "they" are. (McRobbie 1994, 73)

In the interviews, the young women discussed their perceptions of gender inequality and factors they felt limited the choices and opportunities available to them. The suggestion that their options might be limited by external factors was met with a very strong expression of individualism, which reflects what Weeks (1995) identifies as a right to difference.[5] The principle of upholding individual rights and responsibilities was used to critique the suggestion that they might not be allowed to make choices in their lives. This was expressed in terms like, "Don't let anyone tell you what to do," or "You just have to do what you want." It is interesting, however, that this focus on individualism, which has been a defining characteristic of the self-narratives discussed throughout this book, took on a pronounced resonance when tied to the issue of gender inequality. Despite critiques that claim postfeminism contributes toward young women's mistaken belief that equality has been achieved, many of the young women interviewed in this study maintained that gender inequality was still a prominent issue in women's lives. When asked about the limitations that are placed on their own lives, the most frequent answer related to men and women having different opportunities available to them.

Gender relations were generally constructed by these young women as a set of relations in which men have traditionally possessed more power than women, but with a recognition that this arrangement had transformed significantly and would continue to do so through a gradual progression. Thus, traditional power arrangements were seen to be destabilizing, but not to the point where inequality was no longer an issue, as evidenced in chapter 6, in the context of intimate relationships. The main areas identified as resistant to equality and in need of further transformation were sex stereotyping in careers, unequal pay, access to opportunities for advancement in the workplace and in sports, sex stereotyping in domestic roles, and the double standard of sexual practices. To account for why equality had not yet been achieved, many of the young women drew on the notion that traditional, restrictive views about women's appropriate roles intermingled with more progressive opinions. These traditional views were identified as one of the causes of continued resistance to women's equality. Men were not necessarily perceived as a universal category with regard to their beliefs toward women and, indeed, the kinds of attitudes that continued to promote inequality were often attributed to older men. The following comments identify an older generation of men as the primary source of discriminatory attitudes:

Lauren: I think that boys my age are more used to equality because for women there are a lot more choices out there for women as you come through school—you know what you want to do kind of thing. I think they have grown up with it a lot more than the older generation has because the older generation was when women were very limited. So the ones in my generation have grown up with it and they are used to it. *(Lauren, nineteen years old, career guidance center)*

Prea: The guy I am seeing now, he sees me as an equal you know in the sense that anything I want to do he won't say, "That's a man's thing to do" like when I said what job I want to do [police officer] he didn't say that's a man's job but my uncle did. *(Prea, eighteen years old, completing a GNVQ in health and social care at Pearson College)*

While the perception of a generational difference in male attitudes was a dimension evident in accounting for remaining resistance to women's equality, there was also an equally strong assertion that men, both young and old, were generally threatened by women gaining equality because it constituted a threat to male power and privilege:

Lynn: I think that with some of the guys I know they actually get intimidated that a woman can get a lot higher than them now. They feel a bit over whelmed because most of their parents are the typical ones where like the wife stayed at home with kids and the man worked. *(Lynn, eighteen years old, completing a GNVQ in health and social care at Pearson College)*

Kitty: I think with the older men it scares them, makes them feel less powerful because they've always had the power haven't they? They've always been in charge and women are taking control more now and I think that scares them. Some guys my age respect it more. They think, "Good for you" but other ones just try to keep you down. *(Kitty, eighteen years old, career guidance center)*

Mel: I think equality has quite shocked them especially with the Spice Girls and things, the dominance of women and things. I think the men like it up to a point, you know, they've got more assertive women and things but there's a slight worry because you see quite a few stories in the news where they are saying that businesses are now picking women for jobs because they are more intelligent and I think men are a bit frightened by that as well as quite happy. *(Mel, sixteen years old, completing lower sixth form at Greenwood School)*

Mel's comments capture one of the central themes relating to the assessment of the current state of gender relations: that conditions for women have changed dramatically; that young women now enjoy a wide range of choices about how to live their lives; and that they have the right to self-determination. Coexisting with these conditions, however, are those that position women in certain ways that restrict their rights and define them as different—that is, less capable than men—thereby making resistance an issue of ongoing relevance. Posing answers to this dilemma, though, revealed a tendency on the part of these young women to attribute responsibility for a solution to individual women rather than identify with a collective political movement, as the following quotations illustrate:

Shelley: Do you think men and women are equal in our society?

Lianne: No. I think women are getting more respect in what they're doing now and people are realising that we're not just there for cooking and cleaning. We can do just as good as men can do and better but no I don't think we are.

Shelley: How do you think that those existing inequalities can change?

Lianne: Just women taking charge, not listening to, "No you can't do that." You've got to go for it and not listen and if more women started to not listen and just do what they want to do instead of being put down all the time then it'll change. *(Lianne, sixteen years old, career guidance center)*

Shelley: How do you think existing inequality can be overcome?

Sasha: I think it is very hard to change something that has happened over generations but I think women have to stand up a bit more for themselves in a way. I don't know how realistic that is or how many people would do it but they should stand up more for themselves and argue their case. They should just argue or discuss it. If they want it badly enough they should. *(Sasha, seventeen years old, completing lower sixth form at Ripley School)*

Shelley: Why do you think men and women are still treated differently?

AJ: Probably because women still let people treat them like that. If we stood up more because men just think they are in charge but you've got to stand up and say, "No you're not! We've got just as much right!" We've still got to get that confidence to stand up and say we're just as good. *(AJ, twenty years old, YouthWorks program)*

Each of these excerpts expresses recognition on the part of the young women that inequality is still a barrier that women face, but when they speak of women in these accounts, they are referring to *individual* women taking responsibility for what they want. They do not recognize or identify *themselves* as the subject "woman" of feminist discourse, nor is the *abstract* woman they speak of clearly the subject of feminist discourse.[6] Instead, the majority of girls interviewed invoked the right of each individual to do what they want, which then translated into the promotion of individualized solutions. The value of individual rights was clearly apparent in their discussion of role models and ideal female qualities:

Lynn: The only person I've ever looked up to—I know this sounds stupid—is Sharon Stone or Madonna because they always do whatever they want and go against society and everything and I'd like to be able to do that. *(Lynn, eighteen years old, completing a GNVQ in health and social care at Pearson College)*

Raj: My Grandma always encouraged me. If there was something I wanted to do she always said that if you want to do it, just do it for your own sake. *(Raj, twenty years old, completing a GNVQ in health and social care at Pearson College)*

Shelley: What do you think is the definition of the ideal woman?

Alice: Someone that is strong and confident, successful, knows what they want and won't let anyone stand in their way. Professional as well but also be able to have fun and do what they want. *(Alice, seventeen years old, completing lower sixth form at Greenwood School)*

To understand how these comments can be situated or evaluated within the project of feminism, it is useful to examine the feminist discourses that young women have available to them. These discourses provide interpretative frameworks for young women and account partially for their experience. Skeggs (1997, 144) points out that "fragmentation, dispersal and the marketability and notoriety of certain aspects of feminism means that many women only have limited and partial knowledge about feminism." She identifies one accessible brand of feminism that is available to young women as "popular feminism." In the 1980s, Skeggs explains, this form of feminism became separated from professional and academic feminism, its main feature being that it could be marketed:

It is the ability to pull out the individualist aspects—such as sexual power, autonomy, respect, self-esteem—of feminism and make them marketable which has helped to generate ... contradictory effects. These aspects give feminism a popular front which provides selective appeal and reaches across class and "race" divides by speaking to the desire to be autonomous, powerful, confident, glamorous, and so on. But while it does this it detaches feminism from the social and the systematic. It reduces feminism to the solitary individual and linkages across difference and distinction and any sense of collective responsibility are made invisible. (Skeggs 1997, 144)

This appropriation of feminist ideals and the subsequent grafting onto consumable products is an often-identified characteristic of the "postfeminist climate" (Budgeon and Currie 1995; Greer 1999).[7] The marketability of feminist discourse in this popularized form is what renders it so accessible and, therefore, readily available to young women within the context of their everyday lives. Its influence was apparent throughout the course of these interviews, especially when the young women engaged with the notion of rights at the individual level. These discussions revealed a fundamental commitment to the ideals of justice and fairness—values intrinsic to modernity. Indeed, the idea of being treated unequally or unfairly produced a strong response in the young women. The term "postfeminist" is unfortunately too often mistakenly conflated with this form of popular feminism. Thus, it is the responsibility of a postfeminist engagement with young women's voices to acknowledge that the kinds of popular feminist discourse that young women have available contribute to, but do not wholly determine, the formation of their own politics. Therefore, while it would be accurate to characterize their responses as expressions of this brand of highly individualistic popular feminism, to do so uncritically would risk failure of asking important questions and interrogating further the values of its appeal.

What does this popular feminism provide to a postfeminist analysis? The answer to this question involves a closer examination of the link between individualism and popular feminism. While individualism focuses on the worth of the individual rather than an explicit concern with the collectivity, it can also be a source of agency at the microlevel of everyday practices. The young women interviewed expressed virtually no sense of a collective political tradition, but they exercised a politicized agency at the microlevel of everyday social relations, and I propose this to be the focus of retrieval. If we examine this level of micropolitics and the ways in which young women negotiate conflicts, we find a mixture of individualism wedded to feminist ideals. The following interviewee is quoted at length to examine how one young woman uses both discourses to actively challenge the barriers she faces in day-to-day life. The excerpt draws our attention to the embeddedness of individuals within contexts where experiences of those contexts are deeply gendered:

Shelley: Are men and women equal in our society?

Morgan: At the moment it's like up in the air isn't it? It's like women shouldn't be mechanics and men shouldn't be secretaries and you think, "Why?" So I think it's up in the air because you still get that. Like I wanted to be a mechanic and like, "A girl mechanic?" you know. What's wrong with that? Here at careers if you say you want to do a man's job they look at you as if you're stupid.

Shelley: So it's attitudes then?

Morgan: Yeah and just because it's a mucky job it don't mean we can't do it and they say, "Well what about your fingernails? What about your lovely

skin?" and you're like, "I don't care. I want to do it," but you get loads
of looks. We're the little women you know. We've got to have nice little
jobs like beauticians and nursing. No way. If I want to do a man's job,
I'll do a man's job.

Shelley: How do you think that women becoming more equal has affected the
men you know?

Morgan: Women aren't just the little women who sit at home and cook their
husband's tea. Women are not frightened to speak.

Shelley: So how do you think that has affected the lives of men you know?

Morgan: Oh my Granddad won't hear of it! He's like, "Oh I don't agree with
that!" and you're like, "Why?" "Women shouldn't have a say." Then
you say, "You sexist chauvinist pig. I want to kill you!" Yeah it's little
women isn't it? They shouldn't have a say. They should be cooped up at
home with kids, looking after them, cooking, happy little wife, cleaning.

Shelley: What about men that are your age then what do they think of Girl
Power?

Morgan: They think it's stupid. When we say, "Hey it's Girl Power now," and
they say, "What?" They say boy power has been around longer than
Girl Power has and you just say like, "Get a life we're in the nineties
now!" Why shouldn't we have a say?

Shelley: Do you think because you're female that has ever been used to stop you
from doing something?

Morgan: Even worse yeah, take for instance my mate, she went for a mechanics
job, a trainee mechanic and he said quite bluntly you need to be a lad
for this. It's a lad's job and she stood up and just walked out and said,
"I'm not having it." She couldn't do anything about it but he said it's a
lad's job for a mechanic and I say that if I'd been there they'd have pun-
ished him, "Do you know what Girl Power is?" But there is a lot of
things that do stop you like sexism. They might not say it's a woman's
job or a man's job but you tell by how they're going around it. They
won't say it because they know they'll get into trouble for it now. So
they don't actually come out and say it.

Shelley: Do you find you have to stand up for yourself quite a bit?

Morgan: Yeah when you're out it's like someone says, "You will have this drink,"
and you say, "I might not want this drink." Then he says, "How dare
you stand up for yourself." It's just little things like that. "You're a
woman. Shut up. You'll do what I say," and you say, "No I won't." I
won't take it off of them because I don't think it's right. You'll go to the
bar and they'll go, "Right little lady. What do you want?" and you'll say,
"I don't want a drink off you. I want to buy my own." "But why? We're
the men," and you just say "Shut up."

Shelley: Do they seem to be surprised when you stand up for yourself?

Morgan: Yeah. I don't think a lot of women that they know do stand up. But we
do. Girl Power! The Spice Girls brought that out. Stand up for yourself!
(Morgan, eighteen years old, career guidance center)

In this exchange, Morgan is speaking from a position in which she is able to challenge the barriers that she encounters as a young woman situated within unequal gender relations. She draws on a feminist discourse that she deploys at the microlevel of everyday life. Many of the choices that young women negotiate in daily life involve a struggle to assert a self-definition that runs counter to the ways in which they are positioned by competing discourses, practices, and knowledges. One of Morgan's struggles involves the right to make choices for herself, such as pursuing a career regardless of her gender, while another point of conflict is produced by her refusal of a drink from a man in a social setting. In each instance that she recounts in her narrative, she explains how she is positioned in conflict with guidance counselors, her grandfather, boys her own age, and potential employers. This conflict results from her taking up a resistant position that is individualized but is also about structured relations of gendered inequality. Implicit in Morgan's narrative is a realization that these conflicts are about a wider context of structured gender relations that exist prior to her as an individual, but do not necessarily overdetermine the manner in which she will inhabit those relations.

Postfeminism is often critiqued for being apolitical and attractive to young women because it contributes to a belief that gender equality has been won, thereby engendering complacency. I would suggest, however, that the kinds of feminist discourse available to young women in a postfeminist climate allow them to understand their location within social relations and the resistance they encounter in their attempts for self-definition as being due in some part to a gendered struggle over power. In her narrative, Morgan constructs a series of scenarios in which she *actively* positions herself in a conflictual relation to others who seek to define her on the basis of her gender. In telling this story, she reveals how she practices a resistant identity. There are many accounts of such resistance in the research data, which make me reluctant to foreclose on the possibility that social change is happening at this microlevel of daily interactions.

While young women in this study were not involved in activities that feminism would typically constitute as activism—that is, engagement in collective political action—it would be inaccurate to say that they are apolitical or guided entirely by a liberal individualist ethic in the pursuit of individual goals. These young women use an interpretative framework that owes much of its potency to feminism. The result of employing such a framework is the reproduction of a subject position constituted in large part by feminist ideals. It is a position from which young women come to understand how inequality operates in their lives and how they in turn use this understanding to assert their rights at the microlevel. The transformative power of feminist discourse remains, even when the interpretative framework in question may well be derived in part from a brand of popular feminism.

POSTFEMINISM AND LIFE POLITICS

The coexistence of old and new feminism, a situation that the term "postfeminism" encapsulates, can be thought of as characteristic of politics in postmodernity. These two forms approximate what Giddens has designated emancipatory and life politics, each associated with a specific set of historical social conditions. Modernity, driven by the imperative of freeing human social life from preexisting constraints, translates into a political outlook concerned with liberating individuals and groups from conditions that limit their life chances. It is explicitly organized by principles of justice, equality, and participation and is associated with emancipatory politics. Life politics, in contrast, is a politics of lifestyle options where the goal of self-actualization and rights of individualized choice assume that some level of emancipation from traditions and conditions of domination has been achieved. One of the central issues for life politics is access to means of self-actualization (Giddens 1991, 228). Political issues emerge from processes of self-actualization and the decisions that one must confront in reflexively producing a narrative of self-identity. The two forms of politics are not mutually exclusive, and as the example of gender inequality demonstrates, questions arising within one type inevitably pertain to the other as well. The availability of opportunities and the option of "adopting freely chosen lifestyles, a fundamental benefit generated by a post-traditional order, stands in tension ... with barriers to emancipation" (Giddens 1991, 231).

Feminism is fundamentally an emancipatory discourse, as it has its origins in modernity and a liberal humanist political philosophy that emphasizes universal rights to equality. As a movement is made toward postmodernity, however, increasing differentiation along multiple axes problematizes the notion of universality, resulting in fragmentation and the questioning of unity. There is still an emphasis on the right to self-determination and the right to choose, but it becomes increasingly difficult to prescribe in advance the answers to questions about how to live and how to navigate those choices without perpetuating exclusionary discourses.

The boundary between what we conceive as being collective—the category "woman"—and what we perceive as being individual is not easy to demarcate. Within the narratives of self-identity constructed by these young women, the mingling of emancipatory feminism with a life-politics style of feminism is apparent in the ways that gender inequality is defined as a collective problem but with an individual solution. The attribution of the problem of gender divisions to a collective set of conditions in which social relations are structured by gendered inequality is perceived as a problem that affects the life chances of individual women. The young women experienced these constraints as a politics of lifestyle, where inequality meant that their individual choices and life decisions were not always respected. Their choices were being affected by the very fact they found themselves being treated not as individuals but as "women." The point is that individual choices, such as the ones faced by these young women, take place within a context where young women are often treated as a category and not as individuals.

The effects of feminism itself are also part of the wider context within which they confronted various decisions about their own lives. The recognition that these young women were negotiating their choices and constructing their own biographies within social conditions that had significantly been reorganized by the principles of second-wave feminism was apparent in references made to equal-opportunity legislation and women-centered support networks. Louise, in her following comments, attributed awareness of domestic violence to efforts made by the women's liberation movement to bring this form of abuse to public attention:

Shelley: How do you think women are becoming more equal?

Louise: Well, more wife beaters are getting locked up now.

Shelley: Do you think that is the result of the women's movement?

Louise: Well yeah because it used to be seen as normal, just give them a slap. It was part of being in a relationship. *(Louise, twenty-one years old, Youth-Works program)*

These moments of awareness of gender inequality as a collective problem rooted in structural conditions have their strongest resonance in relation to issues surrounding self-actualization. The main issue for these young women was the ways that gender inequality as a particular social relation impeded their ability to choose what they wanted to do with their lives. In the following quote, Kitty interprets the specific educational choices her friend has made as being determined by general male attitudes:

I think it will take time for things to change. A lot of women don't have the confidence to go out and do what they want because of what men will say and once women get that confidence then things will change. I had a friend at school who wanted to be a builder and because of what people would say she did beauty instead. She always wanted to work outdoors but she's still doing beauty therapy training. You see her tottering around in a little white coat. *(Kitty, eighteen years old, career guidance center)*

Because life politics is concerned with self-actualization it appears to be highly individualistic, as does postfeminism, but as Giddens argues, self-discovery is not a celebration of individualism, instead it signals a major transition within late modernity as a whole (Giddens 1991, 207). Postfeminism, as a transitional moment, is located in between two political frameworks incorporating both emancipatory themes and ones more explicitly concerned with individual difference and choices. Thus, two strands run through postfeminist politics. The first strand is defined by themes characteristic of a feminism with its roots in modernity and identification with the universal subject "woman." The second strand is about differences emerging within that category under postmodern conditions and the resulting shift of emphasis onto individual choices as universals dissolve. To think productively about the capacity for postfeminism to be conducive to social change is to think of it as a "politics of becoming" (Rutherford 1990, 14).[8] Identification, if it is to be productive, is about a dynamic interchange between the self and social structures, but "if the object remains static, ossified by tradition or isolated by a radically changing world, if its theoretical foundations cannot address change, then its culture and politics lose their ability to innovate" (Rutherford 1990, 14).

CONCLUSION

Feminism, in all its various manifestations, encompasses a number of tensions and conflicts in late modernity. This is apparent within its continued fragmentation and the escalation of difference between women who are embedded in a diversity of localities, practices, relations, and knowledges. It is also made evident by the recognition that many feminist ideas have become part of the common sense of our culture, yet those ideas are often expressed in a form we barely recognize as feminist (Whelehan 1995, 196). These two issues are interrelated because whether or not we recognize a particular stance as being feminist depends upon our sense of identity within any particular time or space, thus raising the question of who is allowed to construct an authentic feminist position or claim a valid feminist identity. Identity is, after all, always plural and shifting. The contradictory and complex nature of identities makes a politics based upon the representation of a unified identity inherently flawed. Representation seeks to define and thereby fix in place a secure or uniform identity, but one consequence has been the young women's nonidentification with that subject, suggesting that their difference evades this fixing in place.[9]

The challenge presented by difference within the category "woman" has revealed that there are as many ways of becoming a feminist as there are of becoming a woman (Douglas 1994). For feminism, difference has meant trying harder to understand the multiple ways of being a woman and, by implication, the multiple ways of being a feminist. Fragmentation has provided many different ways for women to be feminist, although the positivity of this diversity is rarely represented. Griffin (1989) has asked what it means when a woman says, "I'm not a feminist but ... " and suggests that it is a way of speaking feminism without identifying with it. Nonidentification may display a refusal to be fixed into place as a feminist, but may also be a sign of the inability to position oneself as feminist because of confusing and contradictory messages about what feminism really is (Skeggs 1997, 142). This is a point of major significance. What is feminism? When an answer to such a question is so difficult to produce, it is not surprising that young women don't identify themselves as being feminist.

Within the transformations that feminism is currently undergoing in Britain, it is important to recognize the different ways young women are being positioned and positioning themselves within social relations and conditions that have changed significantly in the past thirty years. Difference is not just about race, class, or ethnicity, but age as well. In a discussion of popular culture and Madonna as a postfeminist role model, Young (1989, 188) argues, "It is too easy to argue that divergence equals dilution, and anyway who claims the authority to say what is and what is not a feminist representation, or who is and who is not feminist?" In effect, the opposition of the categories "feminine" and "feminism" may no longer capture the experience of young women (McRobbie 1993, 409). Indeed, the gap increasingly seems to be between professional or academic feminism and more accessible types of popular feminism (Stuart 1990, 29).

Nonidentification with feminism on the part of young women might signal a collapse of feminist politics, but only if a certain notion of politics and social change is adhered to, namely, a form of feminism that relies upon foundations. A rethinking of the relationship between feminism (as a practice and a discourse) and the subject as an active agent may reveal that recognition does not depend upon identification. Since the young women in this study do not identify themselves as the subjects of feminism, they do not actively incorporate the category "feminist" into their identities. A more subtle affinity is at play, however, as they practice identities informed by feminist ideals, because they do recognize that gender inequality has a bearing upon their lives and their choices. Pursuing the goal of developing a more comprehensive or inclusive notion of the feminist subject that would appeal to young women is not necessary, as this would signify a return to a foundational form of feminism that inevitably relies upon exclusion of those who fall outside the normative constraints of those criteria that constitute inclusion. Within feminist politics, it seems a miscalculated goal to seek to represent in advance all the interests at play when, for instance in this study, feminism appears in the narrative as both a form of emancipatory politics (associated with modernity) and life politics (associated with late/post modernity). The pitting of old against new feminism and the debates about which form of politics is a more accurate representation of young women doesn't seem particularly relevant to the ways that these young women negotiated identities that are inherently contradictory. It is more likely that aspects of both are at play and, as Anna reminds us in the following quote, the contradictions of female identity can provide a source of pleasure:

Sometimes I will just go all out you know. I'll do it just to take the piss and wear the long floating dress and even wear roses in my hair and just be the dead romantic and then I'll wear combat boots because I like the contrast ... the idea on the surface is that you can say, "Look at me! I'm the girlie type" and then when people actually meet you and talk to you they realise that you're as far from that as you ever could be and I enjoy that. I think that is funny. I may be skinny and weedy and be wearing a floaty dress and roses in my hair but you know I've got a bite. *(Anna, eighteen years old, completing lower sixth form at Ripley School)*

A more viable strategy is to relieve categories, in this case "feminist," of foundational moorings and leave them as sites of permanent contest. Such a move leaves open possibilities and avoids potential future exclusions. It also allows one to reach a different understanding of political engagement and what counts as feminist activity. Butler maintains:

If feminism presupposes that "women" designates an undesignatable field of differences, one that cannot be totalised or summarised by a descriptive identity category, then the very term becomes a site of permanent openness and resignifiability.... To deconstruct the subject of feminism is not, then, to censure its usage, but, on the contrary, to release the term into a future of multiple significations ... it may be that only through releasing the category of women from a fixed referent that something like "agency" becomes possible. (Butler 1992, 16)

This strategy provides an effective means of addressing the problem of difference and the difficulties inherent in identity politics. With regard to the young women interviewed in this research, resistance to gender inequality was in operation without the assertion of a clearly recognizable feminist identity by individual subjects. Within a social context transformed by second-wave feminism, this signals the emergence of new feminist identities marked by their own distinct concerns, yet not without a certain affinity with those old feminist identities. These emergent identities borrow what they need from existing discourses, including second-wave feminism, which does address some of their concerns, but does not always allow them to fully articulate their experience; thus, other resources are used in the production of new identities and reconfigurations that are not without contradictions. These contradictions and the lack of unity within the category "women," though, are not about incommensurability, but relationships of complicated entanglement that are not only marked by disagreement, but also overlapping vocabularies, frameworks, and assumptions (Felski 1997). It is important to remember, therefore, that the continued goal for the project of feminism is to learn to practice conflict constructively (Hirsch and Keller 1990).

At times, the failure of a new generation of young women to identify with feminism is seen as a failure on the part of feminism or, more extremely, as the collapse of feminist goals. To think of the way that second-wave feminism has impacted on the lives of young women requires a more positive evaluation. Part of the legacy of second-wave feminism is that young women today not only have more choices available to them, but the very notion of choice is their fundamental right. That they don't acknowledge their debt to feminism is an indication of the extent to which feminism in late modernity is not a marginalized discourse, but has become a basic part of the context in which young women are making sense of their lives. It is part of the interpretative framework employed in the ways they practice their own identities. To say that their identities may be postfeminist is productive insofar as postfeminism is understood as being about a critical interrogation of the limits of second-wave feminism and leaving open the goal of understanding the multiple ways of being a feminist. What can be retrieved from listening to young women is a greater understanding of how agency, informed by feminist ideals, operates as a form of decentralized resistance at the everyday level, contributing to the continuing transformation of social relations as well as to feminism itself.

NOTES

1. "Second-wave" feminism refers to the resurgence of feminism as a social, cultural, and political movement in the 1960s and 1970s. The term is intended to include a wide variety of strands of feminism. Humm (1992, 11) designates the beginning of second-wave feminism as 1949, although this era is not historically discrete from previous feminist movements.

2. The newspaper referred to is the Saturday, March 6, 1999 edition of *The Guardian*, page 9 of the *Review* section.

3. Despite their significant entry into these nontraditional areas, women are still underrepresented in certain subjects, such as the sciences (Furlong and Cartmel 1997, 22).

4. In relation to Butler's arguments, McRobbie (1994, 69) adds the question of how, within the contemporary context, feminism can hope to reproduce itself among a generation of young women.

5. Weeks (1995, 142) refers to this right as the expression of an endorsement of the right to make individual decisions and choices within the larger context of respecting individual differences.

6. This same tendency is discussed by Beverly Skeggs (1997) in a study of young, working-class women.

7. Germaine Greer (1999) writes about how "Girl Power" is constructed and marketed in young women's magazines.

8. Rutherford (1990) makes this point in relation to strategies for transforming left politics, addressing in particular the disadvantages of relying upon identity politics.

9. Difference here is about age, but it is important to acknowledge how young women are positioned through difference in relation to each other according to race, ethnicity, class, disability, and sexuality. One of the main areas of difference that emerged in this study was between young Asian women and the young White women. The Asian women commented specifically on the intersection of ethnicity and gender and the constraints placed upon their choices by both sets of relations, particularly with regard to how both in combination created specific kinds of limitations. Being a young Asian woman is qualitatively different from being either a young woman or an Asian woman.

Chapter 8

Concluding Considerations: No End in Sight

In consideration of the series of interrogations performed throughout these chapters, arriving at a conclusion would seem somewhat dubious, because it suggests a commitment to linear progression toward a goal defined by its finality. Because this project has not been motivated by the desire to reach a specific destination or secure closure, my dissonance toward these connotations renders delivering a conclusion troublesome. However, drawing on the spirit expressed by Elspeth Probyn (1993, 165) in her confession that, "Much as I hate writing conclusions, I do appreciate the conclusions of others," an attempt will be made in this final chapter to draw together some of the main considerations that the project of theorizing the individualization of young women's identity raises.

The aim of this book is to examine the relationship between choice and identity and to explore theoretical strategies that engage with this question. This emerges as a complex task. It has been argued that a reading of identity narratives must first locate the subject within a specific set of sociohistorical elements that constitute a condition of postmodernity. This is a condition characterized by fluidity and heterogeneity, where the myth of a unitary reality is understood as untenable. It is a condition that makes grand narratives increasingly difficult to sustain or justify through either an appeal to reason, progress, or historical necessity. The belief in a rational and self-constituting subject—the universal subject of humanist discourse—has been undermined, and assumptions underlying universality have been laid open to critique by a turn to questions about difference. Subsequently, knowledge production shifts from a position of objectivity to one that is explicitly located in the local and everyday. The constitutive role of language and the movement of meanings across a range of discursive formations become central to the analysis undertaken. Finally, it is a condition in which identity as the expression of an essential interiority is problematized through the location of the subject within a multiplicity of practices, knowledges, spaces, relations, and programs—all of which form specific technologies that work to produce the subject and the enactment of a particular relation to the self.

The extent to which these points describe Western culture at the turn of the twenty-first century has been the source of much debate. Indeed, the problem of what constitutes a postmodern condition is often a matter of degree. These questions, however, are also about how we understand our relation to these conditions. Central to the study of social interactions, relations, identities, institutions, and representations is the task of developing tools, strategies, and methods for theorizing our relation as subjects to this context. This objective has been a motivating force behind this project. Asking what kind of identities or relations to the self are being formed by young women within the specific conditions present at the turn of the twenty-first century also means asking how to adequately theorize these identities and relations. Therefore, thinking through the positioning of young women within this set of conditions requires an engagement with the theoretical tools on hand. Social theory delivers the program set out by theorists of reflexive modernization—most notably Giddens (1991) and Beck (1992). This theoretical position takes as its point of departure the assumption of increased fluidity, fragmentation, and plurality within contemporary social conditions, and it is therefore a reasonable place to commence an investigation. However, many of the ontological assumptions of reflexive modernization prove inadequate for undertaking a detailed reading of the ways young women's identities are constructed within conditions of postmodernity. In the analysis conducted in this study, some of these assumptions are examined and broken apart using principles that implicitly constitute a poststructuralist approach. It is from this exercise that a number of important considerations emerge. Before discussing these more directly, a review of the chapters will set the context for highlighting a set of issues central to theorizing the individualized identities of young women in postmodernity.

The relation to the self that has been under examination here is one in which choice plays a central role. The "choosing self" exhibits the characteristics of the autonomous subject of humanist discourse—that is, a belief in self-determination, a unique and unified interiority, and an essential core that is stable. This conscious sense of self, however, is a specific production. A decentering of this subject reveals that this is a self made knowable through the specificity of its embeddedness. Theories of reflexive modernization place a substantial emphasis upon the subject's conscious or reflexive sense of self as *a self that must choose* to construct her own unique identity. A decentering of the subject allows for the development of an understanding that this relation to the self for young women is an emergent subjectivity. To achieve this understanding, it is fundamental to view this relation to the self as a historical relation. It is an embedded subjectivity, hence an embodied materiality. It is a subjectivity that encapsulates several forms of difference across moments in time and space. Finally, it is a relation that is inhabited in such a way as to allow for agency, self-enunciation, and transformation.

In chapter 2, the assumptions of reflexive modernization are explored in order to begin to indicate where some of the problems with this approach lay. This critique reveals an overemphasis on a conception of the subject as a rational, instrumental, and self-constituting origin of meaning. An over-privileging of reflexivity can contribute to the dislocation of the subject from concrete social and historical contexts and result in the undertheorization of relations organized through localized specificity, heterogeneity, and axes of difference. A poststructuralist decentering of the subject moves the emphasis away from self-constitution toward specific localities, like schools and youth outreach programs, where the organization of knowledges, practices, and relations create the conditions for the production of the subject. This idea is further explored in chapter 3, where narratives of the self produced by young women are read as being indicative of constituting a particular form of selfhood—an autonomous self characterized by a belief in authenticity, independence, and an essential interiority. This is a self that expresses the principles of modernity: individual sovereignty and the belief in being able to submit contingency to human control. This modern form of selfhood, however, was examined by locating it within a specific context of problematizations, authorities, technologies, strategies, and teleologies, thereby revealing it as a relation to the self that arises out of the organization of relations, practices, and knowledges—all of which belong to a historical and local regime of subjectification.

The interrogations of these narratives about choice and life planning revealed that the individual is incited to reflect upon her own conduct in a certain manner and orient further conduct toward reproducing this relation to the self. It was apparent that the narratives functioned to maintain a specific construction of the self, through which the young women engaged with the choices they had available to them regarding decisions about their lives. For example, at the time of being interviewed, both Emilia and Michelle confronted the decision of what to do upon leaving school. Emilia reflects upon herself as someone who always planned to attend a university. Michelle, on the other hand, reflects upon herself as someone who was going to leave school as soon as she reached the age of sixteen. They both approach their decision in view of their past, and the self that has been established in its relationship with parents, peers, teachers, and so forth. For both of them, the question of how to act in this instance is largely answered by the kind of self they are in the process of constructing.

Not only were these narratives embedded within a specific context that made particular constructions possible, but one that also put limits on the kinds of stories that could be told and the kinds of self that could be created. Tensions are created by the discursive positioning of subjects within categories like gender, class, race, and ethnicity, which operate to define statuses that are not chosen as much as ascribed. How the self is rendered thinkable is an effect of these positionings. The young women were aware of their choices being constructed in relation to these ascriptions, which exist external to and prior to the individual that comes to be positioned within these categories. These ascribed statuses often conflicted with the kind of self the young women were constructing, but they also reinforced certain perceptions these young women had of who they were meant to be. For example, Joanne invokes particular images of the categories "working-class" and "single mother" in her narrative. To be working-class is to be employed in manual labor, such as the work performed in a packing factory, while to be a single mother is to get pregnant in order to live off state benefits. Joanne sees these as meanings that have been attached to these categories, yet her belonging to these categories while simultaneously violating their ascribed characteristics means that her narrative is influenced by an implicit understanding of what "someone like her" should be doing with their life.

To understand how the body was related to the identities of the young women interviewed, it was argued again that the subject must be theorized as an embedded subject if the limits of a mind/body dualism are to be transcended. In this analysis, it became apparent that the meaning of the self/body relation is more complex than allowed for by many social constructionist accounts. This discussion also problematized the idea that the body is an object that is reflexively appropriated into the project of the self. Meanings do not simply become inscribed on the body as though it were a blank surface. Instead, they enfold, merge, split apart, mingle, detach, and reattach in a constant process of becoming, in which the body is not an object separate from the subject but an event constituted by its connections with other bodies, practices, knowledges, devices, techniques, and relations. As Grosz (1994, 191) states, the body cannot be understood in terms of a biological entity upon which cultural constructs are founded because it is an "open materiality, a set of (possibly infinite) tendencies and potentialities which may be developed, yet whose development will necessarily hinder or induce other trajectories."

A privileging of the mind (reflexivity) over the body restricts an understanding of how the self and body are implicated in a mutually constitutive but irreducible relation, because to privilege the mind is to suggest that it assigns meaning to the body via the consumption of images and representations. This theoretical perspective reduces the potential for understanding agency in relation to bodily practices and the meanings of these practices in relation to the self. This is particularly problematic for feminism, where women's relation to their bodies has often been constructed as being mediated by an economy of signification that relies upon the negation of the body, materiality, and female corporeality. As such, these approaches suggest that women have a pathologized relation to their bodies. To avoid this move toward reductionism, it is productive, therefore, to locate the body as more than a semiotic problem and instead as a borderline concept—neither pure subject nor pure object. These issues are addressed through an exploration of how young women critically engage with media constructions of ideal femininity and how they position themselves via their engagements in both resistant and disciplinary ways, where the meaning of the self/body relation can convert, fluctuate, and modify, but where any securing of meaning is made temporary by the movement of the embedded self in and out of the technologies that effect its becoming.

To examine how the relationship between the self and others is given meaning, the postmodern principle of difference is analyzed in chapter 5. The tendency in theories of reflexive modernization to posit a universal subject that is seemingly disembedded from social relations limits its usefulness in understanding how postmodernity is a condition in which the concept of difference assumes greater significance. Although difference has been recognized as central to postmodernity to effectively use it as a theoretical tool, it is useful to make a distinction between three dimensions contained within the concept: destabilization, a relational economy of meaning, and experiential diversity. These aspects of difference produce and organize conditions within which axes of identity articulate. The analysis of how the young women and practitioners implicitly used the notion of difference to construct the meaning of and limits to choice revealed that difference is central to understanding the relationship between self and other. In these narratives, social relations like gender and class are structured in specific ways. That is, they are constructed as relations in which difference often meant the recognition of individuals having dissimilar opportunities and choices. For example, what it means to be a young Asian woman was seen to be different from a young White single mother from a working-class background.

Although these categories are somewhat stable, the meanings of these relations shift and alter, as was the case with gender. Shifts in meaning and practice affect the identifications made; hence, the historicity of the identities under construction. To understand how the self and the other are located within these relations, it is useful to understand that identity operates within two fields: first, as a set of social categories where individuals are located on the basis of their "sameness"; and second, as a sense of one's own uniqueness or difference from others. The construction of self-identity involves an interplay within these two fields where social categories that describe a set of relations that exist over time and space are used as the basis for locating the self and others. Self-identification within these relations is due in part to ways in which the subject is produced through experience and one's subjective engagement in practices, institutions, and discourses. Thus, diverse experiential processes provide the basis for making a claim to one's difference and constitute an essential aspect of identity.

In chapter 6, choices about how to live one's life are addressed within the context of transformations to the constraints of ascribed statuses, predominantly the restructuring of gender relations, which has produced a set of social conditions in which self-definition is increasingly important for young women. Compared to previous generations, these young women had a greater diversity of routes available to them with regard to education, training options, and careers paths. The expansion of choice in these areas was seen to produce a number of issues because of the desire these young women expressed to incorporate an intimate relationship into their narratives. The desire to enter into an intimate, committed relationship with a partner produced significant conflict for the kind of self under production—the autonomous self. The construction of an individualized biography, where access to choice is central, demands an active negotiation of the conflicts produced by attempts to reconcile autonomy and connection with an other. In response to this tension, the young women achieved a reconciliation by developing a set of strategies and models for living out intimate arrangements. The strategy most often deployed was defined by the logic of both/and. These young women expressed a desire to have both autonomy *and* connection, and they did not post these as mutually exclusive needs.

The models discussed in chapter 6 reflect the incorporation of varying degrees of what Giddens argues are elements of a pure relationship, for example, an insistence on open communication and negotiation. Yet, these transformations to practices of intimacy coincided with other elements that are more traditional. For instance, these young women identified heterosexual relationships as a space within which male dominance is exercised, thus suggesting that intimacy has not undergone a wholesale transformation but is about both continuity and change. A primary concern for these young women was the maintenance of their independence and their right to difference—that is, the expression of the individual's right to choose how to structure one's relationships. Again, the importance of difference as an analytical tool becomes apparent because autonomy emerges as an expression of one's own unique identity.

The implications of a right to difference also had repercussions for the ways that the young women positioned themselves in relation to collective identities. As a social movement arising in the 1960s, second-wave feminism has fragmented and diversified through the impact of difference held within the category "woman." One source of fracturing that must be acknowledged is age and the effects of generational difference that are apparent throughout these chapters. It was found that this fracturing does not constitute a clear split from the tenets of second-wave feminism in favor of a depoliticized, antifeminist, highly individualized form of individual rights, which is often (mistakenly) called postfeminism. The nonidentification of the self with the collective subject of feminism was apparent in these interviews; however, to understand both the expression of the right to individualism and the right to equality as a form of feminist politics, it is necessary to reconceptualize what constitutes a politicized identity. In chapter 7, the practice of micropolitics is linked to this emergent subjectivity for young women. An exploration of the microlevel of everyday life revealed the engagement of young women in discursively constructed relations that sought to inscribe them in certain ways. Resistance, rooted in the autonomous self, however, is reconceived as a form of political engagement in terms that avoid foundationalism. This move is crucial because the limits of foundational discourses arise from the exclusion of others that the establishment of such foundations relies upon. Postfeminism attempts to address the challenges presented to feminism by a critique of its foundations. The prefix "post" may be attached to feminism to express: (a) the ongoing transformation of gender as a discourse, (b) gender as a set of relations, (c) feminism as a practice, and (d) feminism as a point of recognition rather than identification. It is more useful to use the term "recognition" because it grants agency; as seen in chapter 7, young women recognize gender equality without identifying with feminism.

DECENTERING THE SELF: FUTURE FIGURATIONS

The examination of various strategies for theorizing identity after the demise of the humanist subject of Western metaphysics raises a number of questions for further consideration. If a conceptualization of the subject as the autonomous author of self has been rendered thoroughly problematic, then how can the project of theorizing identity proceed, and indeed why should it? Stuart Hall (1996) embraces this question in an elegantly constructed argument about why identity matters. He raises several points that articulate with the analysis undertaken throughout this book. Deconstruction of the essential, unified, self-sustaining subject has put the very concept of identity under question—or, as Hall states, "under erasure"— to indicate that it is no longer serviceable or adequate to think within its originary and unreconstructed form (Hall 1996, 1). However, without alternatives or a suitable replacement, one is left having to use the concept, albeit strategically. As Hall argues, identity is "an idea which cannot be thought in the old way, but without which certain key questions cannot be thought at all" (1996, 2).

Deployment of the term "identity" is central to the examination of questions about agency and politics, but where both terms have been reconceptualized in ways that do not rely upon a unitary or transparent notion of the subject. Rather, as Hall (1996, 2) argues, given that the subject has been decentered, what is needed "is not an abandonment or abolition of 'the subject' but a reconceptualisation—thinking it in its new, displaced or de-centred position." This requires a way of thinking about identity strategically—not as indicative of a stable core of the self "unfolding from beginning to end through all the vicissitudes of history without change; the bit of the self which remains always-already 'the same,' identical across time" (Hall 1996, 4). Instead, the self as an origin of identity is a particular relation that arises within practices of representation such as narrativization—practices that have been under examination throughout these chapters. According to Hall, identities are about

Questions of using the resources of history, language and culture in the process of becoming rather than being: not "who we are" or "where we came from," so much as what we might become, how we have been represented and how that bears on how we might represent ourselves. (Hall 1996, 4)

This is a question about how the self may be enunciated or spoken and the implications that particular narratives have, for while the self arises through nonessential modes of self-representation, the self under production is not fictional but instead has a "discursive, material or political effectivity" (Hall 1996, 4). Indeed, questions of agency have been central to the analysis undertaken throughout these chapters. The self under production is a located self—one that is embedded within specific historical and institutional sites that are constituted by particular discursive practices, formations, and modes of self-enunciation. What Hall so effectively explains is that while identifications are partial or unstable, they also join subjects into structures of meaning, so there is an enjoining that operates in both directions, to and from subject and structure—never an overdetermination, but always an excess.

Deconstruction of the concept of identity has required ways of theorizing a project of identity undertaken by a subject no longer understood as an origin. The decentering of the self requires what Braidotti (1994, 1) terms new "figurations" of thought—an alternative "style of thought that evokes or expresses ways out of the phallocentric vision of the subject." Braidotti's project is about the creation of a politically informed account of alternative subjectivity informed by an urgency to "learn to think differently about the subject, to invent new frameworks, new images, new modes of thought" (Braidotti 1994, 1). To do this, one must move beyond dualistic accounts and phallocentric devices toward concepts that can accommodate the heterogeneity contained within women's subjectivity. This is what a project that explores young women's identities should do.

It should aim to develop creative ways of thinking about the identities under production and the complexity of levels situated not only within individual subjects, but also those shifting points of identification that flow between subjects. What a project of theorizing the subject and identity requires is the examination of the ontology through which we think ourselves. For Braidotti, the location of the subject at the point of multiple articulations of different axes of identity translates into a particular challenge for feminist theory—"how to invent new images of thought that can help us think about change and changing constructions of the self" (Braidotti 1994, 157).

I agree with Braidotti that a useful way of thinking about the female subject is to invoke the figuration of "nomadic subjectivity." This relies upon an image of the subject as a process—as movement through and around a multiplicity of axes of identity that may inform the joining of the subject into structures of meaning such as gender, race, class, sexuality, and age. Thus, nomadic subjectivity is a way of thinking about the embedded and embodied subject. As such, it is a figuration that implicitly invokes a female subject who is situated, yet not in terms of biological or psychic essentialism. Braidotti (1994, 99) provides a way of thinking about the female subject that is both material and semiotic, institutional and discursive. Nomadic subjectivity is about a new kind of female-embodied materialism situated within a network of simultaneous power formations. Here, Braidotti relies upon the perspective taken throughout these chapters, namely, that the subject is produced within a network of power and knowledge, whereby particular technologies of the self effect a particular relation to the self:

The acquisition of subjectivity is therefore a process of material (institutional) and discursive (symbolic) practices, the aim of which is both positive—because the process allows for forms of empowerment—and regulative—because the forms of empowerment are the site of limitations and disciplining. (Braidotti 1994, 157)

Braidotti's work delivers a way of rethinking the female subject as embodied materiality and allows for a renaming of female subjectivity as a multiple, open-ended, interconnected entity. This way of thinking produces for this project the possibility of theorizing a historicized formation of an emergent subjectivity for young women. Thus, the argument throughout has been that the "choosing self" is a particular relation to the self that is effected by the embeddedness of young women within institutions, like colleges or career guidance centers, and discourses, like gender. Individualized identity characterized by increased choice, a greater degree of freedom from constraints of tradition, and the ability to envision multiple possibilities constitute a "new habitus of gender relations," which these young women inhabit (McRobbie 1994, 157).

The narratives under analysis throughout these chapters are acts of self-enunciation. In the act of confronting choice, a relation to the self is made and remade, generating particular expressions of selfhood. The act of enunciation is about a way of being in the world and inhabiting a particular relation to the self; therefore, this relation is about agency and self-efficacy. To say that the subject is produced through discourse is not to deny a subject with agency, but to understand agency as a capacity created through concrete situations and specific statuses conferred upon particular subjects (Scott 1992, 34). Agency in this figuration is conditional because the subject is both embodied and embedded. As such, the historical nature of experiences that produce the subject are highlighted. It is argued throughout this book that there is no necessity at work in the kinds of identities being expressed by these young women. That is to reiterate that these identities are not essential, but are produced across various historical processes and practices. Scott explains:

Experience in this definition then becomes not the origin of our explanation, not the authoritative (because seen or felt) evidence that grounds what is known, but rather that which we seek to explain, that about which knowledge is produced. To think about experience in this way is to historicize it as well as to historicize the identities it produces. (Scott 1992, 26)

The value of Scott's argument for this project is that historicizing experience allows us to write about identity without essentializing it. Identities that emerge within particular places at particular times are historical events whose contingency demands explanation. As argued by Scott (1992, 33), one must assume that "the appearance of a new identity is not inevitable or determined, not something that was always there simply waiting to be expressed, not something that will always exist in the form it was given in a particular political movement or at a particular historical moment." The conjunction of identity at the point between the personal—that is, what one can claim as one's own experience—and the social means that ways of thinking the self in terms of categories like feminine, Black, middle-class, and so on, always transform, and with them the possibilities for speaking and thinking the self.

In summary, there is a set of social conditions that constitutes the historical moment within which these young women were interviewed about their lives—their goals, attitudes, beliefs, and choices. Their narratives were produced within conditions that have transformed in such a way that new possibilities for constructing a self have emerged—possibilities that undermine the historical marginalization of young women that derives from the combined effect of their positionings with relations organized around age and gender. The expressions of their experience of these conditions support the notion that postmodernity is characterized by a "greater degree of fluidity about what femininity means and how exactly it is anchored in social reality" (McRobbie 1994, 157). These possibilities arise out of the transformations that have occurred within particular meanings attached to relations, most notably gender, which was characterized in the narratives produced here as both a constraining relation and one that was about increased freedom to define the self. Indeed, gender practices and structures appear to be characterized by a degree of fluidity (McRobbie 1994, 157). For these young women, postmodernity means an increased range of choices about who they want to be and how they want to define themselves. In the act of choosing, they are forming a relation to their conditions that has several ramifications. The first pertains to questions about agency. According to Rose:

Agency is itself an effect, a distributed outcome of particular technologies of subjectification that invoke human beings as subjects of a certain type for freedom and supply the norms and techniques by which that freedom is to be recognised, assembled, and played out in specific domains ... agency is, no doubt, a "force," but it is a force that arises not from any essential properties of "the subject" but out of the ways in which humans have been-assembled-together. (Rose 1998, 187–88)

The declaration of confidence made by these young women, their belief in self-efficacy, and their assertion of a right to make choices are expressions of agency made possible by the enactment of this particular regime of subjectification. When this self articulated with discursive positionings that sought to limit choice and freedom, it allowed for a positioning of the self that is resistant to the definitions of others. This was apparent, for example, in the ways that the right to make individual choices was invoked within the context of intimate relationships. Within a broader context, for these young women, this form of selfhood suggests a certain refusal to be located by others; thus, the disruptive moment contained within autonomy. Therefore, the considerable degree of uniformity produced in the narratives was about difference—the right to be whoever one wants to be and the right to be able to make choices. This opens up spaces within which to constitute and live out emergent forms of femininity.

However, this regime of subjectification also produces regulatory effects. It produces a belief that one must become a particular type of subject that may be more difficult to create and sustain for some young women compared to others. In this context, it was much more difficult for the young women who were involved in youth outreach projects to enact self-confidence than for those who were attending Greenwood School. In this respect, this regime of subjectification is embedded in a set of hierarchical social relations and material conditions within which young women occupy diverse locations. The autonomous self is potentially problematic insofar as it operates to obscure this fact and works to individualize failure and make inequality appear as an individual predicament.

An attempt has been made in this analysis to understand the relation these young women had to the choices available to them: how they understood those choices, what they thought those choices meant, and how they actively negotiated those choices and the implications of these processes. In short, the argument made throughout this project is that these questions require strategies for understanding how the conditions that constitute postmodernity effect the formation of young women's identities. The development of this argument contributes to the ongoing project of knowledge production within the context of what is known as the "cultural turn"—the influence that poststructuralism has come to bear on the production of knowledges across a range of academic disciplines[1]—notably, a turn from materiality to discourse, challenges to assumptions about causality and searches for origins, and the centrality of language in the construction rather than conveyance of meaning (Barrett 1992, 202–3).

KNOWING THE SUBJECT

The suggestion in the title of this chapter that there is "no end in sight" refers to the refusal to envision the goal of knowledge production as seeking some form of "truth" or finality. Instead, this project has used empirical data as a lens through which to read and interrogate assumptions of existing approaches to identity. The main points that have emerged are: a challenge against the self-constituting self, the centrality of difference, the importance of relational aspects of identity,[2] a need to acknowledge the microlevel of everyday events and experiences, and the breaking apart of unified categories and binaries. The goal in performing these interrogations has been not to build theory so much as to break it apart, see how it works, and engage in a reassembly of bits and pieces to see what effect might be produced on ways of understanding. This exercise has been conducted within a context where the proposition of the advent of postmodernity produces a certain level of anxiety for intellectuals and has, according to Bauman (1992, 103), "far-reaching consequences for the strategy of intellectual work in general and the traditional business of conducting sociology." He continues:

The form acquired by sociology and social philosophy in the course of what is now, retrospectively, described as "modernity" is indeed experiencing at the moment an unprecedented challenge. While in no way doomed, it must adjust itself to new conditions in order to self-reproduce. (Bauman 1992, 105)

At times, sociology, among other disciplines, has been hesitant to embrace the "cultural turn" because in many respects to do so would undermine many of the premises upon which it has relied in order to theorize its central concerns—the social (systems of social relations and structures), the self (agency), and social knowledge (general approaches to knowledge and conceptions of the role of the academic intellectual).[3] In relation to the influence of the cultural turn in knowledge production, Barrett (1992, 205) asks "whether any given problem can be rethought within the terms of reference of one's existing theory, or whether—in order to proceed—one has to develop a new framework altogether." In response, I would advocate the position taken by Seidman (1997, 37), who argues that new disciplinary possibilities for social knowledge can emerge from a sociology that engages with alternative social knowledges such as cultural studies. It is only through this exercise that the discipline can enact a critical self-examination and reformation. This argument is particularly salient with regard to the decentering of the self enacted throughout the interrogations performed in this book because, according to Seidman, sociology often

Assumes the individual as the foundation of social life and figures the self as an internally coherent, rationally calculating agent. Cultural studies departs from these assumptions by imagining the individual as socially produced; as occupying multiple, contradictory psychic and social positions or identities and by figuring the self as influenced by unconscious processes. (Seidman 1997, 46)

An appropriation of concepts from cultural theory and poststructuralism can contribute to the production of knowledge by inducing a "critical reflexivity in a discipline which sometimes fantastically imagines its conventions and languages of the social as providing a privileged access to the social universe" (Seidman 1997, 54). The goal, according to Seidman, is not to produce the means of arriving closer to a destination called "truth," but to open up productive avenues to asking new questions about the social and the self, thereby creating possibilities for different political interventions. Yet, as illustrated in this research, it is essential to continue to listen to "spoken voices" and to engage with lived experiences—something that is often absent from cultural studies (McRobbie 1994, 178). This project contributes to such an aim—a postmodern reorientation to sociology defined by a self-conscious and self-critical approach that undertakes to both localize and destabilize the ways theorizing is performed. Such a reorientation is guided by the aspiration to reconsider and reconfigure foundations so that creative and flexible responses to sociological questions may be enacted.

NOTES

1. Barrett (1992) effectively explains this turn in relation to the ongoing development of feminist theory.

2. This is Seigel's term (1999, 285), referring to aspects of identity where meanings of subjectivity are organized discursively through operations of language.

3. See Seidman (1997) for a discussion of these three areas of concern and how sociology might develop strategies for rethinking assumptions through an engagement with cultural studies. Although Seidman is making his argument specifically in relation to American sociology, his critique also has implications for sociology outside of the American context.

Appendix

Interview Sites

Interviews were conducted with thirty-three young women and six practitioners across a total of five different sites from April 1997 to October 1998 in a large city in northern England. These sites were specifically chosen to reflect the range of institutions in which young women are located as they navigate divergent routes through adolescence into adulthood. At sixteen years of age, with the end of compulsory education, young women must begin to confront decisions regarding future careers and what type of education and training they wish to pursue. These interview sites indicate to some extent how choices available to young women vary[1] and can be conceptualized as representing the diversity of young women's experiences. The sites can, for instance, be thought of constituting different class contexts, although this is not to say that individuals within sites are being assigned a class designation. The identities that were being produced within these sites are very much site-specific. These sites represent a sociohistorical context and are only a few of the many sites of daily life within which young women engage in formulating their identities. This multiplicity of contexts includes, for example, leisure spaces, consumption spaces, and family spaces. As such, the identities examined in this study must be interpreted as specific identities produced within the context of education, career, skills building, training, and so forth.

SITE 1: RIPLEY SCHOOL

Ripley School is a county secondary school for pupils from eleven to eighteen years old. The school has more than 1,270 students, and the sixth form has more than 200 students, making it one of the largest in the city. In

1974, Ripley was formed in a merger of separate all-boy and all-girl grammar schools. It is now a coeducational comprehensive maintained by the local education authority. The curriculum for students past age sixteen includes a wide range of A-level subjects and GNVQ in business, health and social care, and leisure and recreation. The school was described by the head of sixth form as being located in a very middle-class area that is a highly sought-after suburb to live in. Students from this suburb attend the school, but the traditional catchment area also extends into city center districts that are traditionally working-class areas with low-cost and high-density housing. In the past twenty-five to thirty years, these areas have become established centers for the Asian and African Caribbean communities. The school also provides services to a number of students from a White working-class area of the city. The gender mix is roughly equal between young men and young women.

Although Ripley is attended by a diverse student population, the head of sixth form explained that at age sixteen a lot of children from working-class backgrounds leave the school, with the ones continuing into sixth form being predominantly middle-class and, though not exclusively, White. The number of vocational courses on offer at the school has been expanding over the past seven or eight years in order to meet the different needs of the students; however, the structures of the courses still tend to favor the middle-class students. For students who stay on at Ripley, the academic route of studying A-levels is the norm, with about 28 percent undertaking a vocational qualification. For young women leaving the school at sixteen, further-education colleges in the city are better equipped to offer more vocational options than are possible at Ripley. The sixth-form students, therefore, tend to be on a traditional academic path from GCSEs to A-levels, through to attending a university.

The interviews at this school were conducted in June and July of 1997. The five young women interviewed were all completing their first year of sixth form, in which they were all studying for A-levels. All of these young women planned to attend a university upon completion of their A-level exams.

SITE 2: PEARSON COLLEGE

Pearson College is a further-education college that offers a wide range of different courses of study, including GCSEs, A-levels, and vocational courses. The college has a large catchment area that includes the entire city, as well as surrounding villages. Carol, a course tutor, explained that the young women who come to this college do so for a variety of reasons:

We take girls on from age sixteen. They have to be sixteen to come here and so some are leaving school and see this as a different stage in their education or they feel that school didn't meet their needs so they'll try something else or schools don't do the courses we do so they come here and some see it as a means to an end to get a job after they complete the course because with Health and Social Care it's very specific. And then others do go on to university or to further training or to other courses as well. So again there's quite a mixture there.

The seven young women who were interviewed at this college were in the final stages of completing an advanced GNVQ in health and social care. In addition to the GNVQ, two of these young women were studying for an A-level in psychology. All of them planned to pursue higher education at a university upon completion of the GNVQ, which is a relatively new type of qualification but is fairly well established and recognized. It can be used for entry into higher education and is both vocational and academic in content. The GNVQ course in health and social care at Pearson College tends to be a qualification that young women pursue. Some young men do take the course, but they constitute a visible minority. According to one of the course tutors, most of the young women who come to the college to earn a qualification in health and social care initially want to use it to gain entry into nursing or social work; however, their career goals tend to diversify as they become aware of the range of career options available to them.

The young women who were interviewed expressed a wide range of reasons for pursuing the qualification, and they had a variety of long-term career goals. Many of them saw the GNVQ as more desirable than A-levels because it would provide a broader-based education that was not strictly focused on academic subjects and included work placements. While there is the perception that health and social work is a qualification that appeals to women because of its focus on caring, the majority of these young women wanted to pursue careers that would not fit neatly into this characterization. One young woman wanted to work in probation, one in a prison, and two in the police force. Most of them saw the GNVQ as a route into higher education and the pursuit of long-term career goals.

SITE 3: GREENWOOD SCHOOL

Greenwood School is a private all-girl school located in a small village outside of a large urban center. As a private school, there is no formal catchment area. The head teacher explained that the girls who attend this school are ones whose parents have decided that they want a private education for their daughters and necessarily are wealthy enough to provide this.[2] On the whole, they are middle-class and greatly value education. According to Mrs. Conway, besides education, there is often the added interest of the social kudos of having one's child attend a private school:

I hate to say it because it sounds terribly snobby to say it but it's the nouveau riche who feel this is a way of promoting the welfare of their children but whether it's educational or because of the social thing, whatever, it tends to be girls who are very precious to their parents, very well supported, given almost everything they want and are certainly very solidly backed up by their parents.... the expectation and part of that tradition is that they arrive when they are 3 and they stay with us until they are 18 because of the security and the continuity and all the other things that we have.

The focus of the sixth form is traditional A-levels, but there is the option of doing a GNVQ in business studies. Although some girls will leave at age eleven and age fifteen, the vast majority of the girls who come to Greenwood stay on after age sixteen to do A-levels. The attrition is due more to financial than educational reasons. It is very rare for a girl at this school to leave and drop out. Following A-levels, about 96 percent of the girls from this school go on to attend a university. Nine young women who were in their first year of sixth form were interviewed. All of them planned to pursue higher education upon completion of their studies at Greenwood. The tendency was to speak highly of their experience at this school because of its small size, the individual attention they received, and the sense of security they have there.

SITE 4: CAREER GUIDANCE CENTER

The guidance center is located in the city center and is open during weekdays on a drop-in basis. The organization, which employs more than 100 people, is a limited company that works in partnership with public sector and private organizations. They are responsible for providing comprehensive programs of career education and guidance to young people age fourteen to nineteen within the city under contract to the Department of Education. Services offered include: information on options for school leavers, interviews with career counselors to review career interests, assistance in finding a place in continuing education, employment, or training, assistance in making applications to employment or training, and advice on benefits. Diane, a guidance counselor at the center who works with young people who have left school, describes the client population as follows:

We tend to get the young people who have perhaps fallen out of the system early on in their education and often for reasons of benefits are coming in as a starting point. Then we will tend to see the ones who have dropped out of their first choices and are perhaps debating as to what to do next or felt very sure when they first left school then have either dropped out of the course or dropped out of training or lost the job for whatever reason. We are seeing an increasing number of people who are perhaps in work but want to change direction. They feel they have been doing something for a while but don't want to give it up until they've got something else but really do feel the need to change direction and that's a growing group.

Besides assisting young women with career and training advice, the center is implicated in the administration of state benefits. Young people between the ages of sixteen and eighteen are not eligible to claim benefits unless they register with the career service first as being available for either work or training. If they are estranged from parents, which Diane explained constituted a growing number of young people, then they will be able to claim benefits, but only on the condition of registering. This also means that the career center is involved in the policing of claims, as they are required to give information regarding compliance to the local authority.

For young women who leave school at age sixteen, the options fall mainly into three categories: full-time work, full-time college, or an apprenticeship program. Many of the young women interviewed knew for quite some time that they would leave school as soon as they completed statutory schooling. For others, the center provided opportunities to pursue forms of training other than A-levels. Many school leavers decide to leave school well before they are eleven, and will have dropped out of the pattern of attendance for reasons that might be personal, social, behavioral, or financial.

Nine young women were interviewed at the career guidance center. They had all left school at age sixteen. Three of them had come seeking information about training; two of them were going to start college in a couple of months but wanted to find jobs in the interim; two had completed a training course and now wanted to find work; and two, having just left school, identified finding a job as their main goal. Compared to the young women at both Ripley School and Pearson College, these young women tended to express an antipathy to education:

Shelley: Why did you decide to leave school?

Morgan: I didn't want to do further education from school because I hated the school. I hated school. I did really well in school but I didn't like it. I was bullied and hated it and just everything about it was horrid. I hated it.

Shelley: So why have you come to guidance today?

Morgan: Because I don't know what I want to do for a career. I'm just stuck like, "what do I want to do?" you know. I need to get some advice. *(Morgan, eighteen years old)*

SITE 5: YOUTHWORKS: OUTREACH AND TRAINING PROGRAMS

YouthWorks is a charitable organization that has been in operation for more than ten years. Its main purpose is to provide services to young women who face social exclusion for a number of different reasons. The emphasis in the programs it operates is on building confidence and self-esteem through outdoor pursuits and group activities. Recently, funding was obtained to launch a training program where young women can participate in team-building skills, confidence building, job-search skills, work placements, art workshops, communication skills, and importantly have child-care facilities provided. A promotional pamphlet for this program states:

[The program] came about because we realised there was little developmental provision for the most disadvantaged groups of young women. Women who do not know what their next life choices are or could be but may be at a stage where they are in danger of having choices taken away from them. They may not be ready for a job or formal education is inaccessible or alien to them, they may feel having children gives them no choices or the only choices they have are self destructive. ... The type of woman we work with may have young children, she may have just left prison or care, she may be using drugs, she may be homeless—there are hundreds of reasons why young women need positive role models, practical help and the chance to develop their dreams.

The organization is designed to work with young women from age fourteen onward. Young women may be referred to the organization, but part of its activities center on community outreach, where a number of youth workers make contact with the young women. For example, there is a youth worker whose focus centers upon African Caribbean girls, one who works with Asian girls, and two drug and alcohol workers. A number of the staff also work within other youth provision organizations and may come into contact with young women in this capacity. The activities of the organization are promoted in youth drop-in centers, as well. In general, the young women who become involved in the activities of Youth-Works may come into contact with the organization through a variety of different means.

The main structure of service provision is through weekly group meetings where young women can come for advice and support. The goal for these groups is to work together on the issues that are most relevant to the members. Youth workers mediate the groups and facilitate this process. At various points throughout the year, the groups that have formed will congregate at an outdoor center to participate in activities like rock climbing, canoeing, and abseiling.

Three young women who had involvement with the YouthWorks services were interviewed.[3] Two of them had come into contact with the program when a youth worker came to the "Young Mum's" group they had been attending and told them about the services made available to young women through YouthWorks. They became involved with the Youth-Works program and felt very positive about their experience. The other young woman interviewed was living in a hostel for young women which was visited by one the of the program's workers to encourage young women to get involved with YouthWorks activities. This young woman was struggling with drug addiction, and her daughter was living with her parents under an interim-care agreement. Her immediate priority was to enter into drug rehabilitation so that she might eventually be able to undergo an assessment by the court and regain custody of her daughter.

NOTES

1. All names of the schools described are pseudonyms, as are the names of the young women and practitioners quoted.

2. The cost of fees per term is £1,698 (US$2,748).

3. In general, the young women for whom this organization provided services were extremely reluctant to take part in an interview. Only three young women who were involved in the activities organized by this outreach program would agree to an interview, although more were approached. Their skepticism contrasted significantly with Ripley School, Pearson College, and Greenwood School, where the young women were eager to participate. Indeed, it was very difficult to gain entry into a site that provided services for young women who are marginalized. Various youth workers who were contacted about this project explained that it took an extremely long time for these young women to build a level of trust that would allow them to open up about their experiences.

Bibliography

Abercrombie, Nicholas, Stephen Hill, and Bryan S. Turner. 1986. *Sovereign Individuals of Capitalism*. London: Allen and Unwin.

Alcoff, Linda. 1988. "Cultural Feminism versus Post-Structuralism: The Identity Crisis in Feminist Theory." *Signs* 13 (3): 405–36.

Anthias, Floya. 1999. "Theorising Identity, Difference and Social Divisions." In *Theorising Modernity: Reflexivity, Environment, and Identity in Giddens' Social Theory*, ed. Martin O'Brien, Sue Penna, and Colin Hay, 156–78. London: Longman.

Anthias, Floya, and Nira Yuval-Davis. 1990. "Contextualising Feminism: Gender, Ethnic, and Class Divisions." In *British Feminist Thought*, ed. Terry Lovell, 103–18. Oxford: Basil Blackwell.

Bagguley, Paul. 1999. "Beyond Emancipation? The Reflexivity of Social Movements." In *Theorising Modernity: Reflexivity, Environment, and Identity in Giddens' Social Theory*, ed. Martin O'Brien, Sue Penna, and Colin Hay, 65–82. London: Longman.

Balsamo, Anne. 1995. "Forms of Technological Embodiment: Reading the Body in Contemporary Culture." *Body and Society* 1 (3–4): 215–37.

Barrett, Michèle. 1987. "The Concept of 'Difference.'" *Feminist Review* 26 (summer): 29–41.

———. 1992. "Words and Things: Materialism and Method in Contemporary Feminism." In *Destabilizing Theory*, ed. Michèle Barrett and Anne Philips, 201–19. Stanford, Calif.: Stanford University Press.

Barrett, Michèle, and Mary MacIntosh. 1991. *The Anti-Social Family*. 2d ed. London: Verso.

Barrett, Michèle, and Anne Philips, eds. 1992. *Destabilizing Theory*. Stanford, Calif.: Stanford University Press.

Barthes, Roland. 1972. *Mythologies*. London: Jonathan Cape.

Bartky, Sandra. 1990. *Femininity and Domination: Studies in the Phenomenology of Oppression*. New York: Routledge.

Bates, Inge and George Riseborough, eds. 1993. Youth and Inequality. Bucking-ham: Open University Press.

Bauman, Zygmunt. 1992. Intimations of Postmodernity. London: Routledge.

———. 1993. Review of "The Transformation of Intimacy." Sociological Review 41: 363–68.

———. 1996a. "Morality in the Age of Contingency." In Detraditionalisation: Critical Reflections on Authority and Identity, ed. Paul Heelas, Scott Lash, and Paul Morris, 49–58. Oxford: Blackwell Publishers.

———. 1996b. "From Pilgrim to Tourist: Or a Short History of Identity." In Questions of Cultural Identity, ed. Stuart Hall and Paul Du Gay, 18–36. London: Sage Publications.

Beck, Ulrich. 1992. The Risk Society. London: Sage Publications.

Beck, Ulrich, and Elisabeth Beck-Gernsheim. 1995. The Normal Chaos of Love. Translated by Mark Ritter and Jane Wiebel. Cambridge, U.K.: Polity Press.

———. 1996. "Individualisation and 'Precarious Freedoms.'" In Detraditionalisation: Critical Reflections on Authority and Identity, ed. Paul Heelas, Scott Lash, and Paul Morris, 23–48. Oxford: Blackwell Publishers.

Beck, Ulrich, Anthony Giddens, and Scott Lash. 1994. Reflexive Modernisation. Cambridge, U.K.: Polity Press.

Best, Steven, and Douglas Kellner. 1991. Postmodern Theory. London: Macmillan.

Bhavani, Kum-Kum, Kathryn R. Kent, and France Widdance Twine. 1998. "Editorial." Signs 23 (3): 575–83.

Bordo, Susan. 1986. "The Cartesian Masculinization of Thought." Signs 11 (31): 439–56.

———. 1993. Unbearable Weight. Berkeley, Calif.: University of California Press.

Bourdieu, Pierre. 1984. Distinction: A Social Critique of the Judgement of Taste. London: Routledge.

Bovey, Shelley. 1991. The Forbidden Body. London: Pandora.

Boyne, Roy, and Ali Rattansi, eds. 1990. Postmodernism and Society. London: Macmillan.

Bradley, Harriet. 1996. Fractured Identities: Changing Patterns of Inequality. Cambridge, U.K.: Polity Press.

Brah, Avtar. 1996. Cartographies of Diaspora. London: Routledge.

Braidotti, Rosi. 1991. Patterns of Dissonance. Cambridge, U.K.: Polity Press.

———. 1994. Nomadic Subjects: Embodiment and Sexual Difference in Contemporary Feminist Theory. New York: Columbia University Press.

Bray, Abigail, and Claire Colebrook. 1998. "The Haunted Flesh: Corporeal Feminism and the Politics of (Dis)Embodiment." Signs 24 (11): 35–67.

Brooks, Ann. 1997. Postfeminisms: Feminism, Cultural Theory, and Cultural Forms. London: Routledge.

Brownmiller, Susan. 1985. Femininity. New York: Fawcett Columbine.

Bruch, Hilda. 1979. The Golden Cage: The Enigma of Anorexia. Wells, U.K.: Open Books.

Buchanan, Ian. 1997. "The Problem of the Body in Deleuze and Guattari: Or, What Can a Body Do?" Body & Society 3 (3): 73–91.

Budgeon, Shelley, and Dawn Currie. 1995. "From Feminism to Postfeminism: Women's Liberation in Fashion Magazines." Women's Studies International Forum 18 (2): 173–86.

Burkitt, Ian. 1991. *Social Selves: Theories of the Social Formation of Personality.* London: Sage Publications.

Burr, Vivien. 1995. *An Introduction to Social Constructionism.* London: Routledge.

Butler, Judith. 1990. *Gender Trouble: Feminism and the Subversion of Identity.* New York: Routledge.

———. 1992. "Contingent Foundations: Feminism and the Question of 'Postmodernism.'" In *Feminists Theorize the Political,* ed. Judith Butler and Joan W. Scott, 3–21. New York: Routledge.

———. 1993. *Bodies That Matter.* London: Routledge.

Butler, Judith, and Joan W. Scott. 1992. *Feminists Theorize the Political.* London: Routledge.

Calhoun, Craig, ed. 1994. *Social Theory and the Politics of Identity.* Oxford: Blackwell Publishers.

Castells, Manuel. 1997. *The Power of Identity.* Malden, Mass.: Blackwell Publishers.

Chapkis, Wendy. 1986. *Beauty Secrets.* London: The Women's Press.

Chase, Susan E. 1995. "Taking Narrative Seriously: Consequences for Method and Theory in Interview Studies." In Ruthellen Josselson and Amia Lieblich, *Interpreting Experience: The Narrative Study of Lives.* Thousand Oaks, Calif.: Sage, 1–26.

Cheal, David. 1991. *Family and the State of Theory.* London: Harvester Wheatsheaf.

Chernin, Kim. 1983. *Womansize: The Tyranny of Slenderness.* London: Women's Press.

Coffey, Amanda, and Paul Atkinson. 1996. *Making Sense of Qualitative Data.* Thousand Oaks, Calif.: Sage.

Colebrook, Claire. 2000. "From Radical Representations to Corporeal Becomings: The Feminist Philosophy of Lloyd, Grosz, and Gatens." *Hypatia* 15 (2): 76–93.

Crompton, Rosemary. 1998. *Class and Stratification.* 2d ed. Cambridge, U.K.: Polity Press.

Crompton, Rosemary, Duncan Gallie, and Kate Purcell. 1996. *Changing Forms of Employment: Organisations, Skills, and Gender.* London: Routledge.

Crowley, Helen, and Susan Himmelweit. 1992. *Knowing Women: Feminism and Knowledge.* Cambridge, U.K.: Polity Press.

Davis, Kathy. 1995. *Reshaping the Female Body.* New York: Routledge.

Dean, Mitchell. 1994. " 'A Social Structure of Many Souls': Moral Regulation, Government, and Self-Formation." *Canadian Journal of Sociology* 19 (2): 145–68.

de Certeau, Michel. 1988. *The Practice of Everyday Life,* translated by Steven Rendall. Berkeley: University of California Press.

de Lauretis, Teresa. 1984. *Alice Doesn't.* Bloomington: Indiana University Press.

de Lauretis, Teresa, ed. 1986. *Feminist Studies/Critical Studies.* Bloomington: Indiana University Press.

de Lauretis, Teresa. 1987. *Technologies of Gender.* Bloomington: Indiana University Press.

Deleuze, Gilles. 1988. *Spinoza: Practical Philosophy.* Translated by Robert Hurley. San Francisco, Calif.: City Lights Books.

———. 1992. *The Fold: Leibniz and the Baroque.* Minneapolis: University of Minnesota Press.

Deleuze, Gilles, and Felix Guattari. 1987. *A Thousand Plateaus: Capitalism and Schiz-ophrenia.* Translated by Brian Massumi. Minneapolis: University of Min-nesota Press.

Derrida, Jacques. 1976. *Of Grammatology.* Baltimore, Md.: Johns Hopkins Press.

———. 1978. *Writing and Difference.* London: Routledge.

———. 1982. *Margins of Philosophy.* Translated by Alan Bass. New York: Harvester Wheatsheaf.

Douglas, Susan J. 1994. *Where the Girls Are: Growing Up Female with the Mass Media.* London: Penguin.

Drucker, Peter F. 1993. *Post Capitalist Society.* Oxford: Butterworth Heinemann.

Faludi, Susan. 1992. *Backlash: The Undeclared War against Women.* London: Chatto & Windus.

Featherstone, Mike. 1991. "The Body in Consumer Culture." In Mike Featherstone, Mike Hepworth, and Bryan S. Turner, *The Body: Social Processes and Cultural Theory,* 170–96. London: Sage.

Featherstone, Mike, and Roger Burrows. 1995. *Cyberspace/Cyberbodies/Cyberpunk: Cultures of Technological Embodiment.* London: Sage.

Felski, Rita. 1989. "Feminist Theory and Social Change." *Theory, Culture, and Soci-ety* 6: 219–40.

———. 1997. "The Doxa of Difference." *Signs* 23 (11): 11–22.

Flax, Jane. 1990. "Postmodernism and Gender Relations in Feminist Theory." In *Feminism/Postmodernism,* ed. Linda A. Nicholson, 39–62. New York: Rout-ledge.

———. 1992. "Beyond Equality: Gender, Justice, and Difference." In *Beyond Equal-ity and Difference: Citizenship, Feminist Politics, and Female Subjectivity,* ed. Gisela Bock and Susan James, 192–209. London: Routledge.

Foucault, Michel. 1977. *Discipline and Punish.* London: Allen Lane.

———. 1979. *The History of Sexuality.* Vol. 1. London: Allen Lane.

———. 1982. "The Subject and Power." In *Michel Foucault: Beyond Structuralism and Hermeneutics,* ed. Hubert Dreyfus and Paul Rabinow, 208–27. Brighton, U.K.: Harvester Press.

———. 1986. *The Care of the Self.* London: Penguin.

———. 1988. "Technologies of the Self." In L. H. Martin, H. Gutman, and P. H. Hutton, *Technologies of the Self,* 16–49. Amherst: University of Massachusetts Press.

French, Marilyn. 1992. *The War against Women.* London: Hamish Hamilton.

Furlong, Andy, and Fred Cartmel. 1997. *Young People and Social Change: Individu-alisation and Risk in Late Modernity.* Buckingham, U.K.: Open University Press.

Gatens, Moira. 1991. Feminism and Philosophy: Perspectives in Difference and Equality. Cambridge, U.K.: Polity Press.

———. 1992. "Power, Bodies, and Difference." In *Destabilizing Theory,* ed. Michèle Barrett and Anne Philips, 120–37. Stanford, Calif.: Stanford University Press.

———. 1996. *Imaginary Bodies: Ethics, Power, and Corporeality.* London: Routledge.

———. 2000. "Feminism as 'Password': Re-thinking the 'Possible' with Spinoza and Deleuze." *Hypatia* 15 (2): 59–75.

Giddens, Anthony. 1984. *The Constitution of Society.* Cambridge, U.K.: Polity Press.

———. 1990. *The Consequences of Modernity.* Cambridge, U.K.: Polity Press.

———. 1991. *Modernity and Self Identity.* Cambridge, U.K.: Polity Press.

———. 1992. *The Transformation of Intimacy.* Cambridge, U.K.: Polity Press.

Goffman, Erving. 1971. *Relations in Public.* London: Allen Lane.

Greer, Germaine. 1999. *The Whole Woman.* London: Doubleday.

Griffin, Christine. 1985. *Typical Girls?* London: Routledge and Kegan Paul.

———. 1989. "'I'm Not a Women's Libber But ... ': Feminism, Consciousness, and Identity." In *The Social Identity of Women,* ed. Suzanne Skevington and Deborah Baker, 173–93. London: Sage.

———. 1993. *Representations of Youth: The Study of Youth and Adolescence in Britain and America.* Cambridge, U.K.: Polity Press.

———. 1995. "Review of Sugar and Spice: Sexuality and Adolescent Girls." *Journal of Gender Studies* 4 (1): 110.

Griffiths, Joanna. 1999. "Up for It Girls." *Saturday Review* in *The Guardian,* 6 February, 8.

Grosz, Elizabeth. 1993. "Bodies and Knowledges: Feminism and the Crisis of Reason. In *Feminist Epistemologies,* ed. Linda Alcoff and Elizabeth Potter, 187–216. London: Routledge.

———. 1994. *Volatile Bodies: Toward a Corporeal Feminism.* Bloomington: Indiana University Press.

Hall, Stuart. 1992. "The Question of Cultural Identity." In *Modernity and Its Futures,* ed. Stuart Hall, David Held, and Tony McGrew, 273–326. Cambridge, U.K.: Polity Press.

———. 1996. "Introduction: Who Needs Identity?" In *Questions of Cultural Identity,* ed. Stuart Hall and Paul Du Gay, 1–17. London: Sage.

Hall, Stuart, and Paul Du Gay, eds. 1996. *Questions of Cultural Identity.* London: Sage.

Haraway, Donna. 1988. "Situated Knowledges: The Science Question in Feminism and the Privilege of Partial Perspective." *Feminist Studies* 14 (3): 575–99.

Harding, Sandra. 1990. "Feminism, Science, and the Anti-Enlightenment Critiques." In *Feminism/Postmodernism,* ed. Linda A. Nicholson, 83–106. New York: Routledge.

———. 1993. "Rethinking Standpoint Epistemology: What Is 'Strong Objectivity'?" In *Feminist Epistemologies,* ed. Linda Alcoff and Elisabeth Potter. London: Routledge.

Hartsock, Nancy. 1983. "The Feminist Standpoint: Developing the Ground for a Specifically Feminist Historical Materialism." In *Discovering Reality,* ed. Sandra Harding and Merrill B. Hintikka, 283–310. Amsterdam: D. Reidal.

Harvey, David. 1989. *The Condition of Postmodernity.* Oxford: Blackwell Publishers.

Hassan, Ihab. 1985. "The Culture of Postmodernism." *Theory, Culture, & Society* 2 (3): 119–29.

Hawkesworth, Mary E. 1989. "Knower, Knowing, Known: Feminist Theory and Claims of Truth." *Signs* 14 (31): 533–57.

Heath, Sue. 1999. "Young Adults and Household Formation in the 1990s." *British Journal of Sociology of Education* 20 (4): 545–61.

Heelas, Paul. 1996. "Introduction." In *Detraditionalisation: Critical Reflections on Authority and Identity,* ed. Paul Heelas, Scott Lash, and Paul Morris, 1–19. Oxford: Blackwell Publishers.

Heelas, Paul, Scott Lash, and Paul Morris, eds. 1996. *Detraditionalisation: Critical Reflections on Authority and Identity.* Oxford: Blackwell Publishers.

Hekman, Susan. 1990. *Gender and Knowledge.* Cambridge, U.K.: Polity Press.

Hetherington, Kevin. 1998. *Expressions of Identity.* London: Sage.

Hey, Valerie. 1997. *The Company She Keeps.* Buckingham, U.K.: Open University Press.

Hirsch, Marianne, and Evelyn Fox Keller, eds. 1990. *Conflicts in Feminism.* London: Routledge.

Hollands, Robert G. 1990. *The Long Transition.* Basingstoke, U.K.: Macmillan.

hooks, bell. 1981. *Ain't I a Woman?* London: Pluto Press.

———. 1991. "Sisterhood: Political Solidarity between Women." In *A Reader in Feminist Knowledge,* ed. Sneja Gunew, 27–41. London: Routledge.

Humm, Maggie. 1992. *Feminism: A Reader.* New York: Harvester Wheatsheaf.

Huyssen, Andreas. 1990. "Mapping the Postmodern." In *Feminism/Postmodernism,* ed Linda A. Nicholson, 237–77. New York: Routledge.

Irigaray, Luce. 1985. *The Speculum of the Other Woman.* Translated by Gillian C. Gill. Ithaca, N.Y.: Cornell University Press.

Irwin, Sarah. 1995. *Rights of Passage.* London: UCL.

Jagger, Gill, and Caroline Wright, eds. 1999. *Changing Family Values.* London: Routledge.

Jamieson, Lynn. 1998. *Intimacy: Personal Relationships in Modern Societies.* Cambridge, U.K.: Polity Press.

———. 1999. "Intimacy Transformed? A Critical Look at the Pure Relationship." *Sociology* 33 (3): 477–94.

Jary, David, and Julia Jary. 1995. "The Transformations of Anthony Giddens: The Continuing Story of Structuration Theory." *Theory, Culture, & Society* 12: 141–60.

Jervis, John. 1998. *Exploring the Modern: Patterns of Western Culture and Civilization.* Oxford: Blackwell Publishers.

Jones, Alison. 1993. "Becoming a 'Girl': Post-Structuralist Suggestions for Educational Research." *Gender and Education* 5 (2): 157–66.

Jong, Erica. 1999. *What Do Women Want? Reflections on a Century of Change.* New York: Bloomsbury Publishing.

Josselson, R. 1995. "Imagining the Real." In R. Josselson and A. Lieblich, *Interpreting Experience: The Narrative Study of Lives.* Thousand Oaks, Calif.: Sage.

Joyce, Patrick. 1994. *Democratic Subjects: The Self and the Social in Nineteenth Century England.* Cambridge, U.K. : Cambridge University Press.

Kellner, Douglas. 1992. "Popular Culture and the Construction of Postmodern Identities." In *Modernity and Identity,* ed. Scott Lash and Jonathan Friedman. Oxford: Blackwell Publishers.

Kumar, Krishan. 1995. *From Post-Industrial to Post-Modern Society.* Oxford: Blackwell Publishers.

Laclau, Ernesto. 1990. *New Reflections on the Revolution of Our Time.* London: Verso.

Lash, Scott. 1994. "Reflexivity and Its Doubles: Structure, Aesthetics, Community." In *Reflexive Modernisation,* ed. Ulrich Beck, Anthony Giddens, and Scott Lash. Cambridge, U.K.: Polity Press.

Lash, Scott, and Jonathan Friedman, eds. 1992. *Modernity and Identity.* Oxford: Basil Blackwell.

Lash, Scott, and John Urry. 1994. *Economies of Signs and Space.* London: Sage.

Lees, Sue. 1986. *Losing Out: Sexuality and Adolescent Girls.* London: Hutchinson.

———. 1993. *Sugar and Spice: Sexuality and Adolescent Girls.* London: Penguin.

Luke, Timothy W. 1996. "Identity, Meaning, and Globalisation: Detraditionalisation in Postmodern Space-Time Compression." In *Detraditionalisation: Critical Reflections on Authority and Identity,* ed. Paul Heelas, Scott Lash, and Paul Morris, 109–33. Oxford: Blackwell Publishers.

Lyotard, Jean-Francois. 1984. *The Postmodern Condition.* Translated by Geoff Bennington and Brian Massumi. Minneapolis: University of Minnesota Press.

MacCannell, Dean, and Juliet Flower MacCannell. 1987. "The Beauty System." In *The Ideology of Conduct*, ed. Nancy Armstrong and Leonard Tennenhouse, 206–38. London: Methuen.

MacSween, Morag. 1993. *Anorexic Bodies.* London: Routledge.

Maffesoli, Michel. 1996. *The Time of the Tribes: The Decline of Individualism in Mass Society.* London: Sage.

Marshall, Barbara. 1994. *Engendering Modernity: Feminism, Social Theory, and Social Change.* Cambridge, U.K.: Polity Press.

Martin, Luther H., Huck Gutman, and Patrick H. Hutton. 1988. *Technologies of the Self.* Amherst: University of Massachusetts Press.

Mason, Jennifer. 2000. "Deciding Where to Live: Relational Reasoning and Narratives of the Self." *Centre for Research on Family, Kinship, and Childhood Working Papers.* Leeds, U.K.: University of Leeds.

May, Carl, and Andrew Cooper. 1995. "Personal Identity and Social Change: Some Theoretical Considerations." *Acta Sociologica* 38: 75–85.

McNay, Lois. 1999. "Gender, Habitus, and the Field." *Theory, Culture, & Society* 16 (1): 95–117.

McRobbie, Angela. 1991. *Feminism and Youth Culture.* London: Macmillan Education.

———. 1993. "Shut Up and Dance: Youth Culture and Changing Modes of Femininity." *Cultural Studies* 7: 406–26.

———. 1994. *Postmodernism and Popular Culture.* London: Routledge.

———. 1999. "*More!* New Sexualities in Girls' and Women's Magazines." In *In the Culture Industry: Art, Fashion, and Popular Music.* London: Routledge, 42–61.

Mestrovic, Stjepan. 1998. *Anthony Giddens: The Last Modernist.* London: Routledge.

Morgan, David L. 1996. *Family Connections.* Cambridge, U.K.: Polity Press.

Mouzelis, Nicos. 1999. "Exploring Post-Traditional Orders: Individual Reflexivity, 'Pure Relations,' and Duality of Structure." In *Theorising Modernity: Reflexivity, Environment, and Identity in Giddens's Social Theory,* ed. Martin O'Brien, Sue Penna, and Colin Hay, 83–97. London: Longman.

Nicholson, Linda A., ed. 1990. *Feminism/Postmodernism.* New York: Routledge.

O'Brien, Martin. 1999. "Theorising Modernity: Reflexivity, Identity, and Environment in Giddens's Social Theory." In *Theorising Modernity: Reflexivity, Environment, and Identity in Giddens's Social Theory,* ed. Martin O'Brien, Sue Penna, and Colin Hay, 17–38. London: Longman.

O'Brien, Martin, Sue Penna, and Colin Hay, eds. 1999. *Theorising Modernity: Reflexivity, Environment, and Identity in Giddens's Social Theory.* London: Longman.

Orbach, Susie. 1986. *Hungerstrike: The Anorectic's Struggle as a Metaphor for Our Age.* London: Faber and Faber.

Penna, Sue, Martin O'Brien, and Colin Hay. 1999. "Introduction." In *Theorising Modernity: Reflexivity, Environment, and Identity in Giddens's Social Theory,* ed. Martin O'Brien, Sue Penna, and Colin Hay, 1–16. London: Longman.

Polkinghorne, Donald E. 1988. *Narrative Knowing in the Human Sciences.* Albany: State University of New York Press.

Poovey, Mary. 1988. "Feminism and Deconstruction." *Feminist Studies* 14 (1): 51–65.

Probyn, Elspeth. 1987. "The Anorexic Body." In *Panic Sex,* ed. Arthur Kroker and Marilouise Kroker, 201–12. New York: St. Martin's Press.

———. 1993. *Sexing the Self: Gendered Positions in Cultural Studies.* London: Routledge.

Radley, Alan. 1995. "The Elusory Body and Social Constructionist Theory." *Body & Society* 1 (2): 3–23.

Rapp, Rayna. 1988. "Is the Legacy of Second Wave Feminism Post-Feminism?" *Socialist Review* 97: 31–37.

Rayner, Jay. 2000. "We Want to Be Alone." *Review* in *The Observer,* Sunday, 16 January, 1–2.

Riley, Denise. 1988. *Am I That Name? Feminism and the Category of "Women" in History.* London: Macmillan Press Inc.

Roberts, Kenneth. 1995. *Youth and Employment in Modern Britain.* Oxford: Oxford University Press.

Roger, John J. 1996. *Family Life and Social Control.* Basingstoke, U.K.: Macmillan.

Roiphe, Katie. 1994. *The Morning After: Sex, Fear, and Feminism.* London: Hamish Hamilton.

Rose, Nikolas. 1996a. "Authority and the Genealogy of the Subject." In *Detraditionalisation: Critical Reflections on Authority and Identity,* ed. Paul Heelas, Scott Lash, and Paul Morris, 294–327. Oxford: Blackwell Publishers.

———. 1996b. "Identity, Genealogy, History." In *Questions of Cultural Identity,* ed. Stuart Hall and Paul Du Gay, 128–50. London: Sage.

———. 1998. *Inventing Ourselves.* Cambridge, U.K. : Cambridge University Press.

Rosenau, Pauline Marie. 1992. *Post-Modernism and the Social Sciences.* New Jersey: Princeton University Press.

Roseneil, Sasha. 1995. *Disarming Patriarchy.* Buckingham, U.K.: Open University Press.

———. 1999. "Postmodern Feminist Politics: The Art of the (Im)possible?" *The European Journal of Women's Studies* 6: 161–82.

Roseneil, Sasha, and Julie Seymour, eds. 1999. *Practising Identities.* Basingstoke, U.K.: Macmillan Press Ltd.

Rutherford, Jonathan, ed. 1990. *Identity.* London: Lawrence and Wisehart.

Sarup, Madan. 1996. *Identity, Culture, and the Postmodern World.* Edinburgh, Scotland: Edinburgh University Press.

Scott, Joan W. 1988. "Deconstructing Equality versus Difference: Or the Uses of Poststructuralist Theory for Feminism." *Feminist Studies* 14 (1).

———. 1992. "Experience." In *Feminists Theorise the Political,* ed. Judith Butler and Joan W. Scott, 22–40. New York: Routledge.

Seidman, Steven. 1997. "Relativizing Sociology: The Challenge of Cultural Studies." In *From Sociology to Cultural Studies,* ed. Elizabeth Long, 37–61. Oxford: Blackwell Publishers.

———. 1998. *Contested Knowledge: Social Theory in the Postmodern Era.* 2d ed. Oxford: Blackwell Publishers.

Seigel, Jerrold. 1999. "Problematising the Self." In *Beyond the Cultural Turn,* ed. Victoria E. Bonnell and Lynn Hunt, 281–314. Berkeley: University of California Press.

Sharpe, Sue. 1976. *Just Like a Girl: How Young Girls Learn to Be Women.* London: Penguin.

———. 1994. *Just Like a Girl: How Young Girls Learn to Be Women.* 2d ed. London: Penguin.

Shilling, Chris. 1993. *The Body and Social Theory.* London: Sage.

———. 1997. "The Body and Difference." In *Identity and Difference,* ed. Kathryn Woodward, 63–120. London: Sage.

Shilling, Chris, and Philip A. Mellor. 1996. "Embodiment, Structuration Theory, and Modernity: Mind/Body Dualism and the Repression of Sensuality." *Body and Society* 2 (4): 1–15.

Silva, Elizabeth B., and Carol Smart, eds. 1999. *The New Family?* London: Sage.

Skeggs, Beverly. 1997. *Formations of Class and Gender.* London: Sage Publications.

Smart, Barry. 1992. Modern Conditions, Postmodern Controversies. London: Routledge.

———. 1997. "Postmodern Social Theory." In *The Blackwell Companion to Social Theory,* ed. Bryan S. Turner, 396–428. Oxford: Blackwell Publishers.

Smart, Carol, and Bren Neale. 1999. *Family Fragments?* Cambridge, U.K.: Polity Press.

Smith, Dorothy E. 1988. "Femininity as Discourse." In *Becoming Feminine: The Politics of Popular Culture,* ed. Leslie G. Roman and Linda K. Christian Smith, 37–59. Philadelphia, Pa.: The Falmer Press.

———. 1990. *Texts, Facts, and Femininity.* London: Routledge.

Spelman, Elizabeth V. 1990. *Inessential Woman: Problems of Exclusion in Feminist Thought.* London: The Women's Press.

Spivak, Gayatri. 1987. *In Other Worlds: Essays in Cultural Politics.* London: Methuen.

———. 1990. *The Postcolonial Critic: Interviews, Strategies, Dialogues.* London: Routledge.

Stuart, Andrea. 1990. "Feminism: Dead or Alive?" In *Identity,* ed. Jonathan Rutherford, 28–42. London: Lawrence and Wishart.

Székely, Éva. 1988. *Never Too Thin.* Toronto, Canada: The Women's Press.

Taylor, Charles. 1989. *Sources of the Self.* Cambridge, U.K.: Cambridge University Press.

Taylor, David. 1998. "Social Identity and Social Policy: Engagements with Postmodern Theory." *Journal of Social Policy* 27 (3): 329–50.

Thompson, John B. 1996. *Tradition and Self in a Mediated World.* In *Detraditionalisation: Critical Reflections on Authority and Identity,* ed. Paul Heelas, Scott Lash and Paul Morris, 89–108. Oxford: Blackwell Publishers.

Thrift, Nigel. 1993. "The Arts of the Living, the Beauty of the Dead: Anxieties of Being in the Work of Anthony Giddens." *Progress in Human Geography* 17 (1): 111–21.

Turner, Bryan S. 1992. *Regulating Bodies.* London: Routledge.

———. 1996. *The Body and Society.* 2d ed. London: Sage.

Walby, Sylvia. 1997. *Gender Transformations.* London: Routledge.

Walter, Natasha. 1998. *The New Feminism.* London: Little, Brown, and Company.

Weedon, Chris. 1997. *Feminist Practice and Poststructuralist Theory.* 2d ed. Oxford: Blackwell Publishers.

Weeks, Jeffrey. 1995. *Invented Moralities: Sexual Values in an Age of Uncertainty.* Cambridge, U.K.: Polity Press.

Wendell, Susan. 1996. *The Rejected Body.* London: Routledge.

Whelehan, Imelda. 1995. *Modern Feminist Thought: From Second Wave to "Post-Feminism."* Edinburgh, U.K. : Edinburgh University Press.

Wolf, Naomi. 1990. *The Beauty Myth.* London: Chatto and Windus.

———. 1993. *Fire with Fire: The New Female Power and How It Will Change the Twenty-First Century.* London: Chatto and Windus.

Woodward, Kathryn. 1997. "Concepts of Identity and Difference." In *Identity and Difference,* ed. Kathryn Woodward. London: Sage.

Wright, Caroline, and Gill Jagger. 1999. "End of Century, End of Family, Shifting Discourses of Family 'Crisis.'" In *Changing Family Values,* ed. Gill Jagger and Caroline Wright, 17–37. London: Routledge.

Young, Iris Marion. 1990. *Throwing Like a Girl and Other Essays in Feminist Philosophy and Social Theory.* Bloomington: Indiana University Press.

Young, Shelagh. 1989. "Feminism and the Politics of Power." In *The Female Gaze: Women as Viewers of Popular Culture,* ed. Lorraine Gamman and Margaret Marshment, 173–188. Seattle, Wash.: Real Comet Press.

Index

About the Author

SHELLEY BUDGEON is a Research Fellow in the Department of Sociology and Social Policy at the University of Leeds, U.K.